BACKCOUNTRY BRAZIL

Caracara

Backcountry
Brazil

The Pantanal, Amazon, and north-east coast

Alex Bradbury

Maps and illustrations by the author

BRADT PUBLICATIONS,
HUNTER PUBLISHING, USA

First published in May 1990 by Bradt Publications, 41 Nortoft Rd, Chalfont St Peter, Bucks SL9 0LA, England. Distributed in the USA by Hunter Publishing, Inc., 300 Raritan Center Parkway, CN 94 Edison, NJ 08818.

British Library Cataloguing in Publication Data

Bradbury, Alex
 Backcountry Brazil: the Pantanal, Amazon and the north-east coast.
 1. Brazil. Description and travel
 I. Title
 918.10463

 ISBN 0-946983-44-5

Made and printed in Great Britain by
The Guernsey Press Co. Ltd., Guernsey, Channel Islands.

Cover photographs: Front — Amazon rain forest (Jayne Bradbury) with sloth (Fiona Watson) and piranha (Jayne Bradbury).
Back — Jangadas, North-east coast (Fiona Watson).

THE AUTHOR

Alex Bradbury works as a fisheries biologist in Washington State, USA. He has made three trips to Brazil – the first of which lasted a year – to research this book.

Dear Readers,

Things change so quickly in Brazil that at least one author (Charles Wagley) suggested books on the subject be published in loose-leaf form. Besides that, it would take several lifetimes just to adequately cover the country once. So if you've found changes, errors, or new places you'd like to share, PLEASE write.

And while you're at it, think about sharing those travel adventures, good and bad, that you're bound to have in the backcountry; they may well find their way into the next edition.

Boa Viagem!

Alex Bradbury

This book is lovingly dedicated to Jayne,
my wife and companion on the road.

ACKNOWLEDGEMENTS

First, I owe heartfelt thanks and *abraços* to our Brazilian friends: Silvana de Aguiar, Enrique Aramburu, and Wellington Franklin, who accompanied us on numerous trips and made special contributions to the North-east Coast chapter; Ricardo Silva Pereira and Sheila, who shared their home with us, their insight into Brazilian politics, and who showed us how to play *samba* on tiny wooden matchboxes; Luiz Roberto Sabbato, Hidely, Silvia, Tulio, and Flávia, who shared their home with us for weeks at time and gave us our first taste of the backcountry; Dona Eunice Dantas, who housed us in the North-east and fattened us with her fine cooking; Manoel and Edy de Barros, Edson, Nialva Angela de Souza, Ricardo Gattini, Celso and Casilda Furtado, Hélio Gomes de Amorim, Beré, Eugênio Paccelli, Vicente and Terezinha Neto, Lucídio Silva da Conceição, Tamires Corrêa, Claudio and Rita Costa, Nelson and Graça Torres, Sida and Adalberto, Dondo Ioschpe, René Lana do Amaral Junior, Fernando Celso Junqueira and Silvia, Regina Ramos, and Tarcizo Cirilo. For all of Brazil's natural splendour, it is their warmth, generosity, and patience that made our trips there memorable.

My parents, Bill and Ann, provided both moral and logistical support during our year-long trip, and put up with the cat on numerous shorter journeys.

Veleda Furtado schooled us in Portuguese for well over a year prior to our first trip.

The entire staff of the WWF in Manaus deserves thanks, especially Cynthia Souther, Heraldo Vasconcelos, Raimundo and Alberto. Also in Manaus, Bill Magnussen with INPA graciously consented to take us to his jungle camp without ever laying eyes on us.

This book would never have happened without the support and constant encouragement of editor Hilary Bradt.

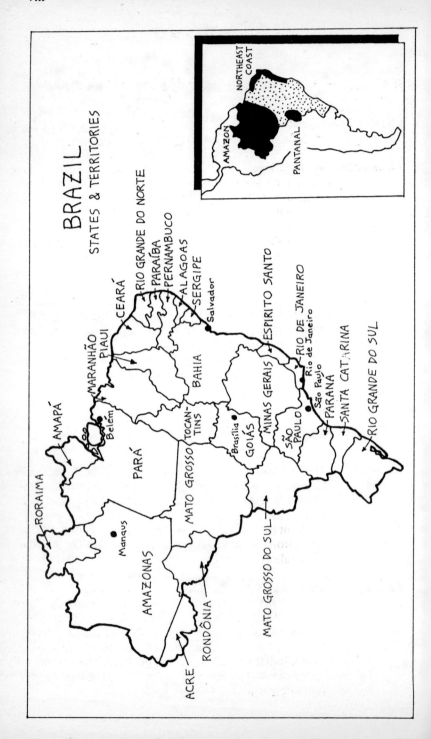

BRAZIL
STATES & TERRITORIES

Contents

GENERAL INFORMATION

BRAZIL

Introduction

In the last few days of 1983, my wife and I quit our comfortable jobs, collected the damage deposit on our rented home, and boarded a Varig jet for Belém do Pará, Brazil. From the air, Belém's urban sprawl hinted at a Brazil utterly tamed by the 20th Century. I half-pictured the beaches lined with condominiums, the jungles leveled by multinational agri-business firms, the swamps drained for airstrips. Our first week did nothing to diminish those fears. As a professional biologist, I insisted on visiting a tiny river town called Peixe-Boi ('fish-ox,' or manatee, the gentle walrus-like mammal of tropical waters). But the townspeople told us — almost proudly, it seemed to me — that they had long ago killed off the remaining manatees. The town was uninspiring. The regional food we'd hungered for consisted of salted crackers and warm Pepsi. What kind of a vacation *was* this, anyway? Where were the palm-thatched fishing villages, the quiet backwaters teeming with bird life, the towering sand dunes undisturbed by man?

We found them, eventually, and this book is the result.

Brazil boasts more undisturbed hinterland than any other country on the continent, most of it accessible to travellers of modest means and limited wilderness experience. This book describes backcountry travel in three regions. Obviously, this approach leaves out much of the country, but to my mind these regions offer the best and most uniquely Brazilian experience for the backcountry traveller: Amazônia for the jungle buff, the Pantanal for wildlife lovers, and the north-east coast for aficionados of deserted beaches and rustic fishing villages.

Every good cookbook admonishes its readers to use the recipes merely as a starting point for experimentation; travel books would do well to offer that same advice. My goal here is to serve up a limited menu of specific backcountry trips within each region — *hors d'oeuvres*, if you will — along with some general tips which you'll find applicable when you strike out on your own — how to see alligators, how to bathe in a fishing village, how to keep mould from fouling your hammock, etc.

Much of the information here is arranged around the concept of 'gateway cities.' These are the cities you'll most likely use as 'base camps' for your forays into the backcountry. Many of these cities are interesting in their own right, but I've deferred the usual sightseeing information and hotel/restaurant listings to other guidebooks. Instead, I've concentrated on getting you in and out of the cities quickly, augmenting this information with the kind frequently missing in the other guides (like where to buy fish hooks, or how to cash travellers cheques).

Obviously, this guide is skewed towards our own particular style of travel. Our river trips, for example, take place aboard small cargo boats or in outboard skiffs piloted by local fishermen. Both the cost and the considerable logistics of transporting a boat through the backlands of South America have so far prevented us from making solo trips in our own boat. Besides, we genuinely value the chance to rub shoulders with the locals, to learn an oldtimer's fishing secrets, or to hear how dolphins make native women pregnant. The social landscape of rural Brazil is every bit as fascinating to us as is the physical one. Likewise, we usually prefer spending the night in a rented hut or slinging our hammocks in a family's back room to pitching a tent. But if you're inclined to thread your way down the Guaporé River in a kayak, camping on your own, you'll still find plenty of useful information in these pages.

You'll also get more than the usual dose of natural history here. Wherever possible, I've included not only the Portuguese common names of plants and animals but their Latin (or scientific) names as well. Don't take this as scholarly one-upmanship; if you ever want to read and learn more about a particular animal, you'll find it much easier with the Latin name than with a score of contradictory common names.

Finally, I've tried to stress conservation. The Brazilian government is beginning to sit up and take notice of the ruckus created by international conservation groups (many of which are listed in the chapter on Amazônia). A recent proposal to reduce Brazil's national debt in return for rain forest protection holds much promise, and the ball is now in our court. Get involved, but don't forget to enjoy the world you're fighting to protect.

Chapter 1

Brazil: Background

GEOGRAPHY

Geographically speaking, Brazil is not a land of many contrasts. Crystalline shield rocks underlie most of the country and make for a landscape of flat horizons, consisting mainly of hilly uplands, plateau, and low-lying mountains. Even before the scientific community accepted the theory of plate tectonics, geologists noted the similarity between landforms in Brazil and southern Africa; we now know that the two continents separated some 65 million years ago.

At the expense of some geological detail, the whole country can be pictured as two vast areas of shield rocks — the Guyana Highlands and the Brazilian Highlands — neatly divided by the Amazon River basin. The Guyana Highlands extend from Venezuela and the Guianas into the northern Brazilian states of Amapá, Pará, Roraima, and Amazonas. The Brazilian Highlands run northward from Argentina to the Amazon River Basin; the two highlands almost touch at Óbidos, where the Amazon Basin narrows to less than 2 km in width.

These highlands represent some of the oldest geological formations on earth, ancient crystalline rocks such as granite, gneiss, and schist. Such shield rocks are easily eroded, and the low rolling topography of both highlands testifies to the work of billions of years of tropical rain. Average elevation of the Guyana and Brazilian Highlands is 900-1200 m, but newer mountains have pushed up in places; the Serra do Espinhaço mountain range in east-central Brazil, for example, boasts the second highest peak in the country (Bandeira, at 2890 m). Pico da Neblina, the tallest mountain at 3014 m, rises out of the Guyana Highlands near the Venezuelan border. More than mere geological curiosities, the Highlands have played a major role in Brazil's boom-and-bust history, for the shield rocks are veined in spots with gold, diamonds, and other semi-precious stones.

From Salvador all the way south to Florianópolis, the Brazilian Highlands plunge to the Atlantic in a series of steep folds. Known as the

Great Escarpment, this mountainous dropoff has historically hampered travel and communication between the coast and interior.

A vast sedimentary basin surrounding the Amazon River separates the two highlands from west to east. The Amazonian floodplain lies perfectly flat for thousands of miles, and geologists estimate that the sediment beneath it may run as much as 4 km deep. The basin is widest at the western edge of Brazil, and slims to a narrow, 2 km-wide ribbon just east of Manaus before expanding again.

There are no volcanic areas in Brazil and, because of the predominance of ancient weathered rocks, no dramatic mountain scenery of the sort seen in the Andean countries.

CLIMATE

Brazil boasts a climate which, like its geography, is remarkably uniform. Draw a line from Recife near Brazil's eastern bulge southwesterly to Paraguay, and you'll have described an area with mean temperatures that vary no more than four degrees Celsius all year long. Only in the extreme south do winter temperatures — and keep in mind that July is the chilly heart of winter down here — plummet to 12°. Frosts occur in parts of São Paulo, Rio Grande do Sul and Paraná — you can buy postcards in Curitiba of their famous 'snowfall' in 1977 — but the areas described in this book rarely get cooler than 22° or warmer than 27° at any time. In terms of temperature, then, 'summer' and 'winter' become pretty meaningless. Daily temperature fluctuations are usually greater than seasonal changes; anyone who has spent an evening aboard a cargo boat in Amazônia can appreciate the old saying, 'Night is the winter of the tropics.'

Rainfall is the chief climatic variable in Brazil. Since everything from mosquito hatches to road conditions to river heights depends on the rain level, much of your itinerary will have to do likewise. The statistics can be deceptive. Judging by annual rainfall alone, Brazil seems neither drenched nor parched. Most of the country receives less than 100 cm, and mean annual rainfall exceeds 200 cm in only a few areas: a thin coastal strip running north from São Luis to French Guiana, portions of eastern Amazonas, and Roraima. Even the notorious 'drought polygon' of north-east Brazil receives, for the most part, between 60 and 100 cm of rain annually. Yet rainy seasons — some more distinct than others, depending on the area — end up dumping much of the year's allotment in a few short months. Precipitation can be surprisingly concentrated even within the space of a single day. Bars and restaurants in Belém do a land-office business during the half-hour of intense rain that drenches the city most afternoons during the wet season. Unfortunately, Brazil's rainfall isn't always so predictable. We've taken boats in the Pantanal because the roads had washed out during the 'dry' season; we've tramped down those same roads, dusty and lined with parched, tinder-dry vegetation, in the 'wet' season. The drought season which normally lasts six months in the north-east had already stretched to four years by 1984. Rainy and dry seasons in Amazônia, the Pantanal, and the north-east coast are discussed in more detail in their respective chapters. Always be prepared for a surprise, however.

HISTORY

Portuguese navigator Pedro Alvares Cabral assumed his ship had been blown off course when he bumped into north-eastern Brazil in April 1500. Cabral was headed for India, and the lucrative spice trade there kept Portugal largely occupied for the next half century. Meanwhile, colonists began exporting *pau do brasil*, a jungle wood which produced both a red dye and a new name for the fledgling colony. By mid-century, wealthy Portuguese colonists in the north-east established sugar cane as a cash crop and imported African slaves to work it. To the south, near present-day São Paulo, Jesuit missionaries and poor Portuguese adventurers began pushing west into the vast interior of Brazil, toward Spanish territory.

Spain and Portugal had already demarcated their claims in South America; the Treaty of Tordesillas ceded most of the continent east of the 45th parallel to the Portuguese crown. The throne was inherited in 1580 by the Spanish, who controlled Brazil for over fifty years. During this period, the Dutch captured a number of important cities on the north-east coast. Portugal regained control of the country, but continued to neglect it for another century and a half.

The feudal principalities established by the crown in north-east Brazil became the most important world source of sugar. But the lower-class colonists near São Paulo had neither the capital nor the desire to establish farms. Instead, they pushed west, searching for gold and Indian slaves. Called *bandeirantes*, these soldiers of fortune clashed violently with Jesuit missionaries protecting the native Indians.

Just as the 17th Century dawned, vast quantities of gold and diamonds were discovered in Minas Gerais. More gold turned up in Mato Grosso and Goiás, and Brazil's first 'boom' began. Gold soon replaced sugar as the colony's economic mainstay; competition from cane-growing Caribbean isles had gradually eroded Brazil's sugar markets. The Portuguese crown took a renewed interest in its colony, extracting heavy taxes on the gold. One particular gold-shipping port assumed preeminence and became Brazil's new capital — Rio de Janeiro.

The Jesuits' success in protecting Amerindians from the slave-trading *bandeirantes* eventually angered the crown. In 1759, all Jesuits were ousted from Brazil. The *bandeirantes* pushed the remaining Indians into the interior; their land was usurped by farmers, gold prospectors, and later, industrialists. São Paulo thus gradually became the wealthiest state in the viceroyalty.

In 1789, Brazilian nationalists under Tiradentes rebelled for the first time against the crown. They failed and were summarily executed, but the stage had been set for independence. When France invaded Portugal in 1808, King João VI sailed to Brazil and from there ruled the Portuguese empire. He returned to the mother country in 1821, leaving his son Pedro in charge of Brazil. A year later, Pedro I refused an order to return and declared Brazil independent. Colonists crowned him constitutional emperor late that year. Brazil is thus the only country in the Western Hemisphere that chose a monarchial system over a republican one following independence.

Pedro I eventually fell into disfavour with the colonists, and they crowned his 15-year old son. Pedro II turned out to be a charismatic and popular ruler, introducing liberal policies, promoting education, and pulling Brazil into a cohesive nation over the next half century. But Pedro's liberalism proved his downfall; his outspoken stance against slavery — abolished in 1888 — alienated the plantation owners, who deposed him and proclaimed the Republic. A series of military and civilian leaders ruled the country for the next forty years, under a 'democratic' constitution which was actually more restrictive than the monarchial one. As for Pedro II, Brazil's most popular ruler died penniless in a French flophouse.

When gold production slowed to a trickle, coffee became the next 'boom crop'. Italian and Japanese immigrants came to work the plantations near São Paulo by the thousands. Amazônia provided the next boom — rubber — and Manaus became the Paris of the Western Hemisphere for a brief time. The end came in 1910, when Asian rubber plantations swiftly out-distanced Brazil's wild harvest.

The military gained control of Brazil during the world depression in the 1930's. Getúlio Vargas ruled for the next 15 years, a popular but iron-fisted dictator who succeeded in setting the country's finances right. He finally permitted elections in 1945, and was re-elected himself in 1950. Corruption marked his second term, however, and Vargas committed suicide four years later.

His elected successor, Juscelino Kubitschek, built the new capital of Brasília and pushed the country near bankruptcy. By 1960, Brazil had become rife with corruption and essentially leaderless, with the military pushing for renewed powers.

The generals made their move in 1964, installing a military dictatorship that would rule for the next 21 years. In 1968, the 'elected' president Marshal Costa e Silva dissolved Congress, exiled the opposition, and censored the press. The succession of military dictators borrowed millions from the International Monetary Fund (IMF), creating an illusion of prosperity and growth. While the world marvelled at the 'Brazilian miracle,' repression and torture came to a peak in the late sixties.

Finally, in 1979, military leaders announced a gradual return to democracry, and Brazil re-opened politically. 1985 saw indirect elections; Tancredo Neves, an elderly and extremely popular statesman, won the presidency over the military's hand-picked candidate. But as Brazilians prepared for a political celebration of Carnaval-like proportions, Neves became ill. He died suddenly on the day before inauguration.

Neves' vice-president José Sarney — a colourless former backer of the military — succeeded him, or tried to. Brazil at that moment was reeling under a series of labour strikes, record unemployment, and runaway inflation that topped 40,000% annually. After an initial period of timid rule, Sarney announced a sweeping economic programme (the Cruzado Plan) similar to Argentina's. He froze prices, abolished the old currency, raised wages and taxes, began implementing land reform, and suspended payment of the huge national debt to the IMF indefinitely. The plan was as flawed as it was bold; black markets sprung up, undermining the plan from the start, strikes accelerated, and Sarney ended up backpedalling on most of the programme.

Brazil's first direct presidential election in 29 years took place in November and December 1989. Fernando Collor de Mello, a wealthy conservative, narrowly defeated charismatic labour leader Luís Inácio da Silva. A former auto factory lathe operator known popularly as 'Lula', da Silva had vowed to suspend debt payments indefinitely.

Brazil currently wavers in economic and political limbo. If anything, things have become worse for the average citizen. In late December 1989, inflation was running at 50% per month, or 600% annually, and in March 1990 Collor de Mello imposed a draconian austerity programme. It is too early to say whether these measures will be successful. Prior to civilian rule, Brazilians could at least cling to the hope that elections would solve their problems; already there are those who support a return to military rule.

It is not overly simplistic to say that all of Brazil's current problems stem from the national debt (*dívida externa*). At US$111 billion, it is the largest in the world, and there is no hope that either interest or capital can ever be repaid. The IMF's 'austerity programmes' only seem designed to extract the bill with recession, unemployment, and hunger. To make matters worse, many creditor nations like the United States have adopted protectionist import laws that prevent Brazil from selling its goods on the open market.

There is only one note of hope in all of this: creditor nations have been discussing recently the possibility of reducing Brazil's debt in exchange for strong conservation measures in the Amazonian rain forest.

PEOPLE

Brazil's population has increased tenfold in the last century, so that it nearly exceeds that of the rest of the continent combined. The 1980 census put the population at 121,077,000, most of whom are concentrated along the narrow coastal strip.

São Paulo, with over 11 million inhabitants, is now the world's third largest city and typifies the disturbing pattern of growth in modern Brazil: rural Brazilians have flocked to the large cities in such numbers that housing, employment, and health needs will never be met. Every urban centre has its *favelas* — pathetic shantytowns, largely populated by refugees from the impoverished and drought-plagued north-east portion of the country.

At the same time, the vast interior states of Pará, Amazonas, Goiás and Mato Grosso contain less than one person per square kilometre. The country's leaders have been trying to lure colonists into the interior for at least three decades now, from the symbolic founding of Brasília near the country's geographical centre to recent land giveaways in Rondônia. They have met with little success.

Brazil is a nation of young people; over half the population is under 20 years of age. Recent surveys indicate that literacy is 76% and that the average life expectancy is 62 years, although both figures seem far too high once you've visited poor rural areas. And Brazil remains a nation of poor people: 1% of the population controls 45% of all the agricultural land; 10% of all Brazilians spend 51% of the national income; and 62% of the work force make less than two minimum wages.

Brazil's cultural mosaic, originally shaped from Portuguese, African, and Amerindian elements, remains unique. Europeans and Amerindians interbred throughout South America, but nowhere else on the continent (with the exception of the Guianas) will you find such a pronounced and widespread African influence. This should come as little surprise: Brazil imported fully 31% of all the slaves sold in the New World while the Spanish-speaking countries together bought a mere 9%. By the beginning of the 19th Century, blacks were the dominant element in the country's population. Whites gradually became more numerous with racial mixing and increased European immigration in the 19th and 20th Centuries. During this period, thousands of Italians, Germans, Poles, and Swiss settled in Brazil, mostly from São Paulo southward. Mosques in cities like Curitiba attest to the country's Lebanese and Syrian immigrants, while the Japanese population of São Paulo is equalled nowhere outside Japan.

Despite this varied racial mix and the sheer size of the country, Brazil has managed to achieve an amazing cultural unity. *Brasileiros* of all skin colours, from Amazonian jungle town to the boutiques of São Paulo, retain a strong and deep-rooted sense of themselves as a distinct people. Along with this goes the national pride in Brazil as the world's greatest 'racial democracy'. Sociologists have been debunking that claim for years, and no objective observer can deny that discrimination and prejudice do exist in Brazil. We've heard some shocking racial slurs levied against '*os pretos*' — often from Brazilians who, in the United States, would themselves be considered coloured!

Still, 'racial democracy' is not entirely a myth. Most Brazilians give at least lip service to the country's strong African heritage. Brazil's most popular author, Jorge Amado, has promoted Afro-Brazilian culture in at least a half-dozen best-selling novels. The words *nego* and *nega* have long been terms of affection, applied to even the blondest of Brazilians. The noticeable lack of racial tension makes far more sense when you realize that Brazilians recognize at least a dozen colour distinctions; a 'black' American, for instance, might be described by Brazilians as either a *morena, morena clara, sarará* or any of ten other names depending on skin colour, hair texture, and facial features. With so many teams playing, it's not easy to choose sides for a racial tug-of-war. And, as a result, there are no Brazilian social classes based on skin colour alone.

The forgotten element in Brazil's 'racial democracy' is the Amerindian. Like all American Indians, Brazil's first immigrants came from Asia some 30,000 years ago via the Bering Strait. The Tupi bands, however, never formed cohesive political units — indeed, many had no concept whatsoever of a leader — and never became "civilized' in the sense of the Mayas, Aztecs, or Incas. Their agriculture, tools, and housing remained primitive; they never developed a written means of communication. Yet it was these Indians who taught the European settlers how to survive in the New World — how to cultivate new crops, how to hunt and fish, how to navigate the rivers and penetrate the jungle. There are now less than 150,000 Amerindians living in Brazil, roughly one-sixth of the estimated population when the Portuguese landed. The now-defunct Indian Protection Service itself was responsible for aerial bombing raids on native villages and other campaigns designed to dispossess Amerindians of their land. The National Indian Foundation (FUNAI), inaugurated in the aftermath of scandals involving the Indian Protective Service, is still largely ineffectual in its attempts to protect native land from gold-seekers, farmers, and ranchers. The tribes themselves have won some recent land battles through demonstrations, road seizures, and the work of charismatic chiefs such as Raoni.

You'll find additional information on Brazilian Indians in Chapter 6.

Chapter 2

Preparations

RED TAPE

Entry requirements

Everyone travelling to Brazil needs a valid passport. Brazil's reciprocal visa requirement means that citizens of countries requiring Brazilians to carry visas (currently including the United States, France, Canada, and Australia) will need a visa *prior to* arriving in Brazil. British, West German, Dutch, Swiss, and Italian citizens do not need a visa, but must show an onward ticket upon entering Brazil (or proof that they can pay for a return ticket, see below. These regulations could change, so check with the local Brazilian consulate before your trip (see addresses below).

Citizens of countries requiring visas must get them by writing or calling the nearest Brazilian consulate. Visas are good for 90 days from the date of entry (*not* the date of issue), and you must arrive in Brazil within 90 days of issuance. Visas allow multiple entries. The consulate will supply you with an application form. To issue the visa, they'll require the following: 1) the completed application form, 2) a passport valid for at least six months from your intended date of arrival, 3) one standard 2 x 3-inch passport photo (colour or b&w), 4) a fee (currently US$10, but this is waived if you apply in person), and 5) proof that you have a round-trip ticket or a means to buy one. This can be either a photocopy of your return ticket, a letter from your travel agent to the consulate stating that you have purchased such a ticket, or a letter from your bank assuring the consulate that you have sufficient funds.

The 90-day visa may be renewed within Brazil for longer stays (but see *Visa Renewals* in Chapter 4 for restrictions).

Other documents

Brazil does not require any proof of immunisation when adults enter the country from North America, Europe, or Australia (children between the ages of three months and six must have proof of polio vaccination). Nevertheless, if you plan to visit either the Amazon or the Pantanal (or if you plan to re-enter Brazil from any country near the Amazon), you should get at the very least a yellow fever immunisation and carry the International Vaccination Certificate as proof (see *Immunisations* in Chapter 3).

If there's even the remotest chance that you'll rent a car in Brazil, bring along your driver's licence — an International Drivers Permit isn't necessary — and a credit card. We've rented before without a credit card, but it required that we furnish the agency with our return airline tickets, a tactic that might not always work (see *Rental cars* in Chapter 4).

Beyond renting a car, credit cards aren't of much use to low- and moderate-budget travellers. See *Receiving money from overseas* in Chapter 4.

NOTE: Make a photocopy of your passport to smooth the way if it's lost or stolen. Also make copies of your return airline tickets; on extended trips, these will suffice in renewing your visa, allowing you to leave the originals with friends or in a hotel safe.

MONEY: HOW MUCH TO BUDGET

Prior to the 1980's, Brazil was one of South America's most expensive countries. The oil crisis, massive foreign debt, and spiraling inflation have devastated the Brazilian economy since then, offering the kind of mixed blessings familiar to all Third World travellers: the same economy which now allows for budget travel is responsible for great suffering on the part of most Brazilians.

Obviously, how much you'll spend depends on your style of travel. Jayne and I generally spend about US$600 per month, or US$10 per day per person; this includes some time spent in both the backcountry and in cities and towns, some camping as well as some paid lodging in houses or budget hotels, all food and drink, transportation by bus, boat, or train, and miscellaneous expenses such as clothing, camping equipment, and entertainment. The most frugal travellers we met in Brazil spent about US$300 per month as a couple.

In towns and cities, a couple can travel almost as cheaply as a single person, since most rooms have double beds and you're charged accordingly. Meals are huge, and as a couple you can often split one, further reducing costs.

Figure that your daily living expenses will be about the same for days spent in the backcountry and days spent in towns and cities. This may seem illogical at first — after all, lodging costs little or nothing at all in the backcountry — but you'll soon find that everything else is pricey as you leave the metropolitan centres. For example, the cost of living in Mato Grosso is double that of São Paulo, due mainly to high food prices. Transportation also gets expensive when you run out of road and have to hire boatmen or four-wheel drive vehicles. Gasoline/petrol is costly in Brazil (they have to import it), and costlier still when it has to be trucked or boated into the wilder regions of the country. Finally, your average price per day will escalate sharply if you plan to rent a car or travel by air.

Average costs of such things as bus travel per kilometre, hotels, car rental, and meals can be found in Chapter 4. You'll find further price information by area in Chapters 5, 6, and 7.

The U.S. dollar is the only reliable medium of exchange in Brazil, whether cash or cheque. Bring the bulk of your money (about 75%) in the form of travellers cheques and the remainder in cash US$. Banks and black marketeers which accept travellers cheques have never once turned down our American Express cheques, and we have exchanged them in virtually every state in Brazil; according to reports, Thomas Cook and Barclays are also accepted, though not quite as widely as American Express. Don't bring anything larger than US$50 in either cash or cheque form. The handiest denominations for exchange are US$20 and US$50 notes and cheques. See *Money Matters* in Chapter 4 for a detailed discussion of currency exchange and receiving money in Brazil.

WHAT TO BRING

Whether you're visiting the Amazon, north-east coast, or the Pantanal, remember that you'll often be hauling your luggage around on foot, cramming it into tiny luggage racks in buses, manoeuvering it through mobs of people, suspending it from trees, and stowing it in small boats. Jayne and I get by with a nylon duffle bag and a small day-pack apiece. Any of the non-rigid nylon 'suitcases' will work, but make sure they've got a comfortable shoulder strap. Internal-frame backpacks are another excellent choice; local prejudice against *muchileiros* (backpackers) seems to be waning in Brazil. Avoid standard (rigid) suitcases, and remember that you can always buy cheap nylon bags in Brazil if you need more space. Our luggage doesn't allow for buying much along the way, so we try to plan our trip with a shopping spree at the very end, purchasing extra bags for the trip home.

Clothes

Most people take far more clothing than they need. Again, remember that you can easily buy extra clothing if you need it in Brazil (shoes larger than size 39 are the single exception). Choose clothing that you can easily wash by hand and which dries quickly; if you spend several months in the backcountry, this routine will quickly wear out your clothes, so don't bring anything you can't part with. We generally throw away or give away half the clothing we take to Brazil by the end of a trip.

Take one pair of loose-fitting athletic trousers made of synthetic fabric. These are cool, they pack well, and dry quicky. Bring also a pair of hiking shorts with pockets, and a pair of nylon jogger's shorts. Avoid blue jeans — they're hot, bulky, they soak up water like a blotter, and you'll turn homicidal trying to wash and dry them.

My favorite shirt for all purposes is a loose-fitting cotton/synthetic blend workshirt with long sleeves and snaps rather than buttons. You'll need long sleeves against the sun and insects, and the snaps never catch and pull off in the rain forest. Take also a couple of tee-shirts for beach use and as layering against the cold at night.

Swim suits are a must along the north-east coast — you'll spend virtually all day in them — and they'll see some use in the Amazon if you're bathing in crowded areas. Women should bring a fairly modest swim suit for use in the backcountry to avoid offending the locals.

Rubber sandals (thongs) are invaluable, especially along the north-east coast where they're all the footwear anyone owns. Except in insect-plagued areas, they're also great for jungle camp use in the Amazon, boat travel, and for much of the Pantanal. Unlike shoes, extra pairs can be purchased in Brazil up to size 44.

Take along a pair of tennis or running shoes; they're practical for everything from muddy jungle trails to sandstone cliffs. Some rain forest buffs, including a number of guides and camp workers, swear by army surplus jungle boots, which feature canvas uppers and thicker soles than running shoes. Leave your standard leather hiking boots at home. As noted earlier, if you wear a size larger than size 39 and plan to spend more than a couple months in the hinterlands, bring extra footwear from home.

It doesn't get cold very often in the three areas described in this book, so you needn't pack bulky items like sweaters. The Pantanal can experience cold fronts in June and July, while the Amazon jungle and river boats get chilly at night. Practice layering with tee-shirts, a sweatshirt, or even light-weight polypropylene long underwear in the Pantanal. In Amazônia, bundle up for the night with extra tee-shirts and a wool blanket (see below).

You probably won't spend your entire trip in the backcountry, so bring one set of nice clothes which need no ironing: a short-sleeved dress shirt and a pair of slacks. Dress shoes take up far too much room when toting a single bag, so I get by with a single pair of black leather tennis shoes for both backcountry and city use. As soon as I hit the city I wash off the jungle mud, let them air-dry, and pay a shoe-shine boy to apply some black polish.

You'll want a cap or visor to shade you from the sun, at least in the Pantanal and the north-east coast.

Toiletries

You can buy most toiletries in Brazil, with the following four exceptions: sun screen lotions, especially with protection factors greater than 8; tampons, which are extremely difficult to find, especially in rural towns; contact lens solutions; and moisturizing creams for use on sunburned skin.

Camping, fishing, and wildlife-viewing equipment

If you can get hold of a hammock from Mexico's Yucatan peninsula, do so; they compress to less than half the size of any other hammock I've ever seen, they dry quickly, and they're lightweight. Otherwise, wait until you're in Brazil to buy a hammock and mosquito net (see Chapter 4). Those who aren't comfortable in hammocks may want to bring along an internal-frame mosquito net for use with a sleeping bag. They can also be placed on a bed in mosquito-ridden hotel rooms, and barely weigh more than 1 kg; Long Road Travel Supply, P.O. Box 638, Alameda, California, 94501 U.S.A. markets several models. Bring along a bedsheet to cover yourself in the hammock. In Amazônia, you'll need a wool blanket to keep warm at night, both in the jungle and aboard cargo boats. We prefer, however, to buy these in Brazil just prior to entering the backcountry; then we give them away rather than have them take up valuable space in our luggage.

You'll want to bring along a flashlight (torch) and extra batteries. Anyone visiting the Amazon rain forest who wants to see animals should also carry a headlamp for night walks (see *Night walks in the rain forest* in Chapter 6). Recreational Equipment, Inc. in the U.S. markets a lithium-powered model with two lamps that operates for up to 8 hours on the highest amperage lamp (17 hours on the lower). It uses two 6-volt lithium batteries, and retails with batteries at about US$60. Ray-O-Vac makes a much cheaper model which utilizes a heavy duty 6-volt lantern battery suspended from your belt.

Binoculars are vital for wildlife-viewing in the Pantanal, and helpful at times in the Amazon. We carry a light-weight (20 ounce) 7x35 model, although serious birdwatchers may want an 8-power model.

A camping stove is by far the most practical way to cook in the backcountry. During our first trip to Brazil we packed along a butane stove, but found few places selling Camping Gaz cartridges. For short trips you may be able to bring an adequate supply from home, but remember that it is technically illegal to check such cartridges aboard aircraft. Unfortunately, many of the camping stoves available in the United States and Europe rely on white gas (paraffin), which is virtually unheard of in Brazil. You can manage burning unleaded gasoline in these stoves, but it will produce a dirty yellow flame of lower heat and will constantly plug up the works. Much more practical are multiple-fuel stoves such as the MXR X-GK, or kerosene-burning stoves such as the Optimus 00. Kerosene (*querosene*) is available throughout Brazil and is

dirt cheap. In a pinch, unleaded gasoline can be burned in kerosene stoves.

Some sort of water purification system is essential if you'll be camping, be it chemical treatment or one of the new filter kits. See *Water sterilisation* in Chapter 3 for a list of options.

A small cookset of nesting aluminum pots, along with silverware and plastic cups completes your camp kitchen. Don't forget a small plastic bottle of dishwashing detergent and a dish scrubber or scouring pad.

Bring plenty of strong nylon cord for tying and hanging things in camp, as well as suspending your hammock. Polyethylene sheeting works well as a dry groundcover and as a roof over your hammocks in the rain forest. Get the kind with metal grommets along the edges, allowing it to be stretched tight with cord. This stuff is quite bulky, so don't unpack it from its original bag until you're ready to use it.

Buy several plastic bottles of insect repellent. The best stuff contains 95% DEET (diethyl-meta-toluamide).

A compass is essential for walking in the rain forest. Practice using it before you leave home. Another aid in finding your way back is plastic flagging tape in bright orange or red; you can buy rolls of it wherever surveying equipment is sold (see *Getting lost* in Chapter 6).

Serious anglers will want to bring fishing gear from home. See page 88 in Chapter 5 for recommended tackle; what works in the Pantanal also works in the Amazon. If you're just out for piranhas, you can easily buy hooks and line in Brazil.

Bring at least one plastic water bottle — they're far sturdier than the litre plastic bottles sold in Brazil, which can puncture or crack in your pack.

Miscellaneous

Don't forget your malaria pills and other medicinal items (see Chapter 3).

Clear plastic Ziplock sandwich bags are a traveller's godsend. We pack everything from matches to pills to dishwashing equipment in Ziplock bags, and they invariably take up less space than the original container. Bring along plenty of extras.

You'll use a pocket knife hundreds of times in a trip; try to get one with scissors. Bring slow-burning candles to cope with the frequent power blackouts in the backcountry towns. Film is difficult to find and very expensive, so bring far more than you think you'll need from home, along with all other photographic equipment, including extra photocell batteries and a tripod (see *Photography* in Chapter 4 for more information).

Buy a fabric money pouch for concealing your valuables under your clothing. These are available in many travel accessory stores, and are far superior to leather money belts worn outside the clothing. The pouch should be large enough to hold your passport, with a thin elastic strap securing it around your waist. See *Safety* in Chapter 3 for more details.

Additional items you may want to bring along include: spare glasses or contact lenses, glasses prescription, sunglasses, Portuguese-English dictionary and phrasebook, photos of your home, family, and friends, postcards from home (your new-found Brazilian friends will want to see these), a sewing kit, pens and notebooks, a hand-held calculator (for figuring currency exchange), a battery-operated travel alarm clock (much wildlife-watching requires that you get up before dawn), toilet paper, and earplugs for noisy hotels or night buses.

Brazil allows you to enter the country with two litres of liquor. If you know anyone living there, take them some good Scotch whisky; the real stuff is a status symbol in Brazil and extremely expensive. Bring a couple of bottles even if you don't know a soul — you're bound to make friends. You can also sell it at an enormous profit, though this isn't quite legal.

LEARNING THE LANGUAGE

With the obvious exceptions of money and passport, the most valuable thing you can possibly take with you on the plane to Brazil is a rudimentary knowledge of Portuguese. Nothing else is spoken outside the large cities.

I once listened in on an American bragging to his breakfast companions that he could communicate virtually anything with body language, gestures, and facial expressions. 'The eyes speak,' he said. As soon as the waiter appeared, however, Mr. Body Language relied on his bilingual Brazilian friend to order breakfast. I was crestfallen; I'd been anxious to see how he was going to order scrambled eggs, toast, and black coffee with those eloquent eyes of his.

This doesn't mean that you have to be fluent before catching the plane. For that matter, we have known gringos who managed to stumble into some fairly remote backwaters with nothing more than hand signals and sheer bravado. Headed out of Santarém on the way to the jungle gold fields of Serra Pelada, we met a German who had somehow found his way there — apparently by bus — without knowing the word for bus station. Then there was the Israeli who'd spent three months in Brazil and couldn't count to ten in Portuguese. When he needed to bargain, he would get out his pen and scribble numbers. When he needed a bathroom, he merely pointed to his crotch.

While it's possible to travel this way — like a pinball bouncing blindly from post to post — it can't be much fun. From a purely practical standpoint, the inability to communicate costs both time and money. There can even be an element of danger involved; the linguistically deficient river traveller may not discover the meaning of the words *cascata perigosa* until his canoe is pitching headfirst down a frothy chute.

Travellers who can speak some Portuguese, on the other hand, will find themselves invited into homes, given lifts, fed meals, and far more importantly, offered friendship. Brazilians are a gregarious people, even more so than most South Americans; if you do more than ask directions in Portuguese, you'll be included in all sorts of cultural activities, the kind of things that transform a mere tourist into a traveller. We've ended up guests at rural weddings and pig barbecues, birthday parties and basketball games, gone catfish fishing and wild-fruit browsing.

Leave your Spanish at the border. Brazilians are fond of saying that 'Spanish is but Portuguese badly spoken,' which fairly sums up their pride in the national tongue. Speaking *castelhano* — as Brazilians refer to Spanish — will neither earn you friends nor get you very far. Many Brazilians can understand rudimentary Spanish, but sadly, it doesn't work the other way around. Even native Spanish speakers throw their hands up in exasperation when forced to decipher spoken Portuguese for the first time. A Mexican friend of ours who boarded a Rio-bound jet Varig jet confident in his ability to understand this sister tongue found himself, within five minutes, begging the flight attendant to speak English. The similarities between the two languages become far more obvious in print; Spanish speakers will have little trouble reading signs, newspapers, and documents in Portuguese.

For a select list of Portuguese grammar books, see the *Bibliography*. I've recommended some tapes and records as well, since they're an excellent way to learn pronunciation. Still, nothing beats a tutor. For US$10 per hour, Jayne and I hired a Brazilian woman to converse with us one hour a week for several months before our first trip. It turned out to be the best travel investment we've ever made.

Not surprisingly, Brazil boasts a number of distinctive regional accents (*sotaques*), but don't let that discourage your language studies. Our first day in the arid badlands of north-east Brazil came as a linguistic shock; sharing the back of a flatbed truck with thirty leathery *sertanejos*, we had to wonder if this was the same language taught by our city-bred tutor from the south of Brazil. It didn't help that the average passenger owned less teeth than a professional hockey player. Nevertheless, they understood *us* perfectly, and before the day was out we had begun to adjust ourselves to their sing-song, hillbilly version of Portuguese.

GETTING THERE

Airline tickets to Brazil vary greatly in price, and you can save enormous amounts by planning your trip well in advance. For example, Jayne and I were just about ready to dish out US$1400 per round-trip ticket to Rio from our home in the north-west United States when we found a fare on LAP (Líneas Aéreas Paraguayas) which cut that cost to US$900 per ticket. Unfortunately, prices and airline routes change all the time, so the information below is necessarily vague.

Work through a travel agent — many specialise in South America and are able to discount tickets bought in bulk. But do your own fare and route research before signing the cheque to make sure you're getting the best deal. Constantly check ads in the travel section of your newspaper;

your travel agent may not deal with a particular airline offering budget fares, and you can either bring such fares to his/her attention or else deal with the agent advertising them. Many agents will assume you want to fly directly to your destination — New York to Rio, for example — even when a two-hour layover in Asunción might save you hundreds of dollars. Ask to see your agent's IATA airlines' schedule book and learn how to use it. Even good agents don't have the time to research creative and unusual routes, and we've discovered some on our own with the IATA 'Bible'. Remember, however, that some budget airlines (including LAP) are non-IATA. In many cases, the cheapest fare will end up being a circuitous route with several airlines rather than a direct one (Miami-Guadeloupe-Cayenne-Belém, for example). Airline fares obey no human laws of logic or reason; never assume that the lengthiest route is the most expensive.

Direct flights from Europe

From London, both Varig and British Airways fly to Rio and São Paulo, the latter twice weekly. Air France flies to both Rio and Recife from Paris. Lufthansa provides service from Germany to Rio and São Paulo. TAP runs flights from Lisbon to Rio and Recife. Iberia, SAS, and Swissair also serve Rio from Europe. Cheap charter flights are reportedly available, especially from Lisbon and Madrid. JLA (Journey Latin America) is an excellent source of bargain flights; telephone 081 747 8315. Also try Trailfinders (071 938 3366), Wexas (071 584 8113) and Viceroy Worldwide (071 627 5959).

Direct flights from the U.S. and Canada

From Los Angeles, both Varig and JAL fly twice a week to Rio (with a stop in Lima) and then on to São Paulo. Pan Am runs a daily Los Angeles-Rio-São Paulo flight. Flying time averages about 13 hours from Los Angeles. Varig, Pan Am, LAP, and Aerolíneas Argentinas all fly to Rio from Miami, though not all directly. Flight time from Miami is about seven hours. You can also reach Manaus twice weekly from Miami on either Varig or LAB; Vasp (until recently a strictly internal carrier) is now running flights from Miami to Manaus, then on to Rio, but this may not continue. Pan Am flies from Dallas and Houston to Rio. Varig offers flights once a week from Miami to Belém, then on to Recife and Salvador. Varig and Pan Am fly to Rio from New York (flight time around nine hours), while Canadian Pacific provides service from Toronto to Rio. Flights from Miami are generally the cheapest, even if you live much closer to Los Angeles, as we do. As mentioned before, be sure to get a fare quote from LAP on their cheap but often overlooked Miami-Asunción-Rio flight. Manaus may well be the cheapest airfare destination in Brazil from the U.S., so even if you're headed to Belém, the Pantanal, or the Northeast coast, you should investigate the cost of a flight to Manaus followed by a domestic flight rather than flying to Rio.

Flights from Australia

No airline currently offers direct flights to Brazil, so it's probably best to fly QANTAS to Mexico City via Tahiti, then change for Brazil. Alternatively, fly Lan Chile from Tahiti to Santiago and change there. I'm told that many Australians combine trips to South America and Europe, since it's scarcely more expensive to visit Europe than Brazil.

Brazil Airpass

While the Brazil Airpass offers flights entirely within Brazil, it deserves mention here because you can only purchase it from a travel agent *outside* the country. For US$330 the Air Pass allows you virtually unlimited flights to all state capitals within Brazil over a 21-day period. There's a second Air Pass option as well, restrictions exist on both of them, and neither one seems particularly worthwhile for backcountry travellers; see page 45 in Chapter 4 for details.

Extended Trips

Most economy airline tickets stipulate a stay of less than 90 days (charter flights often restrict you to three weeks or less), so if you plan to spend more time in Brazil you'll be restricted to standard fares which cost considerably more money. There's no way around it.

For those of us requiring a visa, there's also the problem of the onward-ticket stipulation of the Brazilian government: no return ticket, no visa. 'Open-ended' airline tickets are available for stays of up to a year, but you may have to pay any return-trip fare increases that occur during that time. Obviously, you'll also have to decide ahead of time which Brazilian city you'll be flying from, which puts a damper on free-wheeling travel. Finally, carrying a return ticket around for months on end gets to be a security worry. One solution already mentioned is a letter to the Brazilian consulate from your bank assuring them that you have sufficient funds to get home. Some travellers told us they sold back their return ticket but kept the travel agent's receipt to show the authorities; this ruse may work for the initial 90-day visa, but I can't imagine it would work for a visa renewal within Brazil.

Long-term visitors not requiring a visa were once better off buying a one-way ticket to Brazil and worrying about the return ticket later. As of three years ago, however, the government began charging a whopping 25% tax on international airline tickets sold within Brazil. So you're best off either buying an open-ended two-way ticket at home or else leaving Brazil by overland routes and flying home via another South American country.

Anyone planning a trip over six months should refer to *Visa Renewals* in Chapter 4 before fixing an itinerary.

Overland routes

From Venezuela, the only point of entry is the border at Santa Elena. Overland travellers may take the daily buses from either Carácas,

Ciudad Guayana, or Ciudad Bolívar to El Dorado, at which point the paved road ends and you must catch one of the daily jeeps to Santa Elena (8 hours, US$10). Alternatively, Orinoco operates a direct daily bus from Ciudad Bolívar all the way to Santa Elena (20 hours, US$10). Collective jeep-taxis also leave for Santa Elena from Tumeremo, a town north of El Dorado; travellers report that it may be easier to catch a jeep here than further down the line at El Dorado, by which time it may be full. The trip is scenic but rough, and all vehicles get stopped frequently by Venezuelan border police. Those who want to avoid all this can catch one of the daily flights from Ciudad Bolívar to Santa Elena. An União Cascavel bus leaves Santa Elena daily around 0700 for Boa Vista, Brazil (9 hours, US$5). Exit stamps and other border formalities take an additional two hours.

From Bolivia, travellers may enter Brazil nearest the Pantanal by catching the *ferrobus* train from Santa Cruz to Quijarro; the train used to run three times a week but the schedule varies. Get a visa at the Brazilian consulate in Santa Cruz or you'll be turned back at the border. Taxis, collectives, and buses meet the *ferrobus* in Quijarro and take travellers over the Paraguai River to Corumbá, Brazil. This area is rife with cocaine and alligator-hide smugglers, and plainclothes police on both sides of the border make frequent and often unpleasant searches of baggage and clothing. A second point of entry from Bolivia is at Guayaramerín on the banks of the Mamoré River. Get an exit stamp in town and take the ferry across the river to Guajará-Mirim, Brazil; from there, bus and riverboats travel to the Amazonian metropolises of Porto Velho and Manaus.

The only route from either Peru or Colombia involves a border crossing along the Amazon River (this portion above the confluence with the Rio Negro is known in Brazil as the Solimões). From Peru, riverboats leaving Iquitos are virtually the only option; some cargo boats go all the way downriver to Manaus, but most go only as far as Ramón Castilla, near the border towns of Tabatinga, Leticia, and Benjamin Constant (two days, around US$15). Travellers requiring a visa to enter Brazil should get it in Iquitos; all boats stop for Peruvian exit stamps at a river post called Puerto Alegría, two hours upstream from Benjamin Constant. Canoes run from Ramón Castilla across the river to Benjamin Constant, Brazil. Virtually all boats headed downriver to Manaus leave from Benjamin Constant. Canoes also go from Ramón Castilla to Tabatinga, Brazil on the opposite bank from Benjamin Constant. Entry to Brazil from Colombia is via Leticia; motorized canoes will take you from here to Benjamin Constant.

From Paraguay, travellers headed for the Pantanal may cross the border at Pedro Juan Caballero. The 'border' here is nothing more than a wide, dusty boulevard, and travel is totally unrestricted to Ponta Porã, Brazil on the other side. You must have an exit stamp from Paraguay, however, before going any further into Brazil. Buses leave Ponta Porã daily for Campo Grande, Brazil. A second point of entry is at Puerto Stroessner, a Paraguayan casino town near the Iguaçu Falls and the huge Itaipu dam. Simply take a bus across the 'Friendship Bridge' to Foz do Iguaçu, Brazil.

It's not possible to enter Brazil overland from Suriname. Only French and Brazilian citizens can enter Brazil from French Guiana at Saint-Georges (this according to our friend Robert, an immigration policeman in French Guiana; check in Cayenne to see if things have changed). From Guyana, you must fly first from Georgetown to Lethem (a road is planned in the future), then cross the Takutu river by boat, and finally walk or hitch 3 km to Bom Fim. A bus departs Bom Fim daily in the afternoon for Boa Vista, from where there is daily bus transport to Manaus.

WHEN TO GO AND HOW LONG TO SPEND

The Pantanal, the Amazon — and the Northeast coast to a lesser extent — all have periods of the year when travel is best, mostly weather-dependent. But those periods vary somewhat depending on what you plan to do and see. Read the sections on *When to go* in Chapters 5, 6, and 7 for details by area. In general, the best time to see the three regions described in this book would be between late June and early October, avoiding the rainy seasons as well as the hordes of Brazilians on vacation.

Backcountry travel requires more time than, say, a whirlwind tour of major Brazilian cities. For this reason you probably shouldn't attempt a visit of less than two weeks. Even so, you won't have time to sample more than two of the three regions described in this book on a 14-day jaunt. Jayne and I have never felt it worth our airfare to spend less than a month in Brazil. If you do plan a trip lasting less than a month, you should definitely fly between 'gateway' cities rather than taking the bus.

GETTING INFORMATION

Brazil's National Tourism Authority (EMBRATUR) operates offices in many countries that will mail general information and brochures on request. In the U.S. write or call the Brazilian Tourism Board, 551 Fifth Ave., Suite 421, New York, NY 10176, phone (212) 286-9600; in Great Britain the address is 32, Green St, London W1Y 4AT, phone 01 499 0877. The office in Germany has been temporarily closed at the time of this writing and plans are to relocate.

Brazilian Consulates/Diplomatic Offices
United States
   Brazilian Consulate General, 630 Fifth Ave., New York, Room 2720, NY 10111, phone (212) 757-3080. Consulates in San Francisco, Los Angeles, Washington, D.C., Atlanta, Miami, Dallas, Chicago,

Houston, and New Orleans.

Canada
   Brazilian Embassy, 255 Albert St., Suite 900, Ottawa, Ont. K1P-6A9.

Great Britain
   Brazilian Consulate, 32 Green St, London W1Y 4AT, phone 071 930 9055.

West Germany
   Kennedy Allee 74, 5300 Bonn 2, phone 228 3720 91.

France
   1, rue Miolis, nr. 17, 75732 Paris, phone 1 4568 2900.

Australia
   19 Forster Crescent, Yarralumla, Canberra, ACT 2600, phone 62 73 2372.

Chapter 3

Health and Safety

HEALTH

This section describes only those problems particular to travel in tropical Brazil. All travellers, and especially those spending long periods of time in the backcountry, should also be prepared to deal with the whole spectrum of common ailments and first aid crises. The *Bibliography* section in the Appendix lists a couple of good reference books.

Before you go

Disease patterns and health regulations constantly change, so get the latest information just before you travel. Americans should write to the U.S. Government Printing Office, Washington, D.C., USA 20402, and request a copy of the most recent *Health Information for International Travel* bulletin published by the U.S. Center for Disease Control. British readers should contact MASTA (Medical Advisory Service for Travellers Abroad); among their many services are a Concise Health Brief giving up-to-date advice on health hazards in specified regions. They also operate vaccination centres and sell tropical supplies (telephone 01 631 4408).

Malaria Malaria is far and away the most serious threat to the backcountry traveller's health. Originally a problem in Africa and Europe, the disease hitched a ride to South America on slave ships during the 19th century. Until recently, malaria killed more people per year worldwide than any other transmissible disease. If you're tempted to downplay the threat in this age of prophylactic drugs, remember that malaria was a leading cause of casualties in the Vietnam war.

Four species of tiny, one-celled protozoan parasites cause malaria, but only two are widespread in Brazil: *Plasmodium vivax* and *Plasmodium falciparum*. Both are transmitted to humans via the bite of

infected female *Anopheles* mosquitoes. At least five species of
Anopheles — some of which invade houses and prefer human blood —
are known to carry malaria in Brazil. Once in the bloodstream, the
parasite invades and destroys red blood cells; doctors call this the
primary attack, usually marked by chills, high fever, and finally, as the
attack subsides, by a period of extreme weakness and fatigue. Untreated primary attacks of *vivax* or *falciparum* malaria generally last from
two to four weeks, continuing this pattern of alternating chills and fever
bouts. It is possible to be infected with both *vivax* and *falciparum*
parasites at the same time.

Vivax parasites often disappear from the bloodstream for several
weeks, either naturally or following drug treatment. Parasites that
persist in the liver, however, can cause malarial relapses after this latent
period. The natural duration of this cycle may last 12-18 months, but
sometimes as long as four years. *Falciparum* malaria, on the other hand,
has no latent liver stage; when the parasites are gone from the
bloodstream, they are gone for good — at least until the next bite from
an infected mosquito. Untreated *falciparum* malaria lasts about 7-9
months, sometimes as long as a year and a half, and is frequently fatal.

Falciparum malaria is considered the most serious, partly because of
the dangerous complications it can entail (blackwater fever, cerebral
malaria) and also because this species has developed drug-resistant
strains.

Although no drug can prevent malarial infection itself, there are
several that stave off clinical attacks of the disease and may rid the
parasites from your system should you become infected. *Check with a
doctor specializing in travel health or tropical diseases before deciding on
anti-malarial prophylaxis for your trip*. Be aware that medical recommendations change from year to year as new information is available —
the Fansidar scare is a good example — and that health authorities in the
U.S., Europe, and South America often disagree on what works and
what is safe. Recommendations also change depending on which part of
Brazil you're visiting, since drug-resistant malaria strains are reported
from only certain areas.

As of this writing, the U.S. Center for Disease Control is recommending that travellers in Brazil for less than three weeks take routine weekly
doses of 500 mg chloroquine phosphate (sold as Nivaquine in Europe)
and carry a presumptive (healing) dose of three 75 mg tablets of
Fansidar (pyrimethamine/sulfadoxine). The healing dose of Fansidar is
recommended only in case of fever and only when a doctor is not
immediately available. For travellers spending more than three weeks
in Brazil, the USCDC recommends either the regimen above *or*, in
areas of chloroquine-resistant *falciparum* malaria, routine weekly doses
of both chloroquine and Fansidar. Note the cautions in the next
paragraph.

Fansidar use is still being debated by the medics. Back in the early and
mid-1980's, U.S. health officials were recommending routine weekly
doses of Fansidar in chloroquine-resistant malaria areas. Jayne and I

were among the many that dutifully gobbled down our pill every Sunday, and it was only after a year in Brazil that we read the horror stories about Fansidar reactions. Between 1982 and 1987, 24 cases of severe reactions occurred, including seven deaths. All the reactions occurred after a series of weekly doses, none after a single dose, and the risk of death is estimated at between 1 in 11,000 and 1 in 25,000 users. Jayne and I have been told by the University of Washington Travel Health Clinic that travellers such as ourselves who had taken Fansidar on a routine basis for many weeks need not be worried about using it in the future, since we obviously aren't sensitive to the stuff. But to be on the safe side, the USCDC now recommends weekly prophylactic use of Fansidar only in certain areas of Brazil and only when the traveller is spending more than three weeks in the country. Even in these cases, the USCDC cautions that Fansidar should be immediately discontinued if the traveller develops any unusual symptoms such as itching or redness of the skin or mucous membrane, mouth or genital lesions, or sore throat. For travellers outside the resistant-strain areas or those spending less than three weeks in Brazil, the USCDC recommends Fansidar only as a healing dose in case of unexplained fever when a doctor isn't available. Finally, be aware that Brazil has reported strains of *falciparum* malaria that are resistant to both chloroquine and Fansidar. These can be treated by a doctor with quinine or tetracycline.

Proguanil (sold as Paludrine) and amodiaquine are two other anti-malarials sold in Europe that medical authorities can't seem to agree on. The USCDC does not recommend either as a prophylactic, whereas the Malaria Reference Laboratory in London frequently prescribes proguanil along with chloroquine.

Pregnant women should get special counseling. Both malaria and certain anti-malarial drugs are especially dangerous during pregnancy.

Regardless of the drug(s) your doctor recommends, he or she will have you start them before your trip, generally one or two weeks before entering Brazil. This not only builds up a protective supply of the drug in your body, but allows you to get used to the stuff and to see how you react to it. In almost all cases, you're advised to avoid alcohol and to take the pills with meals or with milk so that you don't become nauseous. Get used to taking them on the same day each week, and don't miss a dose. You'll also be advised to continue taking pills for six weeks after you return home.

Always remember that no drug is 100% effective. If you develop any unexplained flu-like symptoms in Brazil or back at home, get to a doctor specializing in travel medicine. We have a friend whose *vivax* malaria appeared after she got home, but was discounted for a long time by doctors unfamiliar with tropical medicine.

For the latest malaria information, write to the Parasitic Diseases Division, Center for Infectious Diseases, Center for Disease Control, Atlanta, Georgia, USA 30333. Or, in Britain, phone the Malaria Reference Laboratory, 01 636 7921.

Immunisations   As of this writing, Brazil does not require any vaccinations for travellers entering the country from North America, Europe, or Australia. You should definitely check with the Brazilian Embassy or Consulate (see Chapter 2 for addresses) just before leaving on your trip, however. Regardless of government requirements, see a physician and consider getting the following vaccinations as 'insurance'. Don't forget to carry your yellow International Vaccination Certificate as proof.

Yellow fever, a mosquito-borne viral infection, is considered endemic in virtually all of Brazil except the coastal strip. Brazilian health authorities advise that the most infected areas are the states of Acre, Amazonas, Goiás, Maranhão, Mato Grosso, Mato Grosso do Sul, Pará, Rondônia, and the territories of Amapá and Roraima. The disease is especially active during the rainy season in forested, sparsely populated areas drained by tributaries of the Amazon. While yellow fever is serious — fatalities occur in up to 50% of the severe cases — a safe, effective, and long-lasting vaccine has existed for many years. These shots are good for ten years, and every traveller visiting Amazônia or the Pantanal should get one. Indeed, Brazilian authorities sometimes require proof of vaccination when travellers enter from Venezuela, Colombia, Ecuador, and Bolivia. Even within Brazil you may be required to show your immunisation card or be re-vaccinated at certain checkpoints (Vilhena on the BR-364 highway between Porto Velho and Cuiabá is an example).

Hepatitis is an infection of the liver caused by one of several viruses. Travellers in Brazil are mostly at risk from the form known as hepatitis A, which is spread via contaminated food or water. Symptoms may include high fever at the onset, jaundice, weakness, loss of appetite, nausea, and brown or tea-colored urine. There is no specific medical treatment except bed rest. At best, hepatitis A disappears within 4-6 weeks, so it can easily finish your vacation; deaths are extremely rare. Safeguard yourself with an injection of immune (gamma) globulin before leaving home. For prolonged trips, shots are recommended every five months; gamma globulin is widely available from doctors and pharmacists in Brazil when it's time to re-immunise.

Consult with your physician and consider immunisations for tetanus, typhoid, diphtheria, and polio as well.

Water sterilisation   Decide on a water sterilisation programme that best suits your trip and budget (see page 27), and buy the necessary equipment or chemicals before you leave.

Teeth   Have a dental check-up before you go. You can buy an excellent emergency dental kit in Britain which is every bit as useful as a first aid kit.

Insurance   Ask your travel agent about health insurance during your trip. Also write IAMAT (International Association for Medical Assistance to Travellers), 350 Fifth Avenue, Suite 5620, New York, NY,

USA 10001 for advice on this topic and a list of recommended English-speaking doctors in Brazil.

In Brazil
Insects, parasites, and other pleasantries

Teddy Roosevelt wrote: 'South America makes up for its lack ... of large man-eating carnivores by the extraordinary ferocity or blood-thirstiness of certain small creatures.' Unfortunately, the story doesn't end there. Not content merely to sting, bite, and otherwise puncture us, many of these small creatures like to leave us with even smaller, more insidious creatures swimming around in our systems.

Malaria, leishmaniasis, yellow fever, river blindness, and Chagas' disease, among others, are all transmitted by insects. Avoiding contact with host insects is therefore the most obvious way to stay healthy. An ounce of prevention, after all, is worth a pound of cure — especially since some of these diseases are practically incurable. You'll never outfox the mosquitoes, *mutucas*, *piums*, and sandflies 100% of the time; you're dealing with insects that often bite through clothing and invariably find their way inside your mosquito-netting. Nevertheless, not all mosquitoes carry malaria, and not all sandflies carry leishmaniasis; each bite you avoid therefore increases your chances of staying healthy.

Mosquito netting is a must. If you're not using a hammock, consider a lightweight internal-frame mosquito net, which works equally well with a sleeping bag or in bug-ridden rooms over a bed; Long Road Travel Supplies market several models (see the advertisement on page 10). Bring repellent. You may have to apply this under your clothing as well as on exposed skin. Staying inside during the evening helps. In many jungle areas, this is a superfluous bit of advice; you'll be beseiged by an almost opaque mass of mosquitoes as soon as the sun dips below the treeline. Planning your trip to avoid the rainy season can help reduce your insect worries. Finally, some disease-carrying insects such as the *barbeiro* require certain specific environments which you can steer clear of.

Chagas' disease (American Trypanosomiasis)   This one is the work of yet another protozoan, *Trypanosoma cruzi*, transmitted by some six species of biting bugs in rural areas of Brazil. All six species are known collectively as *barbeiros*. One version has it that the striped bug resembles a barber's pole; others claim that the name derives from the bug's habit of biting mostly on the cheek. The *barbeiro* hides during the day, favouring thatched roofs and the deep cracks in mud walls. Naturally enough, Jayne and I first learned of the *barbeiro* only days before we visited a village composed entirely of mud-and-wattle huts with thatched roofs. Jayne finally approached one of the locals and asked the question point-blank: 'Tem barbeiro por aqui?' 'Tem,' nodded the old man, as the blood drained from Jayne's face. Then he added that the gentleman in question lived just up the path and would probably cut our hair for 200 *cruzeiros* a head.

The *barbeiro* — the six-legged one, that is — leaves its hiding place at night, feeding on humans as well as wild and domestic animals. Thousands of *barbeiros* can infest a single house, and bedrooms are normally prime habitat. The *barbeiro* defaecates as it bites, and parasites generally enter the bloodstream when the faeces are rubbed into the wound. The bite itself is often benign, and there may be no immediate symptoms in adults. Trypanosome parasites continue to multiply, however, invading the heart and other tissues. Heart damage and digestive problems may only surface ten to twenty years following infection, and sudden heart failure is not uncommon. Diagnosis is extremely difficult. We've met several people — all Brazilians from rural areas — suffering from Chagas' disease, and health officials estimate that 5% of Brazil's population is infected.

Since there is no drug both safe and effective against Chagas' disease, you'll have to protect yourself from *barbeiros*. If at all possible, avoid spending the night in mud-and-wattle houses; mud houses with smooth plastered walls and roofs of metal or tile are seldom colonized by the *barbeiro*. Hammocks and mosquito nets further decrease the risk, since adult *barbeiros* are poor fliers.

Leishmaniasis 'Leish' is the result of yet another insect-born protozoan, *Leishmania braziliensis*, and a particularly nasty one at that. Three forms of the disease exist, although all involve leprosy-like sores and lesions of the soft tissues, particularly the nose, mouth and lips. Fatal cases are rare, and it is a disease that, unlike malaria, is rarely contracted by travellers. Jayne and I stayed in a jungle camp in Amazônia which had reported 13 cases of the disease within a three-month period in 1987, but all were camp workers who had spent many months at the site. Still, leishmaniasis' hideous toll of disfigurement and its equally unsavoury cure — injections of poisonous sodium antimony gluconate — make it well worth avoiding. The parasite is carried via the bite of the small, creamy-white jungle sandfly *Phlebotomus*. Locals have told us that the bite is painless, and nothing may be apparent until the appearance of small sores on the skin. Once again, prevention is everything; the veteran camp workers in our leish-plagued area of Amazônia entered the jungle only with long-sleeved shirts buttoned at the collar and cuffs, and long trousers with socks rolled up over the pants legs. As a further safeguard, spread a film of good insect repellant on all exposed skin. Any unusual sores or lesions should be examined by a specialist in tropical parasitology immediately.

Onchocerciasis (River Blindness) River blindness is caused by tiny nematode worms transmitted via the bite of either black flies or certain species of buffalo gnats. The disease owes its common name to the fact that immature black flies live attached to rocks in swift-flowing streams, and most infections occur within 10-20 km of such fast water. Untreated, the microparasites often lodge in the cornea, causing blindness. Northern Amazonas state near the Venezuelan border and much of Roraima Territory are considered problem areas. (The Pantanal, since it is a land of mostly sluggish water, does not present much of a threat from river blindness). Adult black flies bite only outdoors and only during the daylight hours. Their bite is painless, however, and insect repellents are reported to be of little value. Thus, there is no way to be certain of avoiding the disease. Fortunately, river blindness is very rarely contracted by travellers. If you begin to develop unusual skin rashes (particularly on the thighs, shoulders, arms, or head) after 12 to 20 months of being in an endemic area, consult a specialist immediately. Chemotherapy is the current cure.

Bicho de pé   These jiggers (alternatively known in Portuguese as *chigões*) are more a nuisance than a threat. That's comforting news, because this tiny flea (*Tunga penetrans*) is quite common on the beaches of the north-east coast, particularly near fishing villages where pigs, chickens, and dogs roam the shoreline. In this kind of habitat, a fertilized female *Tunga* will hop about in search of a suitable host, penetrating any small crevice in the skin. She'll especially favour cracks between the toes, on the soles of the feet, and around the toe-nails, but any part of the body within hopping distance is fair game; more than one beach camper has found *bichos de pé* lodged in their buttocks. Once attached, the female *Tunga* burrows beneath the surface of the skin, swelling to the size of a small pea within 8-12 days and laying her eggs. When the eggs hatch a new generation of *bichos de pé*, the mother flea dies and is expelled, leaving a small sore. I have a biologist friend who finds this so fascinating that he allows the whole process to go unhindered so that he can watch. To avoid turning your body into a parasitology experiment, check your feet daily; enlarge the *bicho's* entrance hole with a sterilized needle and remove her with a forceps. Be sure to get the entire animal, including the burrowing mouthparts, and spread alcohol over the sore.

Botflies   The discovery of botfly larvae growing to maturity in a lump beneath your skin is surely one of the tropics' more repulsive surprises. So you'll be glad to know — if you manage to retain your cool, scientific detachment about the whole thing — that there is nothing particularly dangerous about botflies. Because adult botflies are large and slow-moving, they like to lay their eggs via the bite of other flying insects like the *mutuca*. Swelling and minor discomfort accompanies the growth of the larval flies. Some people remove the larvae with forceps, or by smothering them with Bandaids and airplane glue; in either case, you run the risk of infection. It's best to simply wait until your return to civilization, where a doctor can remove the larvae and sterilize the wound. In Amazonia watch out for the *toucandeiro*, a **black ant** about an inch long whose bite is so supernaturally painful that the Amerindians use it for initiation rites. The *toucandeiros* I've seen always seemed to live at the base of trees, swarming out of their hole when disturbed. There is also a species of biting termite (*cupim*) active at night in Amazônia; if you're inclined to wander in the forest barefoot, you probably deserve an occasional nip.

Other health problems

Conjunctivitis   This infectious disease turns the whites of the eyes pinkish, and is accompanied by itching, pain, and a gritty feeling in the eyelids. Conjunctivitis reaches almost epidemic proportions along the coastal areas of Brazil, but fortunately is not serious. Doctors can prescribe antibiotics, but I've never known anyone in Brazil who actually bothered to treat conjunctivitis; it's one of those irritations of travel that goes away on its own within a week or so.

AIDS   In late 1988 it was estimated that over one million Brazilians had contracted AIDS, placing it right after the United States and France in total number of cases. Any sexual contact, either hetero- or homosexual, puts you at risk. Brazilian-made condoms (*preservativos*) are available at virtually all pharmacies, of course, but quality-control is lax; you are far safer bringing a supply from home. Incidentally, our favorite Brazilian slang for condom is *camisinha de Venus* — 'Venus' little shirt.' If you expect to receive vaccinations in Brazil, consider taking along a sterile needle pack, available from MASTA in Britain (telephone 01 631 4408). These precautions should also safeguard you from hepatitis B, which is contracted in the same way as AIDS.

Sunburn   The equatorial sun can burn right through light cotton clothing and sun shades. Sitting in the shade, we've been burned by sunlight reflected off sand and water. Use a PABA-based sunscreen; don't expect to find sun protection above a number 4 in Brazilian pharmacies, except in Rio and São Paulo.

Traveller's diarrhoea and other intestinal problems   The causes of TD are still at issue. Medical authorities generally claim that TD is due simply to faecally-contaminated food or water, while some of us have a hunch that all kinds of other things come into play: a change in diet, the heat and humidity, the stress of arrival in a strange land. (Witness the fact that visitors from South America frequently get sick when they visit our own, spotlessly hygienic nations.)

Everyone agrees on one point, however: sooner or later, you're bound to get a case of TD. Besides diarrhoea itself, symptoms may include stomach cramps, nausea, bloating, and fever. To lessen your chances of coming down with the trots, most doctors recommend that you follow these simple guidelines: Don't buy food from street vendors or eat at public market stalls. Don't drink tap water (*agua de torneira*) or even brush your teeth with it — drink only bottled water, sterilized water, or soft drinks. Likewise, avoid drinks with ice cubes, locally-made popsicles and flavoured ices, which are generally made from tap water. Avoid salads, dairy products, uncooked fish or vegetables, fly-ridden foods, and any fruit you haven't peeled yourself.

Excellent suggestions, every last one of them. Someday I'm going to meet a backcountry traveller who has managed to follow them all — or even most of them — and maintained his/her sanity.

The problem, of course, is that not only will you miss a good deal of pleasurable eating and drinking following this regimen, but you may well end up sick regardless. There's no need to get neurotic; just exercise a little caution, particularly in the first week or so of your trip, allowing your digestive system to get acquainted with the new local fauna that will be invading it. Likewise, it is almost impossible to avoid tap- or well-water entirely, but don't be drinking tumblers of the stuff if something else is available. When camping in the backcountry, sterilize the water (see page 27). The prejudice against street vendors seems unwarranted to plenty of us who've travelled extensively in the Third World; their food is freshly cooked, sells quickly, and I've never once taken sick after eating it. On the contrary, my few bouts with stomach ailments in Brazil came after restaurant meals. Similarly, editor Hilary Bradt got her only dose of Brazilian food poisoning from Manaus' poshest hotel! As for salads, dairy products, and uncooked vegetables, they're such a welcome treat in Brazil that I prefer to take my chances.

There are perhaps as many remedies for traveller's diarrhoea as there are travellers. The trend nowadays is away from the old 'quick cures' like Lomotil, Kaopectate, Imodium, Enterovioform, Kaolin and the host of other anti-diarrhoea medicines available in South American pharmacies. Most of these simply prolong the problem and may actually make things worse. Tests now show that prophylactic use of the ever-popular Lomotil actually increases the incidence of TD. Enterovioform is responsible for some serious neurological side-effects and its use is being strongly discouraged. And Kaolin apparently interferes with the absorption of the most commonly-used anti-malarial drug, chloroquine.

Doctors now recommend a simple regimen of rest and liquids. Most sufferers have no problem with the first part, since diarrhoea saps energy. But some people have the notion that if they aren't thirsty, they needn't drink. Nothing could be further from the truth. Thirsty or not, you need to replace the massive amounts of liquids and body salts lost during a bout of TD; remember that the dehydration associated with diarrhoea is a major killer of infants in Third World countries. The U.S. Center for Disease Control recommends the following drink for sufferers of diarrhoea: Mix eight ounces of fruit juice with a teaspoon of sugar or honey and a pinch of salt. In a second glass, dissolve one quarter teaspoon of baking soda in eight ounces of water. Alternate sips from these two glasses, and repeat the ritual at least four times a day. Carry plastic sachets or film canisters of baking soda, salt, and sugar just so you're ready.

Drink as much water and/or fruit juice as possible, but avoid alcohol (including beer), caffeine, and foods that are spicy or greasy. Your symptoms should begin to disappear within four or five days; if not, get yourself to a doctor. If a doctor isn't immediately available or your situation warrants it — a long bus trip, for example — go ahead and try Imodium or Lomotil as a short-term 'cork.'

Both fever and cramps are normal during a bout of traveller's diarrhoea. Extremely painful cramps, high fever, and/or blood in the stool, however, may mean that you've got one of various forms of dysentery. As with diarrhoea, drink plenty of fluids, but get yourself to a doctor immediately. Dysentery is serious.

The symptoms of food poisoning often resemble those of traveller's diarrhoea, but they are generally more severe and almost invariably involve vomiting. Fortunately, food poisoning is usually much shorter-lived, often disappearing overnight. Treat food poisoning as you would diarrhoea, with plenty of rest and liquids.

Fungal infections   These are common only in Amazônia, where the oppressive humidity creates ideal conditions for fungal growth. The primary symptom is a persistent itchy rash, and the most common infection sites are the crotch, feet, and armpits. Bathe in cool jungle streams as often as possible, and dust yourself with talc or a fungicidal powder such as Tinactin or Tinaderm. Wear light, loose-fitting clothes made of synthetic fabrics, and no underwear. If the insects allow you, wear sandals in camp. We wear the same clothes every day during jungle treks, but save a second set of dry clothing strictly for camp use. (Remember that in the rain forest, 'dry' is a relative term meaning that you can't actually wring a cup of water from it.)

Snakebite   Snakes are not nearly as common in tropical forests as people would have you believe. As an amateur herpetologist, I consider snakes a lucky find even after exhaustive searching. John Harrison (author of *Up the Creek*) spent eleven months in the Brazilian bush and saw only seven snakes, five of which were swimming. Remember too that only a small percentage of snakes are actually venomous, and those that are don't always inject poison with every bite; after feeding, for example, venom sacs are often depleted. Most snakebites do not cause death in adults even when untreated. Snakes, after all, have evolved their venom systems primarily to stun small mammals and birds.

The most common venomous snake in the Brazilian rain forest is the fer-de-lance (*jararaca* or *jararacussu*). According to the Butantã Institute in São Paulo, fer-de-lances are responsible for 90% of all the snakebites reported in Brazil. Watch your step in the forest — especially near tree-falls — and wear high-topped jungle boots for protection. If bitten, stay calm; almost all snakebite victims recover without any treatment. Cleanse the wound, try to kill the snake for identification, and attempt to get to a doctor. Do not try to apply a tourniquet or open the wound with a razor — both can do far more harm than the bite itself.

Water sterilisation

David Livingstone, the ultimate backcountry traveller, took pride in drinking water 'swarming with insects, thick with mud, putrid with rhinoceroses' urine and buffalo dung.' Livingstone ended up with dysentery, but he needn't have gone to such extremes to catch it; a crystal-clear, swift-flowing mountain stream is just as likely to harbour infectious disease organisms.

Besides dysentery, the most common water-borne maladies in Brazil are hepatitis and giardiasis, and both are present in the backcountry as well as in city tapwater. It's true that many jungle creeks with few people or livestock living upstream are perfectly safe; we've drunk directly from certain Amazonian streams for days without ill effects. Nevertheless, you can never be certain what lies upstream. Don't trust local wisdom on the subject either; in many cases, the inhabitants of small villages are harbouring chronic water-borne parasites such as *Giardia* without even realizing it.

Prevention is clearly the best strategy here. Three general methods of disinfecting water exist: boiling, adding chemicals, and filtering.

Boiling water for 5-10 minutes at sea level should destroy all viruses and bacteria. Since water boils at lower temperatures with increasing altitude, however, you must remember to increase boiling time at higher elevations. A good rule of thumb is to bring the water to a boil for ten minutes and then continue boiling one minute for every 1,000 feet of elevation. This method works without fail, but also puts a big dent in your fuel supplies.

A second option is chemical treatment. Iodine is one of the oldest and most popular disinfectants, since it destroys almost all water-borne organisms and is sold everywhere. One drop of 2% tincture of iodine added to each pint of water will do the trick, but allow the water to sit for at least twenty minutes before using. A somewhat handier form of iodine is Potable-Aqua; add one tablet per litre of water and wait for at least 10-20 minutes before drinking. The same chemical is also marketed as Globaline and Coughlan's, and has proved effective in preventing virtually all water-borne diseases including dysentery, hepatitis, and giardiasis. With either form of iodine, some experts advise longer disinfection times than the traditional 10-20 minutes. To be absolutely certain of destroying the tough cyst of *Giardia*, let the treated water sit for four or five hours if possible. Iodine has two drawbacks as a disinfectant: persons with thyroid problems may be inadvertently poisoned by doses that are perfectly safe for everyone else; and iodine leaves an unmistakable taste to treated water. The latter problem can be solved by adding a pinch of sodium thiosulfate (available in pharmacies and photographic equipment shops) to each litre of treated water. Powdered fruit drink also makes treated water palatable.

Recently, a number of water filters have invaded the backpacking market. If you choose to go this route, however, don't waste your

money on cheap ones. Most U.S. experts agree that the two best are
First-Need (US$42, replacement filter US$24) and Katadyn (US$185).
Though obviously much cheaper, the First-Need system has several
drawbacks that the Swiss-made Katadyn doesn't: its filters cannot be
cleaned, and must be replaced after four hundred litres of water have
passed through it; it also has a larger pore size than the Swiss product
and therefore does not trap as many microorganisms. The First-Need
and Katadyn systems weigh in at 10.4 ounces and 23 ounces, respec-
tively. Both will remove even the smallest *Giardia* cysts from water.
Neither one has yet proved to eliminate viruses, although Katadyn is
still being tested. The best filter on the British market is the Travel Well,
available from MASTA (Medical Advisory Service for Travellers
Abroad, phone 01 631 4408). Some experts advise a combination of
filtration and chlorination: add ten drops of household bleach to each
quart of filtered water, allowing it to sit for at least an hour before using.

A word about Brazilian pharmacies

Like most Central and South Americans, Brazilians tend to be pill-
crazy. Virtually every city block contains at least one *farmácia*, often
more. I once ran across the 'Pope John XXIII Pharmacy,' which seemed
to epitomize the almost religious faith which Brazilians place in pills and
other get-well-quick nostrums. These *farmácias* will be happy to sell
you, without a prescription, a whole spectrum of drugs that have been
banned as unsafe in North America and Europe. They also advertise
injections of everything from antibiotics to vitamins. For many
Brazilians, *farmácias* take the place of doctors; pharmacists regularly
diagnose illnesses over the counter and sell the 'cure' in one sitting. In
short, don't be expecting the detached sort of professionalism that
you've come to expect at home. These people are here to sell drugs, and
the more the better. Antibiotics are especially popular, and are
prescribed in massive doses for all sorts of ailments (including viruses,
for which they are useless).

Following the pharmacist's lead, many Brazilians feel free to offer
their own medical advice at the drop of a hat. When Jayne became sick
in a small town near the mouth of the Amazon, she was beseiged by
well-meaning folk, each of whom insisted on donating something from
their arsenal of pills and potions for her recovery. We could have
opened our own *farmácia* with the spoils. Never mind that Jayne's
problem was a high fever and chills; we were given everything from
antihistamines to cough remedies to tonics for ailing livers!

Natural remedies

Particularly in the backcountry, you'll be offered various natural
remedies for your ills. During her bout with the fever, Jayne graciously
turned down all the free pills in favor of an herb tea steeped in lemon
and garlic. We'll never know whether her subsequent recovery was due
to this nauseating brew, but natural remedies such as this have one big

advantage over pharmaceuticals: even if they don't actually cure you, they tend to be far more innocuous and a great deal cheaper than pills.

Two of the more common natural remedies are *erva sidreira*, a grass that combats insomnia, and *jambu*, a leafy plant which aids digestion. You'll hear Brazilians — especially in Amazônia — sing the praises of energy-restoring *guaraná*, a wild berry-based drink. The source of all that energy turns out to be nothing more exotic than caffeine.

SAFETY

On the eve of our first trip to Brazil, several well-meaning friends tried to persuade us that the place was just too dangerous for travel. Crime statistics seemed to back them up: Rio ranks number ten worldwide in homicides per capita (about 20 per 100,000 residents). São Paulo is close behind at number thirteen. Brazilian newspapers confirmed the fact that lawlessness has risen dramatically with the recent downturn in the economy.

But a closer look should allay your concerns about safe travel in Brazil. First of all, our friends had forgotten to mention that numbers one through nine on the world homicide rankings were all U.S. cities — one of which happened to be their hometown! (For comparative purposes, Frankfurt ranks number 18, with seven homicides per 100,000 residents; London comes in at number 30, with 2 deaths per 100,000.) Secondly, such figures are relatively meaningless to travellers since victims of homicide in any country are virtually all local residents. Much of the truly violent crime in both Rio and São Paulo has in fact been attributed to the police-vigilante groups, the infamous 'Esquadrões da Morte' (Death Squads), known lately as the Polícia Mineira. While certainly regrettable, this violence doesn't extend to foreign travellers. And take comfort in the fact that Brazil, unlike many a South American country, has never had a significant history of political terrorist activity.

In short, the only criminals that you as a foreign traveller need concern yourself about will be purse snatchers, thieves, and pickpockets. Remember too that such crimes are urban phenomena which you'll leave behind, along with the skyscapers and smog, as you penetrate the backcountry. In our travels throughout Brazil, we have had our belongings lifted only once; the thieves ended up with a cheap plastic men's purse containing an address book, a calculator, and a telephone token.

This doesn't mean that you should throw caution and good sense to the wind; every one of our Brazilian friends living in Rio has been robbed at least once. Yet these were all incidents that could have been avoided by following the usual precautions in large cities:

1) Wear a fabric money pouch beneath clothing near your groin, around your neck, or strapped to your leg. Even under the shorts that you'll end up wearing much of the time in Brazil, fabric money pouches are comfortable and very nearly undetectable. Leather money belts

worn on the outside are less practical. An alternative to a money pouch is 'tubigrip,' an elasticized tubular bandage. Very comfortable and safe, it can be put round the calf or thigh to hold money and/or passport.

2) Keep enough spending money in pockets so that you're not constantly fumbling for cash in the money pouch. In the unlikely event that you're confronted by a robber, this can serve as 'mugger's money.'

3) Do not wear expensive jewellery or watches. This is what got our *carioca* friends in trouble (and perhaps inspired the recent glut of punk jewellery in Rio made with metal washers, nuts, and bolts). Nowadays you can buy a perfectly workable plastic watch for US$2, so leave your good one at home. Brazilian thieves have been known to ask couples for the time so that they could assess the best watch!

4) Avoid the areas near fancy tourist hotels. Not surprisingly, thieves who prey on rich tourists frequent these spots rather than the residential areas with economy hotels.

5) Stay with the crowds at night. In the large Brazilian cities, finding a crowd is rarely a problem.

6) At night, take taxis rather than city buses (unless you are certain the bus will be crowded through to your stop and that you won't have far to walk once you're off the bus). Unlike the undergrounds in North America, those in Rio and São Paulo are well-lit, well-patrolled, and quite safe during all working hours (until 2330 or so).

7) Take as little as possible to the beach. Follow the *carioca* example: stuff beer and bus money into your swimsuit, throw on a light cover that can double as a towel and beach mat, and take nothing else. Before going for a swim, bring anything of value to the nearest beachgoers (families and couples are always a safe bet) and ask politely if they might hold it for you. Brazilians themselves do this all the time, and it's a surefire way to meet locals if your Portuguese is at all passable.

8) If you must visit a *favela* (slum), go with an experienced local. If you find yourself in one by accident — it happens — don't panic. Ask directions out of the place; their surroundings may be mean, but *favelados* themselves can be quite gracious.

9) Don't leave valuables in your hotel room. Even most budget hotels have safes (*cofres*), and the owner will write a receipt for your cash, plane tickets, and passports. It's not unusual for thieves to slip the lock on a hotel room while a single traveller is showering down the hall. We've even heard of this happening to travellers who have taken a room with a bathroom, so take your valuables into the bathroom when showering! (Alternately, you can buy rubber wedges to push under the door; this prevents entry from outside and keeps your money dry!)

10) Don't fall for the trick that is the thief's stock-in-trade: artful distraction. Thieves frequently work in teams, one or two diverting your attention by jostling you, asking questions, or even feigning a fight; meanwhile, a third is whisking your purse away.

11) Wear small daypacks in the Brazilian fashion: on your chest rather than on your back. Particularly on buses, thieves have been known to

cut daypack straps with a razor, a feat which is made considerably more difficult if the goods are right under your nose.

12) If you are robbed of something valuable, report it to the police immediately. It's unlikely that the thieves will be apprehended, and a miracle if your stolen goods are returned, but you'll want written proof of the incident from the police for insurance purposes.

13) Make photocopies (*xerox* in Portuguese) of your passports (including the visa pages) and plane tickets. Although our Brazilian friends are horrified that we go anywhere without our passports, Jayne and I rarely carry them with us during day trips unless we need to change money or buy bus tickets.

Crime in the backcountry is virtually nonexistent. Exceptions to this rule are those areas near goldfields, where prospectors (*garimpeiros*) have been known to fire on people they suspected of claim-jumping. The same caution is advised in remote areas of the Pantanal where *coureiros* (alligator hide poachers) operate. In all other backcountry areas, your concerns should be limited to fellow travellers, who do most of the thieving from rented huts, houses, and tents. In these situations, try to have one of the locals watch after your gear while you're off exploring. Usually the person renting the hut to you will be glad to oblige. Keep your money pouch on at all times, even while sleeping. Follow this precaution on river boats as well, although I have never heard of thefts on small cargo boats; travellers on the huge government-run *ENASA* boats sometimes report gear stolen. When beginning bus trips, wait to see that your bags are loaded in the cargo compartment before boarding the bus.

Drugs

Brazil is not the drug haven that some people imagine. Narcotics (*tóxicos*) travel through Brazil from the Andean countries, but very few Brazilians actually use them. By North American or European standards, marijuana (*maconha*) and cocaine (*cocaína*) use is uncommon even in the large cities, and nonexistent in the backcountry. Drug laws are severe, with penalties of up to 15 years imprisonment for simple possession of cocaine. Police searches are rare, but undercover federal police routinely check travellers in two backcountry areas: Corumbá near the Bolivian border, and both Benjamin Constant and Tabatinga near the Colombian smuggling center of Leticia. *Lança perfume*, a mildly euphoric mixture of chloroform and ether that is sniffed through handkerchiefs during Carnaval, is legally a narcotic. While police often turn a blind eye to *lança perfume* use, revellers are occasionally arrested.

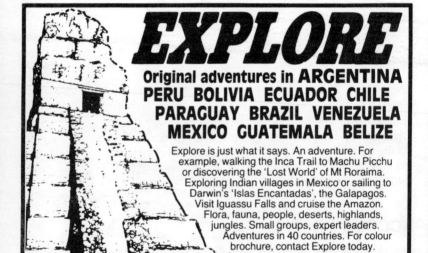

Chapter 4

In Brazil

ARRIVAL

Most *visitors* entering Brazil by air do so via Rio de Janeiro. Galeão International Airport is located on Governor's Island, about 15 km north of the city centre. Whether you leave the airport by taxi or bus, you're far better off paying the fare with *cruzados*; Banco do Brasil located on the third floor will change money (either cash or travellers cheques), and is open around the clock. Change only enough to see you into town and to the nearest *casa de câmbio* — US$20 is more than enough if you arrive on a weekday.

Taxis from the airport to either the city centre or Copacabana are relatively expensive. Transcoopass sells taxi 'tickets' at several counters within the airport, charging about US$9 to Flamengo and US$11 to Copacabana. These rates are good for up to four people, so you may as well share a ride. All prices are posted at the Transcoopass booths. Much cheaper is the 'Alvorada' bus line, run by the Real company, which leaves from the sidewalk outside the terminal every half hour from 0520 to 0010. US$1.50 will take you to the city centre, Santos Dumont airport, Flamengo, Copacabana, and as far as Barra da Tijuca. Along the way are virtually all the hotel districts, cheap, moderate, and expensive. See the section below (*Accommodation in Rio*) for directions to the economy hotel districts when taking the Alvorada bus.

ACCOMMODATION IN RIO

Most economy hotels in Rio are located just south of the city centre in the Lapa, Glória, Flamengo, and Botafogo districts. Lapa is a bit on the seedy side, but the other three are all pleasant neighbourhoods close to the Metrô (underground), main bus lines, restaurants, and shops. You'll spend far less and get a much quieter night's sleep here than in the tourist meccas of Leme, Copacabana, Ipanema, and Leblon. *The South American Handbook* gives a number of economy hotels in these

districts; I'll confine myself to a brief list of streets in the Glória/
Flamengo district with numerous hotels in the US$5-7 range (double
occupancy, with breakfast) from which to choose: Cândido Mendes,
Silveira Martins, Ferreira Viana, Correia Dutra, and rua do Catete. All
of these streets are within walking distance of the Metrô stations at
either Glória or Catete. If coming from the airport on the 'Alvorada'
bus line run by the Real company, ask the driver to let you off in
Flamengo; alternatively, ask him to to drop you off near Cinelândia,
where you can catch the Metrô one stop to the Glória station or two
stops to the Catete station.

If you prefer even cheaper lodging — the kind of room where a bare
light bulb illuminates a girlie calendar on one wall and a tattered poster
of the Virgin Mary on the other — try the Saúde and Mauá districts just
north of the city centre. Mauá is full of sailors' dives, and the best thing
to be said for staying here is that you're right next door to the Federal
Police station where tourist visas are renewed.

The more expensive hotels in Rio are well listed in guides such as
Guia Quatro Rodas, *South American Handbook*, *Fodor's*, and
Michael's.

A final word of caution: Do not expect to find a room in Rio within
three weeks of Carnaval (which falls seven weeks before Easter).

For more information, see *Lodging* in this chapter.

DEPARTURE

If leaving Brazil from Rio's Galeão airport, your cheapest ride to the
terminal is the bus run by the Real company. A flat rate of US$1.50 will
take you there from any of several stops in Barra da Tijuca and
Copacabana. Call the company for a timetable and bus stop locations,
or ask at the fancy tourist hotels in Copacabana. If staying in the city
centre, Flamengo, Catete, Glória, or Lapa, take a short cab ride to
Santos Dumont airport where you can catch a Real bus for US$1.25 to
Galeão International. The first bus runs at 0530.

All travellers leaving Brazil by air must pay a departure tax of
approximately US$10. Travellers cheques are not accepted.

MONEY MATTERS
Currency

In early 1986, the *cruzado* replaced the *cruzeiro* as Brazil's monetary
unit. The move followed Argentina's earlier inflation-busting switch
from *pesos* to *australes*, and essentially involved knocking off three
zeros from the cruzeiro's value. Bank notes at this writing are printed in
10, 50, 100, 500, 1000, 5000, and 10000 cruzado denominations, but
some of the old cruzeiro notes are still circulating. Many, but not all of
these notes have been stamped with the new value; remember to divide
the printed value on old, unstamped cruzeiro notes by 1000 to convert to

cruzados. It's not quite as confusing as it may sound, since the new cruzado bills look identical to the old bills of comparable value which they replaced. Thankfully, all the old cruzeiro coins have been taken out of circulation. Exchange rates vary so much over time due to Brazil's rampant inflation that any mention of them here would become meaningless long before our publication date.

Changing money: banks versus the black market

The black market (*o paralelo* or, less frequently, *o mercado negro*) was, until recently, perfectly legal in Brazil and generally gave the best exchange rate for your dollar, either cash or travellers cheque. Now technically illegal, the *paralelo* still operates quite brazenly; for all practical purposes, nothing has changed. It's still much quicker to change money on the black market — there are seldom the long queues or bureaucratic red tape to wade through. The only disadvantage of the *paralelo* is that it tends to operate only in the larger cities; finding the black markets becomes increasingly difficult as you move inland, and those in the smaller cities may exchange only cash.

The Banco do Brasil, on the other hand, operates branches in most towns with a population over 10,000, changing both cash and travellers cheques. Travellers cheques are not discounted at banks; they receive exactly the same exchange rate as do cash dollars. The big disadvantage to changing money in a bank is the exchange rate itself; banks change money only at the official rate (*taxa oficial*). This rate is set by the government and does not vary among banks or localities as it may in other South American countries. Not surprisingly, the *taxa oficial* is almost always lower than the black market rate. From 1984 through 1988, the difference between official and black market exchange rates varied from 1% to as much as 30% on the dollar, but hovered around 25% most of the time. As mentioned above, banks also involve a great deal more bureaucracy than the *paralelo* — we once waited nearly an hour for a banker in Ponta Porã to okay a US$20 travellers cheque.

In short, change money in a bank only as a last resort when you can't locate a local black market.

Finding the black market is ridiculously simple in most large cities. State or city tourist agencies can usually point you in the right direction, as will most hotels. In downtown Rio de Janeiro, at least eight money and cheque changers (*casas de câmbio*) operate out of prominently-marked offices on the avenida Rio Branco in the city centre. You'll find a similar concentration of offices near São Paulo's Praça da República. Black market exchange rates in such a situation are generally all within a few cents of each other, so don't waste too much time comparison-shopping. In smaller towns, try inquiring at travel agencies, even if they don't advertise themselves as money-changers (pilots and other travel professionals generally act as conduits for black market currency) or simply ask other gringos. We've changed cash and cheques at furniture stores, hotels, perfume shops, men's clothing stores, veterinarian's offices, and even an undertaker's! Virtually all black marketeers operate openly out of respectable shops; those without a shop will change money in your hotel under the watchful eye of the owners. Don't change money in alleys or cars, and never hand money over to someone who promises to 'be right back.' Accept only cash. Count your cruzados, although we've never once been shortchanged in literally hundreds of transactions.

In 1984, 1985, and 1988, we never encountered a difference between black market exchange rates for cash and travellers cheques amounting to more than 20%, with the average difference being about 6%. In short, travellers cheques can buy a lot of peace of mind at very little cost in purchasing power. For this reason, we generally carry about three-quarters of our money in the form of travellers cheques and the remainder in cash.

You will be required to show your passport when changing travellers cheques on the black market. Sign the cheque in front of the buyer, but never date it — they add the date later when *they* sell it.

Black market exchange rates (as well as the official rate) are published daily in many newspapers; *O Jornal do Brasil* and *O Estado de São Paulo* are good bets (look in the section labeled *Câmbio*). Alternatively, watch the national news on TV Globo —both official and *paralelo* rates are announced on a regular basis. Keep in mind that these black market rates reflect the estimated going price for cash in São Paulo or Rio; the rate you receive may vary slightly.

As you move away from the major cities, black markets will disappear and you'll find yourself having to rely on the banks to change your money. Banco do Brasil, the national bank, is virtually the only bank that changes either travellers cheques or cash. Branches in some of the smaller towns may not always change cheques. We generally check the *Guia Quatro Rodas* to determine if a town we're headed to has a Banco do Brasil; if not, we either stock up on cruzados or hope the town has a black market.

Remember that exchange rates change almost daily in Brazil, so don't change too much money at any one time.

Brazil instituted the 'Tourist Dollar' in 1989, a program whereby travellers can exchange cash and travellers cheques at Banco do Brasil at a rate higher than the official. The black market still gives a better deal, but the Tourist Dollar programme may come in handy where black markets don't exist. All foreign credit card transactions are now being figured using the Tourist Dollar exchange rate.

Receiving money from overseas

There are several ways you can receive money from overseas, none of them ideal. This is why: Brazilian government regulations require in each case that all foreign currencies be converted to cruzados at the current official rate before your money is handed over. It is equally impossible to buy foreign-currency travellers cheques in Brazil with overseas funds. So unless you are receiving only small amounts of money — US$50, for instance — this conversion will saddle you with a huge fistful of cruzados that will rapidly devalue. A service charge, sometimes substantial, is also involved. Nevertheless, there may come a time when you'll need an emergency transfusion of cash from home, so here are your options:

American Express card-holders may draw the equivalent of up to US$250 on their personal checking account at any of the company's five offices in Brazil (Rio, São Paulo, Belo Horizonte, Recife, and Brasília). You must have your American Express card, a personal cheque, and your passport. A fee of about US$25 is charged for this service.

Before leaving, discuss the trip with the manager of your bank; Banco do Brasil does business with most major world banks, so that you may telex a request for money during your trip. Your bank will in turn telex the funds to the local Banco do Brasil branch. Particularly if you've laid the groundwork at home for such transactions, you can receive a fresh transfusion of cruzados within 24 hours.

Finally, if you're willing to gamble, there is a simple way to receive cash from home without having to convert it to cruzados: have a friend back home mail you US$ notes care of the local *posta restante*, or better yet, your embassy. Although we've met folks who claimed to have success with this method — receiving a single US$50 note per envelope — I have never been willing to risk it.

Miscellaneous money problems

Be sure to liquidate any leftover cruzados before leaving Brazil; they can rarely be exchanged beyond the border towns of neighbouring countries. If you have changed money on the official market and remembered to save your bank receipts (*recibos*), you may recover up to one-third the sum in foreign currency.

Brazilian law won't allow non-citizens to purchase foreign currency; even Brazilians must show a plane ticket before they can buy foreign money. This means, for instance, that if you fly to French Guiana, there is no way for you to buy *francs* prior to your arrival at the Cayenne airport — where, naturally enough, there is no currency exchange booth! To get foreign currency you'll have to find gringos coming the other way with spare cash.

Change (*troco*) is a constant problem in Brazil. Do as the Brazilians do: when buying something, never relinquish your small bills — nor even admit to having them — unless you absolutely must. Let the seller find change. It gets to be a tiresome game, but one you must play if you want to keep your change for bus rides, snacks, etc.

Watch local papers for news of impending bank strikes. Strikes at the Banco do Brasil choke the flow of cash everywhere, including the most reliable black market money changers. At the first rumour of a strike, stock up on cruzados.

NOTE: Numbers in Portuguese are always written using reverse notation. For instance, a car rental costing seven thousand one hundred and fifty cruzados would be written Cz$7.150,00.

VISA RENEWALS

Anyone requiring a tourist visa to enter Brazil (see *Red Tape* in Chapter 2) will need to renew the visa if planning to stay beyond 90 days from the date of arrival (*not* the date of issuance). You'll need to visit one of the larger cities to do this, preferably a state capital, and you should allow at least a half day to deal with the red tape. Visas are renewed at the offices of the Polícia Federal, who will hand you a blank application form. In most cities, you'll then be sent to one of several nearby offices that, for a small fee, will type your application (handwritten forms are not generally accepted). Next you'll have to go to a bank of the Polícia Federal's choosing — usually the Banco do Brasil — to pay the visa fee (about US$10). The Polícia Federal will issue your new 90-day visa when you present the receipt. Depending on where you renew and who's behind the desk, you may be asked to show a return ticket and/or 'sufficient funds' to continue your stay. I've never been asked myself.

If you renew your visa for the full 90 days, then leave Brazil, you will have to wait until the 90 days have elapsed before returning. In this case, ask for a shorter-term renewal.

Visas are renewed only once; if you're planning to stay longer than 180 days, you'll have to leave Brazil before the second visa renewal runs out and then re-enter the country. This means that you should plan to be somewhere near a border at the six-month juncture of your trip — the Pantanal, for example, or even portions of Amazônia, but not the north-east coast! The Brazilian government takes visas very seriously, and the fine for overstaying can be substantial. Once again, be prepared to show a return airline ticket (or photocopy) and 'sufficient funds.'

In theory at least, it is supremely easy to get a fresh visa after a six-month stay in Brazil. You simply step across the border, have your passport stamped, then walk back to Brazil and apply for a visa. That's not quite how it worked for Jayne and me in the Paraguayan border town of Pedro Juan Caballero. Already stamped out of Brazil a few miles up the road, we made the mistake of arriving on a Paraguayan holiday. And there we waited in political limbo for two days and a night while Brazilian bureaucrats argued that we couldn't possibly return to Brazil because, although we had clearly left Brazil, they had no proof that we'd actually been to Paraguay, and surely you understand, *senhor*.

MAIL

In the large Brazilian cities, you'll find a post office (*correio*) in nearly every neighbourhood. Rio, for instance, has at least a dozen small post offices in the city centre alone; simply ask someone in the street. In tiny backcountry towns, the *correio* — if it exists at all — is likely to be a private home or small store. Our favourite Brazilian post office is located on stilts above the floodwaters of the Paraguai River in Porto Esperança, Mato Grosso do Sul. A casual kind of place, complete with bare-chested postmaster and a parrot on the railing.

Post offices in the cities are generally open from 0800 to 1800 with no midday breaks. In small towns, hours vary according to the habits of the postmaster. Post offices are closed on weekends and national holidays.

Don't place mail in public mailboxes in small towns; it may not be picked up for weeks. Wait until you're in a large city or near a post office.

Don't mail anything but letters, postcards, and aerograms from Brazil back to your home. Postal rates are extremely high for overseas packages, and they have a way of disappearing en route.

To receive mail, have your friends back home address it to you care of the Posta Restante in the town you're visiting (for example: Alex BRADBURY, Posta Restante, Cuiabá, Brasil). Make sure they print or type your last name carefully to avoid confusing the postal officials, who are easily confused by foreign names. Posta Restante mail ends up at the main branch of the post office in cities which have more than one branch. To claim your mail, bring your passport. Postal clerks will often file your mail variously under your first name, last name, or even 'M' for Mr or Mrs, so ask them to check all the possible combinations and permutations. Sometimes you can convince a clerk to let you go through the file of letters yourself. *Posta restantes* will keep mail for 30 days before disposing of it.

You can also have mail sent to any of the five American Express offices in Brazil if you're a cardholder or have their travellers cheques. Some embassies will also hold mail for a limited time. If you're having mail sent to you care of a friend living in Brazil, the notation for 'in care of' is a/c (*ao cuidado*).

It takes about a week for letters to go between Brazil and either the United States or England.

TELEPHONES

Local calls can be made at the pay phones known colloquially as *orelhões* ('big ears', after the bulbous plastic hemisphere that encloses your head as you speak). All pay phones operate on tokens (*fichas telefônicas*) rather than coins. You can buy a handful of *fichas* from either newsstands or street vendors nearby. Buy several; it's a short call that costs only one *ficha*, and *fichas* bought in one city are always good in another. Long lines are common at pay phones, probably because two out of every three phones seem to be inoperable!

Long-distance phone calls within Brazil can be made at offices known as Postos Telefônicos DDD. After telling the cashier what city you want to call, you'll be handed a numbered key corresponding to one of the phone booths in the office. Make your call, turn in your key, and the cashier will have a computerized bill waiting for you. The Posto Telefônico generally has phone books encompassing the entire country. Don't make long-distance phone calls from hotel rooms (in the unlikely event that your room will even *have* a phone!) because of the expensive surcharges.

You can phone long-distance overseas from a DDD office as above, or collect (reverse charge), (*ao cobrar*) from most pay phones. To make international calls with operator assistance, dial 000111. Dial 000333 for information on placing overseas calls.

NOTE: Whenever reciting phone numbers (or addresses, for that matter), Brazilians invariably use the word *meia* ('half', as in half a dozen) instead of *seis*, to mean 'six.' This presumably avoids confusion with the word *tres*, but many foreigners who thought they could decipher at least the numbers in Portuguese have been left completely baffled by this custom!

TOURIST INFORMATION

Each of the Brazilian states promotes tourism via its own government agency. The larger cities like São Paulo and Rio also fund municipal tourist agencies. Services are free, although sometimes you'll be charged for a map. Sadly, few of these offices provide useful information for the backcountry traveller. In everything from hotel lodging to river travel, you'll be steered toward the expensive and the pre-packaged. Understandably, Brazilians are proud of their country's technological advances, and they would like to spare you as much discomfort as possible.

In some cases, the staff at these government agencies is enthusiastic but woefully uninformed. Jayne and I once spent a half hour convincing a young woman at the Paratur office in Belém that we preferred to ascend the Amazon on a small cargo boat rather than the government's *ENASA* ships. She finally shrugged her shoulders and told us how to reach the cargo docks by bus. As we left, an older man with a push broom who was apparently the office janitor quietly motioned us over. He'd overheard our conversation and wanted us to know that the young woman had us headed for the wrong bus. And in five minutes, he told us more about boat schedules on the lower Amazon than we'd learned in half an hour with the official.

Despite these misgivings, we always stop off at the government tourist bureaux. They can usually tell you where to change money on the black market and they'll often call hotels for vacancies and current rates. Occasionally, they can help in planning a trip. If they tell us that a particular spot on the map is accessible, we can be certain that is it is indeed accessible. And if they tell us that it isn't ... well, we ask someone else.

For information on river travel it's a good idea to check with the local Capitania do Porto. These are the offices which control commercial river traffic, and they are usually a good source not only of information on cargo boat sailings, but also on river conditions.

Likewise, try the state offices of the IBDF (Delegacia Estadual do Instituto Brasileiro do Desenvolvimento Florestal), which manage the national parks and biological reserves. These are located in state capitals and, depending on who's sitting behind the desk and how you present yourself, can be either very helpful or a total waste of time. Sometimes these offices are staffed by bureaucrats who've never set foot in territory wilder than the local zoo.

TRANSPORT
Interstate buses

Brazilians, like all South Americans, still make the sign of the cross when beginning a long journey by bus. Yet buses (*ônibus* is both the singular and plural) in Brazil are probably the safest and most reliable anywhere in South or Central America. While logging some 35,000 km throughout the country, we've experienced only two minor break-downs, and not a single cliff-hanging nightmare of the type you often hear about. Buses run almost everywhere, all have toilets aboard, fares are cheap (expect to pay about US$1 per 100 km), and they are spotlessly clean. Veteran travellers in Spanish-speaking Latin America may already be shaking their heads in disbelief, so prepare for yet another shock: Brazilian buses run on time.

Of course, all this comfort and convenience comes at the expense of some regional colour. You won't be able to regale your friends back home with tales of pigs, chickens, goats, and parrots frolicking down the bus aisles. Nor will you see ornate painted filigree, jewelled crucifixes, or carved Saint Christophers surrounding the driver. Only once, outside Teresina, have I ever seen a pig aboard a Brazilian bus — and it had to ride alongside our luggage in a separate compartment, trussed and squealing.

In most Brazilian cities, the various bus companies are all centralised in a single bus station (*rodoviária*). In large cities the *rodoviárias* resemble busy airports; restaurants, snack bars, magazine stands, public restrooms (some with showers), information booths, and even record stores all vie for space with scores of ticket booths. At least one city — Natal in north-eastern Brazil — proudly sells picture postcards of its *rodoviária*. If you're headed for a small town anywhere within a 500-kilometre radius of the *rodoviária*, you'll probably find a bus going there.

All bus stations have some sort of facility for storing your baggage while you scout the town for lodging, eat a meal, etc. Price per bag per 24-hour period generally runs about US$0.25 at the *guarda volumes*. Generally you'll check your bags with a clerk, but some of the newer bus stations have installed *guarda volumes* which are nothing more than oversized gym lockers; to unlock and lock them, you'll have to buy a token (*ficha*) at one of the nearby magazine stands. We've never lost anything at a *guarda volumes*, but avoid checking money or passports with your baggage.

Most bus companies post their schedules and prices inside the ticket booth (*caixa*). Since neither prices nor service vary much between competing bus companies, time schedules will largely determine which bus you choose. Depending on the destination, you can generally buy tickets a day or two in advance. Although there are usually plenty of buses to most destinations, I highly advise buying tickets at least a day in advance to avoid disappointment. Plan your bus travel around the Brazilian holidays. Don't, for instance, try to buy tickets for the Easter weekend when all of Brazil is standing in line at the *rodoviária* doing that very thing. The busiest holidays are Easter, Christmas, and Carnaval. Have your passport ready; it'll be required now and then. Virtually all seats on the interstate buses are sold on a numbered, reserved-seat basis, and occasionally you'll be asked for a seat preference. Don't pick seats in the rear or you'll be stuck near the toilet door. Before leaving the booth, check your tickets for accuracy; each ticket should list the destination, departure time and, in large bus stations, the departure gate (*portal*).

Interstate buses are generally classed as either *comun*, *leito*, or *executivo*. *Leito* buses are an option on the longer runs to large cities; they provide extra-large reclining seats for almost double the fare of a regular bus (*comun*). We find that we sleep just as well in the *ônibus comuns*. *Executivos* are generally air-conditioned, with piped music, 'free' snacks served by a *rodomoça* (stewardess), and other luxuries that we can easily do without on a bus trip.

An attendant will tag and load your bags shortly before departure. On the short runs, you may find yourself the only ones with baggage that won't fit in the overhead racks; in this case, simply ask the driver (*motorista*) to stow your bags in the lower luggage compartment. In either case, it's a good idea to watch your baggage until it is safely stowed and the luggage compartment has been shut. Theft is unlikely, but it isn't unheard of for luggage to become mislaid on the crowded medians between departing buses.

Every couple of hours, interstate buses will make a 15-20 minute stop at restaurant/snack bars along the highway. These tend to be clean though somewhat overpriced, so bring your own food if on a tight budget. At some of these roadside restaurants, you'll be given a blank receipt (*ficha*) as you pass the door; even if you end up ordering nothing at all, hold on to the *ficha*, because you'll be required to return it on leaving or else pay a set fee of several dollars. At the busier roadside stops, keep an eye on the bus and/or *motorista*; he'll usually count his passengers before pulling out, but don't rely on it.

Buses also make brief stops at smaller *rodoviárias* along the way. There, you'd be well advised to stay in your seat. Once in a while, new passengers are permitted to board an already full bus, and any empty seat becomes fair game.

On long bus trips, we always take a canteen of purified water or a plastic bottle of mineral water and two bedsheets — nights on the road can get surprisingly chilly in the tropics. Some travellers, who figure they're not missing anything by tuning out that hungry baby or that spirited conversation at two o'clock in the morning, add earplugs to the list.

City buses

Buses are by far the cheapest way to get around town — unless you happen to be in Rio or São Paulo, both of which have excellent underground railways. Stops, unfortunately, are rarely marked, so you'll have to ask locals where to flag down the *ônibus*. City buses can also be insanely crowded; if you're carrying a backpack or other bulky baggage, try to board the bus near the beginning of the line and make a beeline for the seats furthest in front. Once the bus begins to fill, it can become almost impossible to get both yourself and your luggage off if you're seated in the rear (although passing your bags out the window is an option favoured by many Brazilians). Enter city buses from the rear door (except in Curitiba) and pay the *cobrador* before passing through the turnstile. There will generally be a placard above the *cobrador* announcing the fare. The *cobrador* will answer questions, call out your stop to the driver, and make certain you get off at the proper spot.

Taxis

Although buses run 24 hours a day in most cities, we prefer to play it safe and take taxis late at night. Many Brazilians do likewise. Taxis are also the only way to reach the airport in some Brazilian cities such as Santarém. While taxis are cheap by European and American standards, many first-time visitors to Brazil assume they're being cheated when it comes time to pay the fare. Remember that meters cannot keep pace with inflation, so the cabbie must refer to a printed table which adjusts the meter price upward. These tables, authorised by the city government and regularly updated, can usually be found taped to the left passenger window. If you don't find one prominently displayed, ask the driver to show you his copy of the *tabela* before the ride begins. Don't accept a photocopied *tabela*; the official one is printed in several colors. Make sure also that the meter is running. Airport taxis generally don't fall under these regulations, so make your fare arrangements with the driver before leaving. Most cabbies are scrupulously honest, but there's no point in losing your temper with those who aren't — just ask to see the table. Faced with wealthy gringos, wouldn't you be tempted to ignore the government's fare tables every now and then?

Hitchhiking

Brazilians generally fall all over themselves to help a traveller in their country, so it came as a surprise when we learned that thumbing a ride was next to impossible. Combine big families and little cars with the rising crime rate, and you'll understand why it's usually a waste of time to hitchhike (*pedir uma corôna*) in Brazil. Even if you manage to catch a lift you may be asked to contribute gas money. In oil-poor Brazil — where gas prices are double those in the United States — that can make a large and unexpected dent in your wallet. If you must hitchhike, try the gas station/restaurant/hotel complexes (*postos*) that are located on the highways several miles outside major cities and towns. Truckers (*camioneiros*) stop here during the day for gas and meals, and can occasionally be talked into taking you aboard. If you arrive at the *posto* late in the evening, be prepared to spend the night — that's what most of the truckers are doing.

Difficult as hitchhiking is in most of Brazil, there are a few notable exceptions such as the Transpantaneira highway, (see Chapter 5).

Trains

The rail system in Brazil has never been very extensive, and backcountry travellers won't be taking the train often. Most of the country's 30,000 km of track runs south and west from Rio and São Paulo — nice country at times, but hardly wild. Even many of these lines are being closed by the government. Of the three areas described in this book, only one is served by rail: the RFFSA runs from Bauru (in the interior of São Paulo state) westward across the Mato Grosso all the way to Santa Cruz, Bolivia. Along the way, the train grazes the southern edge of

Brazil's vast swampy plain known as the Pantanal. Here, green and yellow parrots flit by the windows. Alligators bask along the tracks. And backcountry travellers can revel in the knowledge that they're riding the line known colloquially as the Trem da Morte: the Train of Death. For details, see Chapter 5.

Boats

Particularly in the soggier parts of backcountry Brazil — Amazônia and the Pantanal — boat travel is often the only option from A to B. Even if it weren't, most adventurous travellers wouldn't hesitate to choose a boat over faster but more mundane modes of transport. What traveller can stroll the docks of Santarém, crowded with a riotous assortment of scruffy cargo boats being loaded to the scuppers with bananas, jute, Brazil nuts, and Coca-Cola, bound for places with names like Oriximiná, Faro, Nhamundá, and Urucurituba — what real traveller can walk past such a scene and resist racing back to the hotel for a hammock and backpack? Even if Point B turns out to be singularly uninspiring, the trip itself is reward enough for most river vagabonds: nights spent lolling in hammocks, sharing a gourd of *mate* tea with grizzled gold prospectors; days spent gliding past an impenetrable green wall of jungle.

Your choice of river craft isn't limited to Amazonian cargo boats, either. Resourceful travellers can find berths (of a sort) aboard cattle boats, cement barges, and even Brazilian Army boats bringing fresh troops to jungle outposts. In those cases where public transport can't take you from A to B — or when you simply want to do some fishing, camping, or alligator watching on your own — there are usually local boatmen (*barqueiros*) for hire.

Occasionally, hikers making their way along the beaches of the north-east coast will need to hop a small ferry to cross the mouth of a river, or even hire a local boatman to make the crossing. But with that exception, boat travel isn't nearly as common in the north-east as it is in Amazônia and the Pantanal. On the other hand, coastal villages fairly bristle with the masts of primitive fishing rafts called *jangadas*, and if you can talk yourself aboard one, you'll have savoured a living piece of Brazilian folklore.

Boat travel has more than its share of disadvantages. The food ... well, let's just say that veteran river vagabonds tend to be on the lean side. Travel is slow, and frequently interrupted by everything from engine breakdowns to shallow sand bars. On cargo boats, passengers are a secondary consideration; you may find your hammock wedged tightly between crates of manioc flour and a brand new Volkswagen. But perhaps the most insidious problem with extended boat trips is boredom. Don't expect alligators, toucans, and native rubber-tappers to appear around every bend, even on the best of days. Until you've tried it, don't sign on for a week-long cruise. And bring plenty of books.

More so than any other type of travel, river travel demands a working knowledge of Portuguese. Finding a boat, bartering with the captain, and chewing the fat with your fellow travellers will be a great deal easier if you've taken the time to learn some of the local tongue. The alternative is to travel like the group of four South Africans we met on a trip up the mainstem Amazon from Belém; two days into the journey it dawned on them that the word 'Santarém,' a word which had been bandied about so much by both passengers and crew, was indeed the name of a city — a city which was not only our boat's final destination but one which was some 700 km downriver from the city they had assumed they were heading for!

Specific information on boat travel in the Pantanal and Amazônia can be found in Chapters 5 and 6.

Rental cars

Why would anyone but the certifiably insane rent a car in Brazil, where cheap public transportation extends to virtually every backwater, where a litre of gasoline costs double what it does in the United States, where spare parts may take weeks to arrive? I had plenty of time to ponder these and other questions while coaxing my rented Fiat Uno down the Transpantaneira, 140 km of red-dirt highway in the Pantanal. Three days, several headaches, and many dollars later (I ripped the car's rear bumper off in a particularly nasty pothole), I was still at a loss for answers.

To rent a car, you'll need a valid driving licence from home or an international licence, your passport, and a major credit card such as American Express. We once rented a car without a credit card, but had to convince the agency people that our return plane tickets would be adequate collateral.

In addition to the basic daily charge (ranging from US$15 to US$50), you'll pay a mileage charge (anywhere from US$0.07 to US$0.14 per kilometre), insurance (from US$5 to US$12 per day), and a 5% service tax on everything. And it doesn't end there; in many parts of the interior and the north-east, you'll be charged a 'regional tax' of another 10% in view of the poor road conditions. These, of course, are the very areas where a backcountry traveller is most likely to want a rental car. An additional daily sum is charged for air conditioning, and air-conditioned cars may well be all that are available. In most cases, you must return the car to the city where rented; a 'return tax' is charged if you leave the car in another city. As mentioned earlier, you'll be paying for fuel (generally alcohol) yourself. In mid-1988, a litre of alcohol cost US$0.30 and gasoline ran US$0.45. And finally, be forewarned that rental agencies frequently won't have the cheap models (VW sedans, Fiats, and Chevettes) advertised in their brochures.

The insurance (*seguro*) you buy will in most cases give you only partial coverage. Be sure you understand exactly how much you would pay and how much the agency would pay were the car to be damaged or stolen.

Costs vary of course, but the final bill for a 24-hour, 352 km trip of ours in 1988 came to US$77, not including fuel and damages to the car.

If you've taken all these costs into consideration and still feel you're better off renting a car, sign the papers. Someone from the agency will check the car for damage and defects before you drive off. Make sure you note every defect, lest you end up paying at the end of your trip.

Ninety-five percent of all Brazilian-made cars (this includes Fiats, Opals, and Volkswagens) run on sugarcane alcohol. Underneath the hood you'll find a small reservoir filled with real gasoline to get the car started in the morning. Simply press the button on the dashboard labelled with a drawing of a gas pump, and don't forget to turn it off immediately after the car starts. Always check this reservoir when refueling; it is damned near impossible to start a cold engine on alcohol alone.

The general word for auto fuel is *combustivel*, and prices for alcohol, gasoline, and diesel fuel are fixed by the government. This means that you won't pay any more for fuel in a distant backwater town than you would in the state capital.

Check on the availability of fuel as you head out into the backcountry. Since towns deep in the interior are served mostly by trucks, it often happens that only gasoline and diesel fuel are available there. Ask a truck driver; they're usually the best source of information on this topic.

Internal air travel

The four national airlines — Cruzeiro do Sul, Varig, Transbrasil, and Vasp — offer regularly scheduled flights to all state and territorial capitals, as well as a number of other Brazilian cities. While far costlier than bus travel, flying has two advantages for the backcountry traveller: first, those on a tight schedule can spend more time in the hinterland and less time on the highways. Secondly, a number of areas in Amazônia are simply not accessible by bus or even boat on a year-round basis. If you plan to strike out into the backcountry from these cities — notably Porto Velho and Rio Branco — you may be ahead to fly directly from either Rio, Manaus, or São Paulo rather than waste weeks on the road or river.

The Brazil Air Pass offered by all three national airlines is a popular and cheap way to see lots of the country quickly. For US$330, the pass allows you virtually unlimited air travel within Brazil for 21 days. You must buy the pass outside Brazil, however, and no city may be visited twice (except at the start and finish of your trip). Also offered is a 14-day version of the Air Pass which costs US$250. With this pass you can only fly to four cities not including the one you start from. Your travel agent at home will sell you an MCO (Miscellaneous Charges Order) redeemable in Brazil for the Air Pass. Despite the popularity of the Air Pass with foreign tourists — most of whom want to visit as many Brazilian cities as possible — backcountry travellers should think twice before purchasing one. Since you'll probably need at least two weeks to really penetrate areas like Amazônia or the Pantanal, the value of a 21-day airpass is dubious.

If you're anxious to get into the backcountry quickly, don't forget small charter planes. If it's got a runway (or even a reasonably flat pasture) and you've got the money, you can fly there. This is particularly true in Amazônia, where hundreds of pilot/entrepreneurs fly *garimpeiros* in and out of the goldfields daily. The best places to locate small charter flights are in the Manaus and Belém airports. The Brazilian-made Bandeirante, a twelve-seater, is now the most common plane on charter runs.

An airport departure tax is charged on all domestic flights. This varies somewhat depending on the airport, but generally runs about US$2.50.

Miscellaneous

If there isn't a bus, taxi, plane, or boat going there, don't despair. This is Brazil, after all, where they will *dar um jeitinho* ('find a way'). Four-wheel drive owners often hire their jeep out as a sort of informal collective taxi; you'll pay a flat fee, but you'll also have to wait until the driver has a full load of paying passengers. In the north-east, you can still ride a genuine *pau-de-arara* ('parrot's perch'), a huge flatbed truck designed to carry both passengers and cargo. These tend to operate out of very small towns on loose schedules; see Chapter 7 for a description. And finally, there is four-legged transport — donkeys, usually — along the north-east coast.

Deserted beach in Rio Grande de Norte (North-east coast)

LODGING

City lodging

Even the most ardent backpackers end up spending a fair number of nights in hotels. Hotels in Brazil run the gamut from cheap flophouse to four-star palace. Virtually all of them include breakfast (*café da manhã*) in the cost, but be sure to ask before checking in. We prefer hotels in the US$5 per night range (price is for a double, with breakfast included), although we've spent as little as US$2 and as much as US$22. At these prices, bathrooms and showers are often shared. Many hotels feature both *quartos* (simple rooms with a washbasin but shared toilet and bath) and *apartamentos* (rooms with private bath).

Pensões (singular *pensão*) and *pousadas* were originally cheap, simple lodgings with some meals included. Nowadays, few serve anything but breakfast, and the term *pousada* is often applied to quite expensive hotels near the beach. *Hotel familiar* generally refers to a cheap hotel which allows you to wash and dry clothes on the premises, and sometimes provides all meals. Unless your definition of adventure travel is somewhat broader than ours, you won't be staying in *moteis* (singular *motel*); motels in Brazil serve strictly as hideaways for extramarital affairs, complete with circular waterbeds, porn video, and hidden parking.

For hordes of young Brazilians, student residences are a popular and cheap alternative to hotels. These are usually called something like the *Casa dos Estudantes*, and are the Brazilian equivalent of a youth hostel. All state capitals have at least one university, and most have a student residence nearby. I've never heard of one that actually required you to be a student — or asked that you be young, for that matter. Most of the travellers in a student residence do tend to be Brazilians in their twenties on holiday, however. These places are big barracks or dormitory style-affairs, and men and women bunk separately. Don't plan on getting to sleep early; especially during school holidays (January and July), parties can erupt spontaneously in your bunkroom. Unlike a hotel, a student residence doesn't generally provide breakfast, nor will it be centrally located in most cities. Despite these disadvantages, *casas dos estudantes* are popular because they're dirt cheap and because they're a good place to meet other travellers, both Brazilian and foreign.

Guidebooks such as the *South American Handbook* and the *Guia Quatro Rodas* are invaluable for locating reasonably-priced rooms (although the latter favours the more expensive hotels, at least in the large cities). Remember, however, that the time lag involved in publication often means that prices can change dramatically. In some cases, hotels listed in a guide may no longer even exist. Rather than following the guidebooks slavishly, we look for patterns in hotel addresses; most budget hotels tend to be concentrated in certain neighbourhoods, so watch for street names that appear often in the guidebooks and head there to begin hotel-shopping. (When arriving in a

strange city by bus, we always check our bags in the *rodoviária* and then
set off to search for lodging.) Central bus stations, by the way, are
invariably surrounded by cheap hotels — although they are often
located in the seedier portions of town.

Some state-run tourist bureaux will have a listing of hotels, and may
even phone them to check on vacancies and current prices. This service
is especially convenient when the information desk is located in the bus
station.

The easiest way to locate a good hotel in a strange city, however, is to
ask fellow travellers who have been there. In most cases you'll be better
off asking foreign travellers; Brazilians themselves will tend to recommend the type of place with four stars and a uniformed doorman.

Insist on looking at hotel rooms before checking in, and be sure to
check that the fan, toilet, and shower are in working condition. Test the
bed if you have trouble sleeping on a marshmallow-soft mattress. As an
alternative, some hotels in northern Brazil have hooks (*ganchos*)
installed in the walls from which to hang your hammock. Look for
potential irritations such as noisy streets or bars. (We once learned,
somewhere past midnight, that our budget room in Belo Horizonte
faced an all-night *discoteca*! On another occasion, we had to endure the
squawking of the family macaw; while perhaps more authentically
tropical than disco music, the bird had a smaller repertoire of noises and
was equally disturbing.)

Many hotels and *pensões*, particularly those in the smaller cities
where nightlife is practically nonexistent, close their doors after
midnight. If you plan to return late, be sure to ask the staff what the
procedure is after-hours. You may be given a pass key, or simply told
which window to rap on to get someone's attention.

Most hotel rooms are cooled by fan (*ventilador*); air conditioning
costs more, and, once you've acclimated to the tropics, may give you a
nasty cold. If you end up with air conditioning, you may in some hotels
have to phone the front desk every time you want it turned on or off.
Economy hotels in northern and central Brazil never have hot water —
nor will you need it.

Toilets in budget hotels — as well as most homes — cannot flush toilet
paper. Drop used tissue in the box or basket next to the toilet.
Unsanitary as it may seem, this practice is much preferable to a plugged
and flooding toilet.

Be sure to leave your key at the desk whenever leaving the hotel;
otherwise, the maid won't change linen and clean the room.

When checking out, we follow the lead of our Brazilian friends and
give the maid a ten percent tip. Hand it to her personally, since a tip left
with the front desk may not always trickle down the chain of command.
You may also want to leave a tip with the people at the front desk if
they've been of special help.

A final note on hotel security: we have never had anything stolen from
a hotel room, and we credit that largely to our preference for small,
family-run hotels. A single, well-watched entrance and conscientious

owners can make all the difference in the world where security is involved. Most hotels, large and small, also have a safe (*cofre*) where you can store passports, money, and airline tickets during your stay. Be sure to fill out a receipt when placing money in the safe; we've never had a problem nor heard of one in this regard.

Lodging in the backcountry

As the pavement begins to run out, so do the well-marked hotels, *pensões*, and *dormitorios*. Don't be discouraged — as long as there are still two bricks stuck together in town, there will be a place to stay. Just ask around.

The simplest option is either to take a room or hammock space in a house where the owners will cook meals for you. A breakfast and dinner arrangement allows you to wander off during the day, providing your own lunch. Everry small village seems to have a household that can put travellers up in this manner. Feel free to haggle over the price, but in most cases you'll be paying less than US$3 per person, food included. Be sure to ask if there are any special rules of the house you should know about. We learned at one house where we'd decided to rent a room that the owner unleashed her huge watchdog every night at 2300, and that we'd best be inside by then.

The big advantage to this arrangement is that you'll cease to be a tourist; before long you'll feel like part of a real Brazilian family. Chances are you'll be invited along when the locals go fishing, or dancing, or firewood collecting. The food will be simple but hearty. We've tasted plenty of unusual, home-made dishes that you'll never see in cafés or restaurants, things like sweet avocado pudding, tapioca cakes, and stingray soup. Living conditions will be simple, often crowded. We once spent several nights in the same room with our host's children — all seven of them. Each night in the dark, I tried manoeuvering silently through an obstacle course of hammocks slung at crazy angles, and each night I managed to wake the whole room. Bathrooms will usually include nothing more than a pit toilet and a hand-operated water pump. Finally, don't expect much peace and quiet; we've been awakened by roosters, pigs, and even on one occasion by a donkey that wandered into our sleeping quarters. And then there was the night we spent with our hammocks slung in the village billiard parlour and dance hall ...

A second option that is particularly popular along the north-east coast is simply to rent a house. These tend to be mud-and-wattle or simple wood houses built by local fishermen. Once again, ask around town and be prepared to bargain a little. Sometimes you'll have a propane stove, a water pump, and a bathroom. In most cases, though, you'll end up with a bare house, no water, and a pit toilet. Ask the locals where you can bathe, wash clothing, and get water. Either cook with a camping stove or make arrangements with someone in town to feed you at breakfast and dinner.

If you don't have a hammock, it's an easy matter to find someone who will rent you one (see *Camping* below).

STORING GEAR

Travelling as lightly as possible means that you'll frequently need to store excess gear while you're in the backcountry. This is particularly true if you make numerous short trips into rural Brazil from a central town or city. Assuming that you don't have Brazilian friends living there, the next best solution in cities is to leave excess baggage at a hotel. I've never been refused, especially since it guarantees that I'll give the hotel my business for at least a day or two upon my return.

Safest bets are small hotels run by families and/or those where you've come to be a 'regular.' Offer to help carry your gear; that way you'll know exactly where it is. Leave a generous tip, both when you stash the gear and upon your return. It's wise to indicate a rough date for your return, but we know one Welshman who cached five different knapsacks (all of which contained money) in hotels throughout Brazil without any idea where his travels would take him. After a year of travelling, he reported no problems claiming his gear. I wouldn't be so cavalier; at least one traveller has reported a bag stolen by someone claiming to be a friend of the owner — complete with note to that effect and a description of the bag. It's easy enough for a thief to claim his own bag and while doing so check out other travellers' luggage. You may avoid this by putting your passport number on the bag and stipulate that it should only be claimed when the passport is presented.

The *guarda volumes* desks at interstate bus stations provide a more formal way to store gear for a small, fixed price. Be careful, though; some have limits on the length of time they'll hold onto your belongings.

CAMPING

Organized campgrounds are common in Brazil. The most popular are those run by the Camping Clube do Brasil, which has some 45 sites in 13 states. These and other campgrounds are listed in Quatro Rodas' *Guia de Areas de Camping*, an annually updated book on the order of their popular *Guia do Brasil*; you'll find it at most magazine and book stands. Organized campgrounds in Brazil tend to feature far more creature comforts than do their North American counterparts. Some actually have swimming pools, restaurants, electrical hookups and gift shops! A second disadvantage is that the vast majority of campgrounds are accessible only by car; seldom are they located along a bus line. While they won't put you in the backcountry, organized campgrounds have some advantages if your idea is simply to save money.

Along the north-east coast, you can feel free to camp just about anywhere on deserted sections of beach. Avoid pitching your tent or hammock directly beneath a coconut palm and be conscious of the high

tide mark. In small villages, you'll generally be permitted to set up camp
on someone's land for free; ask first, of course. We've even seen people
pitching their tents directly in the dirt main streets of small fishing
villages. In national parks in Amazônia and the Pantanal, you are
generally free to camp anywhere. Check in at the local IBDF outpost so
that you aren't taken as poachers. Never camp too close to small creeks
in the jungle — they can become raging torrents in a matter of minutes.
Remember that much of the jungle and lowland in both these areas is
farming or cattle-raising land; ask permission from the local ranchers,
and you'll usually be allowed to stay.

Never bring any type of firearm while camping in the Pantanal, lest
you be taken for poachers by the IBDF or army patrols.

We've cooked over both wood and charcoal (*carvão*) in Brazil, but a
small backpacking stove is most practical. See *What to Bring* in Chapter
2 for stove and fuel recommendations.

As far as I'm concerned, a good hammock (*rede*) is the only way to
sleep when camping in the tropics. Hammocks are less bulky and thus
more easily packed around than either sleeping bags or blankets.
Suspended above the ground, you won't be troubled by dampness, ants,
snakes, or spiders. It's also a very comfortable way to pass the night; the
Amerindians, who were introduced to hammocks by Portuguese and
Spanish explorers, claimed that sleeping in one was akin to being
wrapped in a mother's arms.

As mentioned in Chapter 2, my favorite hammocks for travel are
those made in Mexico's Yucatan peninsula. Brazil produces excellent
hammocks at bargain prices, however, and their only real disadvantage
is that they are somewhat bulkier and slower to dry than the Yucatecan
variety. The best places to buy hammocks in Brazil are the big cities in
Amazônia (Manaus, Belém) and Fortaleza on the north-east coast. The
text dealing with these cities mentions places to shop for a quality
hammock. Don't bother hammock-shopping in Rio or São Paulo;
cariocas and *paulistas* don't sleep in hammocks, so the ones you'll find
for sale will be expensive tourist mementos. Be sure to check the size of
the hammock against your body before buying — remember that
Brazilians tend to be much shorter than most gringos.

As long as you're buying a hammock, pick up a mosquito net
(*mosquiteiro*). Get the finest mesh available, since some of the coarse
meshes allow mosquitoes inside. Have the clerk show you how to hang
the *mosquiteiro*. You'll also need some rope (*corda*) with which to hang
your new hammock. For some reason, stores selling hammocks don't
often stock rope, so have the clerk direct you to the nearest hardware
store.

Hanging a hammock is relatively easy, but it takes a few moments of
practice for the uninitiated to learn the proper way to lie in one. First,
put some weight on the hammock to test that both your knots and
whatever you've tied to are stable. Then gently climb in at about a 30-
degree angle. Beginners commonly try to lie down with their body

parallel to the long axis of the hammock, a sure way to spend a sleepless night and stretch the *rede* out of shape.

On the north-east coast, we sleep in our hammocks under a light cotton sheet. In the Amazonian rain forest you'll probably want a light wool blanket at night (hard to believe, but true!).

When camped near a village, it's always easy to rent a hammock. Just ask around. At the beginning of our first trip to Brazil, this proved so convenient that I wondered why anyone bothered to buy and tote around their own hammock. That was before I spent a nearly sleepless night in a tiny, rented hammock of coarse fibres. The next day, upon closer inspection, it proved to be a trawl net for fishing!

If you're worried about insects creeping into your hammock, spread a film of repellent on the loops at each end.

Store your hammock in a plastic sack, carefully folding the ends so that the small strings don't become tangled. Particularly in Amazônia, be careful that your hammock doesn't get mouldy or mildewy. There is no way to prevent a hammock from soaking up a good deal of that moist rain forest air, but the problem occurs when you pack it for travel. Unless you air-dry the hammock at your next stop, you can wind up with a smelly, mildewed bundle of cotton within a single day. Make a practice of unpacking your hammock immediately upon reaching a new camping site so that it has time to air. When you've left the jungle and returned to civilization, hang the hammock in your hotel room for as many days as possible before repacking.

FOOD

Eating in restaurants

Food in Brazil tends to be a bland and monotonous combination of white rice, beans, and either fish, chicken, or beef. While gourmet fare can be fashioned from these most prosaic of ingredients — Mexican cooks, after all, have been doing just that for centuries — Brazilians prefer a simple diet that steers clear of any seasoning other than salt. There are regional exceptions, of course; the African-influenced cuisine of Bahia, rich with palm oil, dried shrimp, okra, nuts, and hot peppers, is a celebrated national treasure. Don't expect to see such exotic foods outside the large coastal cities, however.

On the bright side, you won't starve in Brazil. From posh restaurant to seedy riverfront café, the portions are huge — so huge, in fact, that Jayne and I generally split a single plate of food when we eat out.

Brazilians eat three meals a day; breakfast (*café da manhã*) is a simple affair of french bread, butter, occasionally a piece of fruit, and coffee. In the north-east, especially in the countryside, expect chewy tapioca cakes instead of bread. Lunch (*almoço*) is a scaled-down version of supper — rice, beans, and either fish, chicken or beef — eaten sometime between 1100 and 1400. Large, extended lunches aren't common in

Brazil as they are in some other Latin American countries. Supper (*jantar*) is the big meal of the day, and it's eaten anywhere from 1800 to 2300 — earlier in the country, later in the city. *Jantar* is again based on rice, beans, noodles at times, and either fish, chicken, or beef.

Desserts are uncommon, but coffee always follows the meal. Brazil outdistances all other countries in coffee production, but to watch Brazilians down the stuff you would wonder that there's any left to export. The whole country seems to run on *cafezinhos*, thimble-like servings of sweet, syrupy black coffee taken throughout the day until bedtime. Finding an unsweetened *cafezinho* isn't always possible; often it is brewed with copious amounts of sugar mixed in with the grounds. Coffee is something of a national ritual, and we've been offered *cafezinhos* everywhere from posh government offices to tin shanties in the north-east. Unfortunately, backcountry travellers will frequently have to make do with powdered Nescafe.

The cheapest eateries in the towns and cities are the so-called *lanchonettes*. Most serve a variety of *salgadinhos* (deep-fried snack food), sandwiches, and the ubiquitous hamburger. Many *lanchonettes* also whip up excellent fruit juices (*sucos*), freshly-blended from local fruits such as mangoes, papayas, oranges, limes, pineapples, water-melons, and passion fruit. *Vitaminas* are juices fortified with milk. *Lanchonettes* generally require that you order and pay first at the cashier where you're given a receipt (*ficha*) to claim your food.

If you're in need of something more substantial, there is no lack of small cafés and restaurants. The most economical meal is the *prato feito* (sometimes known as the *prato commercial* or the *prato do dia*) which features meat, rice, beans, and spaghetti for around US$1.50. Bra-zilians liberally sprinkle such a plate with *farinha* (ground manioc flour), which resembles coarse cracker meal. *Farinha* that has been lightly toasted in butter or oil is known as *farofa*. By far the most popular restaurants are the *churrascarias*, serving salted beef grilled on a spit. *Churrasco* is Brazil's true national dish — despite *feijoada's* flimsy claim to the title — and you'll find at least one *churrascaria* in every town big enough to show up on a map. *Rodízios* are specialized *churrascarias* where you can eat your fill of grilled meat for a fixed, reasonable price. The *rodízio* is a vegetarian's worst nightmare: an army of waiters continually parade past the tables, hefting huge slabs of smoky, skewered meat which drip gobbets of fat and blood on the tables as the diners make their choices. One of the most prized cuts is known as *cupim* — the fatty, dorsal hump of the zebu steer.

Beer is the national drink at lunch and supper, sharing the spotlight with Coca-Cola. Brazilian beer generally comes in 600 ml bottles, with Antárctica, Brahma, Skol, and Malt 90 the popular brands. If the waiter pauses before opening your *cerveja*, he's expecting you to test the bottlecap with index and middle finger for the proper icy chill. Draft beer (*choppe*) is particularly common in the larger cities. All restaurants carry bottled water (*agua mineral*) and soft drinks (including *guaraná*, a sweet and mildly stimulating soda made from a native Amazonian berry.) Brazil's raw sugarcane rum goes by the name of *cachaça* (or *pinga* in the south); mixed with sugar and limes, it becomes a *caipirinha*. (Some *caipirinha* purists further insist that the limes be crushed with a freshly-cut chunk of sugarcane). Avoid the highly-refined *pingas* such as São Francisco and stick with the cheaper brands (Pitu, Tatuzinho, or Velho Barreiro), all of them redolent of raw cane and a bargain at US$0.55 a bottle. And finally, there is Brazilian wine. The best thing that can be said about local wine is that it is not actually poisonous. If you must have wine, order Chilean or Argentinian.

Vegetarians won't find much to eat in either restaurants, cafés, or private homes. Green vegetables are virtually non-existent in the Brazilian diet, and I've actually heard locals claim that they were harmful! All-you-can-eat, buffet-style vegetarian restaurants can now be found in most large cities, but they are generally open only for lunch. Chinese restaurants (also common in most of the larger cities) may be able to serve you a plate of crispy greens, but a vegetarian's best bet is the marketplace.

A service charge (*serviço*) of 10% is generally included on a restaurant's bill; leave a tip otherwise. Service can be lackadaisical, and it is not considered at all impolite to call a waiter with a loud hiss (more a '*psyoo*' than a hiss).

Buying your own food

Food stores in Brazil run the gamut from huge *supermercados* to tiny *mercearias* that stock little more than crackers and Coca-Cola. Shops in the backcountry often specialize: for beef or pork you'll have to locate the *carniceria*, for chicken the *galetaria*, and for fish the *pescaria*. The best place to lay in stores for camping, however, is the local marketplace (*mercado municipal*). The *mercado* is the focal point, socially speaking, of many small towns, and often occupies the geographical centre of the town as well. Here you'll find a dizzying array of tropical fruits and vegetables that rarely find their way into cafés, restaurants, or middle-class kitchens. Prices for all items are usually displayed per kilogram, but occasionally you'll see fruit put up in small batches called *lotes*. If prices aren't displayed, we usually hang around within earshot until a local buys the product we're interested in; you may find yourself paying a wildly exorbitant price otherwise. Food prices generally aren't haggled over in the marketplace, and will vary only slightly from vendor to vendor. Don't be shy about asking for samples, however — most vendors are eager to prove that they've got the sweetest papayas or mangoes or starfruit, and will gladly slice you off a chunk to taste. Bring a large bag or knapsack to carry your produce; there will be children selling large plastic shopping bags if you forget yours.

Bakeries (*padarías*) are often completely sold out of bread by ten o'clock in the morning, so do your shopping early. And if you plan to buy beer, remember that there is a substantial deposit levied on the bottles (*cáscaras*), often as much as a third the cost of the beer.

FISHING, HUNTING AND FORAGING

My advice to those who plan to eat off the land in Brazil is simple: forget it. Contrary to popular myth, the jungle is not laden with succulent fruits dangling from every tree. Nor is there wild game at every bend in the trail. If you doubt this, reflect for a moment on the lives of the Amazonian Indians, whose daily routine is a constant struggle to find food. Travellers in extremely remote areas for extended periods may have to ignore this advice; John Harrison managed to augment his dried and tinned food during river trips by hunting, fishing, and foraging, all of which he describes in his book *Up the Creek*.

Foraging

Most of the tropical fruits found in the marketplaces are cultivated rather than wild. In some cases these fruits aren't even native to South America; take for instance the banana, originally imported from Southeast Asia. This means that you should think twice before picking that ripe *caju* fruit or that football-sized *jaca* (jack fruit) during your stroll in the 'jungle.' Chances are good they were planted by a local who can ill afford to have his food stolen by wealthy gringos. When in doubt, check the area for any sign of cultivation, fences, or nearby huts. Remember that Brazilian 'orchards' are not the neatly manicured affairs that you're used to seeing, and can look a good deal like untamed jungle. If people live nearby, ask politely if you may pick some fruit in the area. You'll rarely be refused. The fruit of the cashew (*caju*) tree is an unexpected delight to those whose only acquaintance is with the nut. Pop the nut off the fruit, squeeze it until soft, and suck out the juices from the hole left by the nut. The nuts can then be roasted in a pan until they pop and sizzle, allowing the husk to be discarded. Other treats include mangoes and coconuts; we've visited areas in the north-east where coconuts and mangoes grew so plentifully that the locals fed them to pigs. Always, however, offer payment.

Fishing

Fishing is, in most cases, a far more rewarding method of supplementing your store-bought foodstuffs than either hunting or fruit-foraging. It's possible to catch saltwater fish with simple hook-and-line gear along the beaches of the north-east, but freshwater generally provides the easiest fishing for beginners. Many rivers and creeks in both the Pantanal and Amazônia teem with easily-hooked fish; see Chapters 5 and 6 for more detailed information on techniques and local species.

Fishing gear can be hard to come by in Brazil. Don't expect to be able to buy, for example, monofilament line or barbed hooks in most backcountry towns. Local fishermen will be understandably reluctant to part with their gear. Chapters 5 and 6 list some suppliers in the large cities like Cuiabá and Manaus. Your best bet is to bring an assortment of lines, hooks, and gear from home (see *Fish and Fishing in the Pantanal* in Chapter 5 for tackle recommendations).

Fishing licences aren't required for beaches along the north-east coast nor for Amazônia. Two government agencies control sport and commercial fishing in the Pantanal: the Instituto de Preservação e Controle Ambiental (INAMB) in the the state of Mato Grosso do Sul, and the Instituto Brasileiro de Desenvolvimento Florestal (IBDF) in the state of Mato Grosso. These agencies issue fishing licences, but primarily for big-time sport anglers after the really prized game fish. Backcountry travellers, most of whom will be filling a modest creel with piranhas and small catfish, will not require a licence. See Chapter 5 for more details.

When in doubt as to the best fishing locations, time of day, or techniques to use, just sidle up to one of the locals and politely ask. Anglers worldwide are a secretive bunch, and while Brazilians are no exception, they'll generally be pleased to let you, the *estrangeiro*, in on a few local secrets. After all, they know you won't be staying long enough to compete with them or drive a species to extinction. They also know that you'll be perfectly happy with the less prized types of fish, such as piranhas. And finally, they know that their fishing secrets are buying a great afternoon's entertainment. On one occasion, local fishermen practically begged Jayne and me to reel in catfish after catfish that they had hooked in the Paraguai River.

Hunting (Shooting)

Hunting in Brazil is primarily a sport of wealthy São Paulo businessmen who can afford guided trophy hunts into the hinterland. There are, of course, countless subsistence hunters among the Indians and *caboclos*, but even with their expertise in the ways of the forest, hunting is an uncertain existence. All hunting is expressly forbidden in the Pantanal, and there are no game animals to speak of along the north-east coast. That leaves Amazônia, where the thick rain forest automatically precludes most hunting as we know it. Even as a supplemental source of food, hunting isn't usually worth the trouble.

If you absolutely insist on hunting, you'll need a shotgun, since rifles and handguns are impractical in the forest. No firearms may enter the country, meaning that you'll have to buy one there. Visit the Polícia Federal to apply for a permit; they'll have suggestions also on where to purchase a gun.

PHOTOGRAPHY

Supplies

As noted earlier, film is extremely expensive in Brazil. If you find that you've run out, your best bets in terms of availability and price are São Paulo and Rio. In Rio, an excellent source of photographic equipment is Kartel, rua Senador Dantas, 44. Nickel-cadmium batteries for light meters are tough to find even in the city, so bring extras from home.

Care of equipment and special techniques

The Pantanal presents no unusual challenges for photographers, at least during the dry season. The north-east coast and Amazônia, however, will test both your skill and equipment.

Along the beaches of the north-east, you'll need to protect your gear from the destructive influence of sand and saltwater. Don't underestimate the corrosive power of fine, windblown salt spray on the beach; keep your camera in its case at all times except when actually taking pictures. You may even want to cover the entire camera with a plastic bag, leaving only the lens uncovered. Secure the plastic bag around the lens sleeve with a rubber band. Use an ultraviolet filter to protect the front lens element, and wipe salt spray off frequently with a rag dampened in fresh water or alcohol. Don't change film or open the camera for any reason on the beach; all it takes is a single grain of sand to destroy your film and possibly your camera.

The same clear blue skies and white sand that make deserted beaches so attractive also present some photographic challenges. With the sun overhead, the beach tends to lose all textural detail, and photos taken at midday look bland and formless. Avoid this by shooting when the sun is at a low angle — early in the morning or late in the afternoon. Huge expanses of white sand and water reflect so much light that through-the-lens meters and especially automatic-exposure cameras are easily fooled. With all that sun, the ironic result is frequently an underexposed photo. Try increasing the exposure by about one aperture stop; for important pictures, bracket your exposures by two stops on either side. Alternatively, you can use a light meter that takes incident readings off the subject rather than registering the entire sun-washed scene. A polarizing filter can help restore colour and contrast dulled by the effects of heat haze.

The Amazonian rain forest is perhaps the ultimate challenge for a photographer. Humidity is always above 80%, ever eager to seep into your camera and wreak havoc. The enemy is not only moisture in the air; some jungle photographers have had their gear ruined by fungal growths. There is no drying out a fungus-infested camera, and fungal growth on lenses can actually etch the glass forever. Keep cameras and lenses in two tightly-sealed plastic bags at all times except when actually shooting. And don't try to get away with just one bag! If you have a camera case with a good silicone rubber gasket, so much the better. Whether you've got a case or decide to cheap it out like we do with plastic bags, you'll want to surround your camera with plenty of silica-gel packets to absorb moisture. These can be dried in an oven or even over a campfire when they've become sodden.

Film requires as much protection as do cameras in the rain forest. Never open film canisters until you are ready to load the film. As soon as the roll is exposed, reseal it with some silica gel and keep it as cool as possible. This generally means keeping it in the shade. Do not put exposed film on ice or in cool streams, because you'll run the risk of condensation.

Taking pictures in the rain forest is always difficult. It becomes absolutely impossible unless you've brought that one vital piece of equipment: a tripod. You'll be amazed at how little light actually penetrates below the forest canopy until you consult your light meter. Four-second exposures are not at all uncommon with slow-speed films (ASA 64 and 100), and some situations may require even longer exposures. We favour a lightweight tripod that can easily telescope into a backpack. The disadvantage with lightweight tripods is that you cannot trip the shutter yourself and expect a sharp picture; the forest floor, strewn with leaf litter, assures that your feather-light tripod is going to wiggle. We circumvent this problem using a cable shutter release. Be forewarned that sunny days actually pose more picture-taking headaches in the rain forest than overcast days. The contrast between deep shadows and sun-dappled foliage, striking as it may look to your eyes, is far too variable for any film to capture. Neither electronic flashes nor high-speed film will solve the problem. Your best bet is simply to wait until clouds move in to create a more uniform light situation. In the rain forest, you won't be waiting long. A very similar problem arises when shooting near creeks or rivers in the jungle. The contrast between brightly-lit water and shadowy foliage results in some truly bizarre photographs. Once again, wait for clouds and bracket your exposures.

Some photographers try to outfox the perpetual dark of the rain forest by using high-speed films. If you are satisfied with the inherent graininess of these films, bring some along. Even with ASA 400 film, however, we have had to resort to the tripod on occasion.

We highly recommend an electronic flash for both night photography and for closeups of insects and plants in the jungle. Let's face it, most of your wildlife photography in the rain forest is going to be confined to small, relatively immobile objects anyway: flowers, butterflies, beetles, snakes, frogs, and spiders. With a flash, you can leave the tripod behind and take these sorts of pictures easily. Don't waste your film trying to take wide-angle shots of the jungle with a flash, however; hand-held flash units don't pack nearly enough punch to light such large areas, and they'll leave all but the foreground in deep shadow.

It would take another book to teach wildlife photography, and Jayne and I won't be writing it; we've filled this guide with drawings of animals rather than photographs for a very good reason! As just mentioned, it is relatively easy for rank amateurs such as ourselves to take good shots of insects and reptiles, particularly at night. Only trained wildlife photographers are likely to get shots of larger animals in the jungle, however. Most of your glimpses of large animals will be fleeting. Both the thick jungle foliage and the gloomy light situation discourage action shots of animals fleeing you in the rain forest. For the beginner, the wide-open expanses of the Pantanal make a much easier studio for wildlife photos than does the Amazonian rain forest. Even so, you'll need lots of patience, luck, most likely a local guide, and the right equipment. A good telephoto lens is essential for wildlife photography. Even with most zoom lenses, you'll be hardpressed to pick out the animal from the background in the finished photos. Jayne was once able to drift incredibly close to a basking alligator along a tributary of the Paraguai River, snapping the shutter just before the beast plunged into the water. She'd zoomed her telephoto lens in all the way, and we were so close that our aluminium canoe was splashed with water. Nevertheless, the finished picture looked as if we'd been on the other side of the river, and no one much believed our tales of nearly becoming part of the food chain.

Developing/Storing your film

Unless you are staying in Brazil for a long time — over a year — it's probably best to simply hold onto your exposed film and develop it upon your return home. Processing can be shoddy; and mailing film, like mailing anything else from Brazil, is very risky. If you do decide to mail film home, mark the package accordingly to avoid its being x-rayed at customs. Remember that exposed film is more vulnerable than unexposed film to the tropical heat and humidity. Keep your exposed film sealed, dry, and as cool as possible without actually chilling it (which can cause condensation). Placing your film on concrete floors will cool it a few degrees, as will burying it in the ground. Unexposed film should be treated with the same respect, although it can be refrigerated safely when you're in the city. Most hotel owners will let you store film in their coolers, even if they cast some quizzical glances your way.

Photographic etiquette

A few words about taking pictures of people, advice that is perhaps just plain common sense and courtesy:

Remember that backcountry folk tend to be fairly shy. Candid shots of what to you is their colourful way of life may make them extremely uncomfortable. Use discretion, and when in doubt, don't take out your camera. Jayne and I once came upon a tiny fishing village during a hike along the north-east coast. During our fifteen-minute chat with the villagers, we realized that there was an exceptional photograph staring us right in the face: the sun setting on thatched huts, primitive nets hung up to dry, barefoot children smiling coyly from behind their mothers' skirts, the whole thing framed by coconut palms. But we couldn't do it. We just couldn't whip out the camera and reduce these shy, trusting folk to picturesque curiosities.

If we had really wanted that shot — and wanted to retain our self-respect in the bargain — the thing would have been to return the next afternoon, chat some more, invest a bit of ourselves. But we didn't, and consequently we deserved to miss the shot. Too bad … it would have made one hell of a cover.

Photo opportunities abound in the public markets. Both picturesque vendors and their wares make great travel photos. Once again, however, don't barge in and simply start shooting. Even if what you really want is a shot of the colourful old fishmonger himself, praise first his fine selection of groupers, mullet, and sardines. Ask for a small fillet of his cheapest fish, adding that you'd love to get a picture to remember the moment. You can always give the fish away later. This method ends up costing a little money, but you won't have to sneak furtively through the market, nor will you feel that you're taking advantage of your subjects. Taking 'people shots' with a telephoto lens is decidedly sneaky, but sometimes it's the only way to get an unposed shot.

Incidentally, we have never been asked for money by Brazilians whose pictures we've snapped. If you're solicited in this manner, chances are you're not in the backcountry.

JOBS

To work legally in Brazil you must first obtain a work permit. This involves a great deal of time, money, and bureaucratic red tape, which probably explains why no one bothers to get one. If you'd like to try, visit the Ministério de Trabalho, avenida Presidente Antônio Carlos 251 A, ground floor, in Rio.

Most travellers who want to earn money in Brazil become language teachers. It seems as if every Brazilian wants to learn English, although there is some work for German and French teachers. For professional teachers it's an opportunity to practice the craft under unusual but rewarding circumstances. Unfortunately, virtually all the work is in large and relatively uninspiring cities: São Paulo, Belo Horizonte, and Porto Alegre top the list. Don't bother applying at the established schools such as Yazigi and Cultura Inglesa; they'll probably require a work visa and will pay next to nothing. Smaller schools may be worth trying, however. Most foreigners simply free-lance, advertising locally and eventually drawing students by word of mouth. Average pay for a conversational class runs about US$5 per hour.

Foreign musicians are always in demand in Brazil; a few years ago, American country and western bands were the rage in São Paulo.

CUSTOMS, ETIQUETTE, AND OTHER TOUCHY SUBJECTS

To the traveller accustomed to Spanish-speaking South and Central America, Brazil will come as something of a cultural anomaly. At the risk of some oversimplification, let it be said that Brazilians are a lot more casual than their Latin neighbours. (Brazilians, by the way, often refer to the rest of the continent as *latino*.) They are noticeably more gregarious, quicker to begin a conversation with foreigners, more direct in their speech, and more physically expressive. Sexual codes are also more relaxed in Brazil. Brazilians say it best themselves: they are *quente* — 'hot.'

All this means that you as a traveller need not be quite so concerned with propriety as you might in other South American countries. As in any foreign country, however, recognize that you are a guest and act accordingly. Recognize also that customs do differ; take your cues from the locals before becoming an active participant in their world. What follows is a random list of do's and don'ts:

Dress and groom yourself as neatly as possible. Like all South Americans, Brazilians pride themselves on their appearance, and nothing repels them more than an affluent foreigner dressed in tattered, faded jeans, sporting a three-day growth of beard, and smelling like the Manaus fish market at noon. Obviously, you and your clothing are going to get pretty rumpled camping along the Transpantaneira; but clean up before you hit the streets of Cuiabá again, or even before visiting that farmhouse to ask permission to pitch your tent. It can't be over-emphasized — slovenly dress harkening back to the hippie era is probably the single most common cultural *faux pas* committed by foreign travellers in Brazil.

Never enter churches in shorts and/or tee shirts.

Brazilian women do indeed wear the tiniest bikinis in the world — the *tanga*. And *tangas* are getting smaller, if that's possible; a new variation is being called the *fio dental* — 'dental floss'! Topless bathing, however, is not at all common in Brazil, and nude bathing is unheard of. Unless you are totally and completely secluded, keep your bathing suits on. Keep in mind that villagers along the primitive north-east coast are not nearly as accustomed to seeing the *tanga* as are more cosmopolitan Brazilians; wear a modest cover when returning to the village. Public beaches near Amazonian river towns are fairly conservative; Rio-style *tangas* are too immodest here and should be avoided.

Along the north-east coast, dress is extremely casual. Shorts, tee-shirts, and sandals are quite acceptable wear for both men and women at all times of the day and night. In the cities (except at the beach itself) and from Rio south, long pants and dresses are *de rigeur*. In general, however, Brazilians are far less offended by beach wear away from the beach than are other South Americans.

Be especially conscious of your appearance when meeting with government officials for a favour (such as permission to visit a biological reserve). Even in the equatorial zones, wear slacks and a long-sleeved shirt, and shined shoes if you have some. Business cards and/or letters of introduction on letterhead stationery are a real bonus during such meetings. Anything official-looking will do.

Always greet a stranger with a '*bom dia*' or '*boa tarde*' before asking a question. To get someone's attention or to move past them in a crowded bus, say '*licença*.' If you've stepped on their foot, say '*desculpe*.'

Strangers should be addressed with the formal '*o senhor*' or '*a senhora*' at least in the beginning of a dialogue. As soon as you hear them use the informal '*você*' or '*tu*', feel free to follow suit. Brazilians themselves don't always follow this rule, particularly if they consider the person being addressed as belonging to a lower economic or social class, but you can't go wrong being overly polite. In the same vein, avoid calling waiters and domestic help with the somewhat demeaning '*moço*' (boy), even though Brazilians do it all the time. Professional people are often addressed, even among friends, as '*doutor*.' No knowledge of medicine is required; an architect, a lawyer, an engineer, even a lowly biologist is referred to as '*o doutor*.'

Brazilian men shake hands on meeting. Once a friendship has been established — and that can happen over a beer in Brazil — the *abraço* or hug is used for greeting and taking leave. Take your cues from the Brazilians you meet as to what to do.

Women and men who are acquainted always kiss upon meeting and taking leave. Kissing is also the standard greeting between women. The Brazilian *beijo* consists of a light hug and a quick peck on first one cheek, then the other, and frequently a third kiss as well. Total strangers often kiss upon being introduced. Once again, just take your cues from the Brazilians. You'll end up doing a lot of kissing in Brazil — tough as it is, you must learn to accept the local customs!

There are almost never lines (*filas*) for city buses or trains. Push and shove your way like everyone else if you want to make it aboard. I have very rarely seen men give up bus seats to women, even elderly women. Pregnant women are an exception.

Brazilians are typically late. Let's be honest — they are *always* late. It is considered somewhat rude, in fact, to arrive on time for a dinner or party. Get used to what is proudly known as the *hora brasileira* (Brazilian time).

Brazilians never decline invitations to parties, dinners, or other social functions; this is considered rude. If they have other plans or aren't interested, they accept nonetheless and simply don't show up. This isn't considered rude.

Don't expect Brazilians to understand your occasional desire to be alone for a while. As far as they're concerned, you're either very depressed or very rude to want to be by yourself.

Our common hand symbol for 'OK' — thumb and index finger forming an 'o' — is an obscene gesture meaning anus in South America. Stick your thumb up instead.

Politics aren't taken as seriously in Brazil as they are in, say, Argentina. But they are freely discussed throughout the country. Even before the military stepped down, Brazilians were openly derisive of the generals. We heard the military government blamed for everything from potholes to poor fishing. There are no real political tender spots, but foreigners, especially Americans, can expect some ribbing about the FMI (World Monetary Fund) and the debilitating national debt.

Women Travellers

Jayne assures me that Brazil is the easiest country in either South or
Central America for the lone female traveller. A number of women
we've met on the road agree. It's rare for a woman — even a blonde —
to hear the catcalls that are so common in Spanish-speaking America.
It's not that *machismo* isn't firmly entrenched in Brazil. It is. Yet
Brazilian men, even in the backcountry, seem more sophisticated
around single foreign women than do their Spanish-speaking counterparts. I can't explain it; perhaps by acting blasé, they're actually pushing
machismo to new limits.

Still, if a woman has a choice, she'll have a much easier time of it by
travelling with a male friend or with a group of women. In a country
where no one would consider vacationing alone, any single traveller of
either sex is considered an oddity.

Common sense dictates that women dress modestly in the
backcountry.

Beggars

Brazil is a riddled with poverty, and Brazil's poor are far worse off now
than ten years ago. Once in the backcountry, you will rarely if ever see a
beggar; even if the standard of living is dismally low, the rural poor take
care of their own, here as in other countries. It is in the cities that
begging has become a way of life. Dealing with beggars is obviously a
personal decision, but keep one thing in mind: unlike our own societies,
Brazil has no welfare system whatsoever to care for the poor or
disabled.

We follow a few simple rules: we give money to beggars when we
notice other Brazilians doing the same, and we never give money to
children; you can be sure that any adult begging for money sincerely
needs it to survive, whereas the same is not necessarily true for children.

Gift-giving

Plenty of travellers like to play Santa Claus when they hit a remote town
in the backcountry, passing out candies, bubblegum, balloons, and
trinkets of all kinds to the local children. I have no proof of this, but I
suspect that many of these same people balk at giving money to needy
beggars in the big city. In any case, it's a detestable practice.
Backcountry folk are amazingly self-sufficient; they don't need these
gifts — at least until they've been habituated by a string of gift-giving
foreigners — and may even resent them. What most rural Brazilians
really want from you is an insight into your strange way of life. Sit down
and talk with them, show them photographs of your family back home,
play a song for them or teach them a dance ... do anything but play
Great White Father.

The preceding advice applies strictly to the backcountry. You can and
should give gifts to urban Brazilian friends. Alcohol — especially real
Scotch whisky from home — is highly prized.

Vitória Régia waterlilies outside Porto Jofre, Pantanal

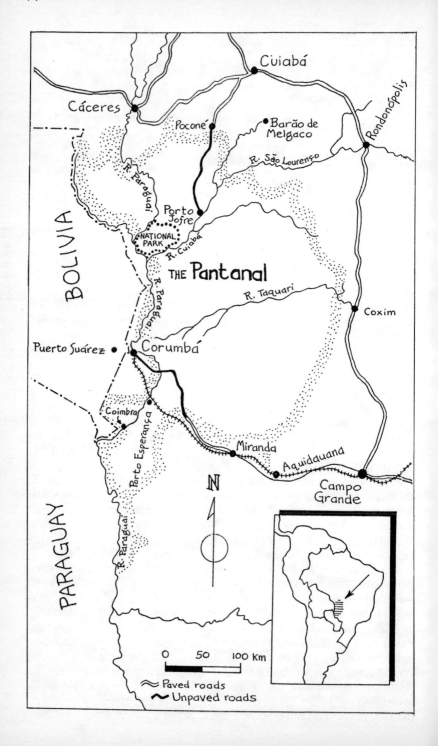

Cuiabá

Cáceres

Poconé

Barão de
Melgaco

R. São Lourenço

Rondonópolis

BOLIVIA

R. Paraguai

Porto
Jofre

NATIONAL
PARK

R. Cuiabá

THE Pantanal

R. Taquari

Coxim

R. Paraguai

Puerto Suárez

Corumbá

Coimbra

Porto Esperança

Miranda

Aquidauana

Campo
Grande

PARAGUAY

R. Paraguai

N

0   50   100 Km

≈ Paved roads
∿ Unpaved roads

Chapter 5

The Pantanal

Big empty spaces are invariably the most intriguing part of a map for any backcountry traveller. Such a space appears on the *Guia Quatro Rodas* map where the Bolivian and Paraguayan borders toueh Brazil. Larger than a hand, this portion of the map is covered entirely by those tiny blue dashes which signify marshy ground. Except around the perimeter, there are no roads, no rail lines, no towns.

This is the Pantanal, an immense swampy plain encompassing some 230,000 square kilometres along the upper reaches of the Paraguai River. The chief draw here is wildlife; the Pantanal is home to more than 600 species of birds, 300 species of fish, and a wealth of terrestrial wildlife that includes alligators, monkeys, deer, capybaras, and the flightless, ostrich-like rhea.

True, there are other areas — Amazônia, for instance — that are richer in terms of both species and sheer numbers of animals. But unlike the thickly-jungled Amazon, the Pantanal keeps its wildlife largely on display. The terrain is open and veldt-like, the perfect setting for animal-watching. Once a vast inland sea, much of the Pantanal still floods with up to three metres of water during the rainy season. This further concentrates both wildlife and cattle on the remaining dry 'islands'. It is not at all uncommon to see the white, humpbacked steers known as *nelore* sharing an 'island' with a group of basking alligators.

The proximity to Bolivia and Paraguay has driven much of the Pantanal's human history over the past five centuries. The entire region was originally ceded to the Spanish following the Treaty of Tordesillas in 1494, but explorers didn't reach the interior until the 1520's. Spurred by tales of gold and silver, groups of hardy fortune-seekers from the São Paulo area cut their way as far west as the Paraguai River. Known as *bandeirantes*, they battled fiercely against both the Spaniards and the Portuguese Jesuits, enslaving Indians captured from the Jesuit missions. (Contrary to popular belief, the Jesuits had no qualms about the institution of slavery itself; they often fought to the death to protect their Amerindian converts, but were perfectly willing to see blacks enslaved.) As in the rest of Brazil, only remnant groups of Bororo Indians survive today in the areas bordering the Pantanal. Gold was discovered in the early 1700's. By 1719, Cuiabá had been founded to the north, and the area now known as Mato Grosso and Mato Grosso do Sul was made a royal captaincy by King João V of Portugal in 1748. Within thirty years, strategic forts protecting Portuguese land claims had sprung up on the Paraguai River near present-day Cáceres and Corumbá.

When the gold boom slowed, cattle ranching gradually took its place as the new economic mainstay of the area. That much hasn't changed to this day. Huge ranches, known variously as *fazendas* or *estancias*, make up virtually every square inch of the Pantanal that isn't under water the entire year. Many ranch owners live cosmopolitan lives far from their land and cattle; we visited one *fazendeiro* at his luxurious suburban home in Campo Grande, complete with swimming pool and a bar stocked with imported Scotch whisky.

Agriculture has played a part in the Pantanal's economy since the 1950's. You'll find rice, soybean, sugarcane, and coffee plantations scattered around the perimeter of the Pantanal. Industry has made inroads in the area as well; sugarcane alcohol, cement, and manganese mining may someday vie with cattle-ranching as the prime economic movers in this part of Brazil.

How to get there The Pantanal — more properly the Pantanal Matogrossense, since it spans the states of Mato Grosso and Mato Grosso do Sul — is accessible via the gateway cities of Campo Grande, Corumbá, Cuiabá, and Cáceres. Varig, Cruzeiro do Sul, and Vasp all run daily flights to Cuiabá and Campo Grande from Rio and São Paulo. Vasp has flights to Corumbá. Buses run daily to Cuiabá and Campo Grande from most state capitals throughout Brazil. From São Paulo, you can catch the Fepasa train daily to Bauru, then buy a ticket for the afternoon RFFSA train (leaving at 1545), which runs to Campo Grande and on to Corumbá. The train takes about 24 hours to reach Campo Grande, counting the layover in Bauru; make sure before leaving São Paulo that you'll be able to catch the afternoon train from Bauru, otherwise you're stuck there for the night.

Getting around Many visitors never get much farther into the the the Pantanal than the perimeter cities of Corumbá, Cuiabá, and Cáceres. The Pantanal itself is largely roadless, and public transportation is virtually nonexistent. Commercial truck and river boat traffic tends to be irregular. Faced with these problems, frustrated travellers often sign on for the type of four-hour boat 'safari' touted by the local hotels. They generally leave the Pantanal several cruzados poorer and just as frustrated. Penetrating the Pantanal takes time and a little initiative; the less of the former you have, the more of the latter you'll need. Either make up your mind to wait for that cargo boat — it may be days — or search out a boatman who will take you where you want to go on short notice. For those on a very tight schedule, there is still another alternative: the growing number of fishing lodges and ranches catering to tourists. You can arrange well in advance to be boated, trucked, or flown in to these places, and transportation from the lodge to good fishing or wildlife-viewing sites is readily available once there. The catch, of course, is that this is the costliest option for penetrating the Pantanal.

Where and how to see wildlife   In general, the best and easiest way to see lots of animals is to cruise the smaller rivers by canoe. Doing this with oars allows you to sneak up on animals that might flee the approach of a noisy gas motor. Even with a motor running, you'll suprise plenty of wildlife, but if you're with a guide insist that he cut the engine every now and then. During the bird mating season, a canoe trip to the breeding areas — usually dead-end channels — is a must. Walking the riverbanks also produces some fine wildlife-viewing, although it's not always possible; you're often cut off by meandering side-channels too deep to wade, or the underbrush gets too thick. You'll also make a good deal of noise thrashing about, noise that can frighten animals a lot more than the unexpected ruckus of a boat approaching from the middle of the stream. Walking the roads, few as they are, is an excellent way to spot wildlife, as is a hike along the railway. A number of ranches and lodges rent horses (usually accompanied by a guide); this is a great way to cover lots of ground — including marshes that would be difficult on foot — although you won't see quite as much wildlife on the grassy plains as along the small waterways. As a rule of thumb, your best animal-viewing will occur near dusk and near dawn. The sections below on birds, mammals, and alligators give more detailed advice.

When to go   There is no single 'best time' to visit the Pantanal. The rainy season runs from about late October through March. During this time, the rains which fall in the north of the Pantanal drain to the south, and huge expanses of grassland become completely covered with water. Floods often disrupt travel on the dirt roads around the perimeter of the Pantanal and even on the railroad itself. The floods bring on mosquitoes during January, February and March, with January the worst month. Despite these problems, there are a couple of advantages to visiting the Pantanal during the rainy season: first, it's warm, generally in the mid-20's. Secondly, as the waters rise, both cattle and wild animals are forced to cluster on the few remaining dry 'islands' (*cordilheiras*), where they are easy to see and photograph. Thirdly, the Pantanal's incredible array of flowering trees, water lilies, and water hyacinths all blossom during the wet season; February and March are best for these species, while orchids flower later (October or November).

If it's your first visit and you have the choice, however, you should probably visit the Pantanal during the dry season, which runs generally from late June to early October. This is the nesting and breeding season for thousands of egrets, storks, herons, cormorants, and ibises.

Particularly along calm oxbows in the rivers, you'll see tree after tree swarming with birds returning from their daytime feeding binges. The dry season also makes for better fishing, since gamefish tend to be concentrated in the remaining water. Fishing for many species is best between May and September, though several of the most important gamefish can be caught through December (see *Fish and Fishing in the Pantanal* in this chapter).

There are only two disadvantages to visiting during the dry season. One is the temperature; during June, July, and August, southerly winds sometimes bring cold Antarctic air to the Pantanal, plunging temperatures to near freezing. September and early October, while still dry, usually boast warmer temperatures. A second possible disadvantage to visiting the Pantanal during the dry season is the fact that navigation on the rivers is sometimes impeded by low water. If your itinerary includes river travel, you may want to avoid the driest months (July through September).

Finally, don't always expect the rainy and dry seasons to comply faithfully with the neat timetable above. We've seen roads washed out during the 'dry' season; we've hiked over river banks that were baked hard as concrete during the 'wet' season.

CAMPO GRANDE

Campo Grande is the state capital of Mato Grosso do Sul, founded in 1889 and now boasting 290,000 residents. It doesn't actually border the Pantanal; in fact, the nearest marshy land lies 130 km away near Aquidauana. Nevertheless, Campo Grande rates as a 'gateway city' because it's the terminus for buses and trains that run through the Pantanal on their way to Corumbá. The museum and state tourist office are also well worth visiting prior to a trip in the Pantanal.

Arrival   The bus station is located at rua Joaquim Nabuco 200, an easy two-block walk from avenida Calógeras, the main thoroughfare where most budget hotels are located. Daily buses run to Rio de Janeiro, São Paulo, Belo Horizonte, Brasília, Corumbá, Cuiabá, Ponta Porã, Rondonópolis, and many other smaller cities and towns. If you prefer to check your baggage while scouting for a hotel, the bus station has a *guarda volumes* desk. It's also a fairly easy walk from the bus station to the train station; just head up either rua Barão do Rio Branco or avenida Afonso Peña until you hit avenida Calógeras, then take a left and walk five or six blocks to the train depot.

Getting around   Virtually everywhere you might want to go in Campo Grande is within walking distance of the downtown area.

Changing money   If you have cash, ask at the reception desk of large, fancy hotels like the Campo Grande, Fenícia, and Jandaia for black

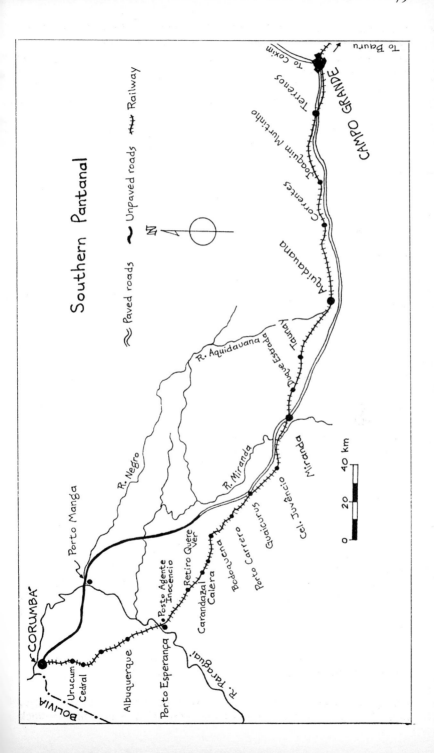

market rates. With travellers cheques, you're probably limited to the official rate at the Banco do Brasil, avenida Afonso Peña 2202.

Information   The MSTUR office at avenida Afonso Peña 3149 (phone 382-3091) is perhaps the best place in either Mato Grosso or Mato Grosso do Sul for information on Pantanal trips. They keep a notebook of all lodges within the Pantanal, complete with current prices and services. In addition, they'll provide information on fishing, and some advice for those travellers wishing to strike out on their own. They may be willing to part with copies of their fine colour travel posters of Pantanal wildlife.

Museum   Anyone seriously interested in the wildlife of the Pantanal should spend a few hours prior to the trip at the Museo Regional Dom Bosco, rua Barão do Rio Branco 1843. Here you'll find several rooms devoted entirely to stuffed birds, mammals, reptiles, and fish of the Pantanal. It's also a great way to learn their local Portuguese names. Along with the regional animal exhibits, there are collections of local Indian artifacts, sea shells, insects, and minerals. The museum is open daily, 0700-1100 and 1300-1700. The entrance fee is ridiculously low.

Shopping   The Casa do Artesão, avenida Calógeras 2050, has a good selection of local handicrafts for sale: carved and painted wooden animals, dried and lacquered river fish, homemade fruit liqueurs, leather, ceramics, Indian headdresses, spears, and arrows. Open Monday-Friday from 0800-1200 and from 1400-1800.

Trains   The train station is located at the corner of avenida Calógeras and avenida Mato Grosso. It's from here that most people catch the RFFSA train to Corumbá, known locally as the *Trem da Morte* ('Train of Death'). Two trains make daily runs to Corumbá: the night train, leaving at 2010 and arriving at 0640; and the day train, leaving at 0815 and arriving at 1930. Since both these trains originate in Bauru, some 650 km away, they tend to arrive in Campo Grande a bit late. It's not unusual for the morning train to leave Campo Grande at 0900. Obviously, the only way you'll see any of the Pantanal is to take the day train. Tickets are sold only on the day of travel. The ticket booth inside opens daily at 0645. First class tickets are US$2.75, second class cost US$1.90. With this minute price difference, there is absolutely no reason to ride second class. When the morning train arrives, it's a mad scramble for the remaining seats (remember, many passengers boarded between Bauru and Campo Grande). If you're travelling with a partner, do what the locals do: send one person — preferably the most aggressive — to claw his/her way into a likely-looking first class car, then pass baggage in through an open window once a vacant seat's been located. If you're left standing or separated, you'll probably find a seat when local travellers disembark in large towns like Aquidauana or Miranda.

Bring plenty of food and water for this trip. Vendors stroll the aisles periodically, selling *cafezinhos*, beer, and sandwiches at fairly inflated prices.

The train from Campo Grande to Corumbá doesn't enter the Pantanal proper until the Carandazal station; from there to just beyond the Paraguai River, a distance of about 40 km, many people get their first (and sometimes only) taste of this magnificent landscape and its wildlife. Unfortunately, the sun is usually setting just as the Campo Grande-Corumbá train reaches the river.

CORUMBÁ

Corumbá lies at the southwestern margin of the Pantanal, a sleepy port city of 81,000 people overlooking the Paraguai River. A huge cement factory operates here, as do manganese and iron works. But it is the river that dominates Corumbá. A broad blue-gray ribbon at the north end of the city, the Rio Paraguai flows past so languidly that it's nearly impossible to tell which direction is upriver and which is downriver. The city matches that languid pace; on our first trip, we'd expected a bustling port, not unlike Manaus, with scores of boatmen eager to take us into the Pantanal. We found instead a single row of cargo boats, only one of which was within a week of sailing. The closest that Corumbá's waterfront came to bustling occurred when a solitary fisherman pushed a wheelbarrow of freshly-caught catfish up the street.

Arrival/Departure   The train station is an easy walk from the city centre; follow the crowds, taking the dirt path through the large open field just north of the station; take a left on the first street, walk two blocks to rua Frei Mariano, and take a right. Frei Mariano is the main street in Corumbá, with a number of hotels and restaurants. If you have lots of baggage, take a taxi or horse-drawn carriage into the city centre.

The RFFSA trains for Bauru (via Campo Grande) run twice daily. The day train leaves at 0715, arriving in Campo Grande at 1830. The faster night train leaves at 2055, arriving at 0700. Fares are the same as the Campo Grande-Corumbá run, US$2.75 for first class and US$1.90 for second class.

There is no bus station *per se* in Corumbá. If arriving by bus, you'll be let off at the corner of rua Antônio Maria Coelho and rua América, in the city centre just a few blocks from the main street (rua Frei Mariano). Buses leave for Campo Grande (via Miranda and Aquidauana) and Puerto Suarez (Bolivia) from this same corner. A small storefront labeled Agencia Andorinha sells tickets. They keep irregular hours, generally opening shortly before scheduled departures. The daytime bus leaves for Campo Grande at 1130. During the rainy season, bus services may be halted for days or even weeks; try the train, which is rarely washed out.

The airport is 3 km from the city centre. VASP has daily flights to and from Rio, São Paulo, Cuiabá, and Campo Grande. A small charter plane is run by ETAPA, with a booth at the airport.

Police   Every foreigner leaving Corumbá by either train or bus can count on receiving a polite but very thorough search of both clothing and baggage by plainclothes members of the Polícia Federal. They approach bus travellers about 30 minutes before scheduled departure, and will have you empty your bags in a nearby storefront. On the train, they'll often wait until just minutes before scheduled departure to make their checks. These guys are dedicated; I was asked to remove my well-worn and highly pungent tennis shoes during one particularly exhaustive search.

Getting around   Everything but the airport is within walking distance in Corumbá. To reach the waterfront, take rua Frei Mariano all the way to its end, then walk down the steep street to the left, which will wind to the right and put you on rua Manoel Cavassa along the water.

Changing money   Black market rates for cash are available at the reception desk of the Hotel Santa Mônica, rua Antônio Maria Coelho 345. The Banco do Brasil, rua 13 de Junho 914, changes travellers cheques at the official rate.

Information   The state-sponsored tourism authority, MSTUR, operates out of the former local jail at rua Dom Aquino Correa 405.

Fishing gear   Try Sr. Orozimbo's shop at rua Manoel Cavassa 61.

BOAT TRIPS FROM CORUMBÁ

Guided trips

Virtually every hotel in Corumbá offers day excursions on the River Paraguai. Travellers are often tempted by these trips because they are easy to arrange, require but a day, are relatively cheap, and run on schedule. The flip side of all this convenience is that you won't really experience the Pantanal. Travellers usually return from such boat trips with nothing more than a sunburn. They will have taken a snaphot or two of the Vitória Régias (giant water lilies), but the chances of actually seeing an alligator or a capybara are slim indeed. Few wild animals, after all, opt to live within earshot of a city of 81,000.

Another option is to hire a local guide and a small boat, travelling up the River Paraguai and into some of the smaller tributaries and side channels for a day. Best known of these guides is an American expatriate named Bill Seffusatti, or simply 'Senhor Bill.' Bill speaks English, French, Spanish, and Portuguese, runs his own guide service (California Boats), and is fairly easy to find; ask at the Bar El Pacu on the waterfront, or try his home on Travessa Mercúrio, a small side street near the docks (phone 231-4834). Bill used to hire out primarily as a fishing guide, but now does at least an equal amount of business with wildlife watchers. For a day trip, expect to pay about US$30-35. This is a flat rate for up to four people; you don't pay any less if you're going alone, since the real cost of any boat excursion is the gas and oil. The problem with day trips — and Bill is brutally honest about it — is the lack of wildlife close to Corumbá. As an alternative, Bill has a cabin up the river for overnight trips. He'll take you there and tour you around the first day for about US$32 (once again, flat fee for a four-person boat). The cabin (bunk beds, ice chest, and a three-person rowboat) overnight costs US$4 per person. He'll charge about US$16 to ferry you back to Corumbá the following day. Be forewarned that Bill makes all of these trips *only* during the dry season.

Commercial boats

The best option for those with an open-ended schedule is to find upriver passage on a small cargo boat. This is more ambitious, time-consuming and downright frustrating than a guided day or overnight trip. Then again, it is the cheapest alternative and often the most rewarding.

In general, you have a choice of two types of boat: large cement boats or small cargo boats. Cement produced at the huge factory in Corumbá is shipped upriver during the wet season as far as Porto Jofre and Porto Cercado in the state of Mato Grosso. The final destination is generally Porto Cercado rather than Porto Jofre, although brief stops are often made in Porto Jofre. The route follows the River Paraguai for about 160 km and the Cuiabá River for another 105 km to Porto Jofre; Porto Cercado lies another 105 km upriver. Along the way, the cement boat skirts the southern border of the National Park of the Pantanal Matogrossense. Depending on river conditions, the trip from Corumbá to Porto Jofre takes about six days. The boats are large (35-40 metres), with simple showers and bathrooms. There is no cabin space for passengers as in many Amazonian cargo boats; you sling hammocks wherever there's room.

Cement boats are operated by the firm Empresa Navegação Miguéis. They have two offices in Corumbá: one on the waterfront itself, at rua Manoel Cavassa 1, phone (067)231-3683 and the other at rua Delamare 612, phone (067)231-2451. Ever since 1984, when a boat capsized and killed a young mother and a student from São Paulo, the company has been reluctant to take on passengers for the run upriver. You should try first at the offices above, but you're likely to be handed the official company line (i.e., that passage is impossible). Don't give up. Go down to the dock itself, way at the end of rua Manoel Cavassa. A guard is posted at the gate, but he'll let you in if you explain that you're looking for upriver passage. Once inside, ask to see the *capitão* of the cement boat. At last accounting, this was a gentleman named senhor Vandil. Senhor Vandil recited for us the official company policy at first, but then told us to enquire at the Capitania do Porto in town for permission to book passage. (Other travellers have reported success in approaching the captain for a berth.) If you are sent to the Capitania do Porto and they give you the bureaucratic runaround, don't despair. Keep on reminding yourself that this is Brazil, where 'no' never really means 'no.' Talk to either senhor Bill (see above) or the German-born owner of the Bar El Pacu on the waterfront. Among backcountry travellers, Hermann is surely the best-known local character and information source in Corumbá. He washed up on the shores of the River Paraguai after years as an expatriate in Argentina. He speaks German, Spanish, Portuguese, and English — often all in a single sentence. His Brazilian wife is a fountain of good information, and also happens to make the best piranha soup in Corumbá. They'll be able to provide you with information on local sailings of cement boats and other cargo vessels. They can also suggest ways to avoid the restrictions on passenger travel; one popular ruse is to hire a small boat to ferry you upriver, just out of the Capitania do Porto's jurisdiction. Cargo boats commonly pull over and board passengers at this point.

Cost is negotiable with the captain, but generally runs about US$15-20 per person for the Corumbá-Porto Jofre cement run. Food of sorts is provided; if you want anything more exotic than beans, rice, and manioc flour, bring it yourself. Drinking water comes directly from the river, as does bathing water. Bring bottled water if you're at all squeamish on this point. Ask about eating utensils, plates, and cups — they are not always provided. A hammock is essential, along with two lengths of rope to hang it. Sometimes you can rent a hammock from the crew; if you're making a round trip, Hermann at the Bar El Pacu (see above) rents hammocks for a nominal fee.

Your second option is one of a number of smaller cargo boats. These generally run downriver from Corumbá, then ply the smaller rivers such as the Taquari or the Miranda, bringing food and supplies to the Pantanal's isolated cattle ranches. These are invariably round trips, returning to Corumbá in about 3-7 days. No one leaves the boat. Sometimes they transport cattle back to Corumbá on the return trip. These small cargo boats run more frequently in the wet season, but even then their schedules are highly irregular. You may wait, as we did, for many days past the scheduled sailing while the boat is being 'loaded.' The largest company operating these boats is the Serviço Navegação Bacia da Prata SA, with three offices in Corumbá: rua Frei Mariano 684 (phone 231-1615): rua Colombo 231 (phone 231-1718); and rua 14 de Março 134 in Ladário, about ten minutes out of town on the Ladário bus (phone 231-2561). You should also ask at Portobrás, on rua Manoel Cavassa (no number) along the waterfront (phone 231-2913). Cost is negotiable with the captain, but generally runs about US$3-5 per person per day. See Hermann or his wife for advice and suggestions on prices and sailing schedules.

A ferry boat provides an irregularly-scheduled service from Porto Esperança on the River Paraguai (accessible via the train) to Coimbra, 60 km downriver. This ferry transports army infantry to the jungle outpost in Coimbra, but ends up taking more civilians than soldiers. Wives, relatives, and friends crowd the boat as it leaves the tiny dock in Porto Esperança; foreign travellers not connected with the military are also welcome, but be sure to ask when the ferry returns and add a few days for the inevitable delay.

LAND TRIPS FROM CORUMBÁ

The very cheapest and easiest way to see a slice of the Pantanal is to ride either the bus or the train to Campo Grande. Both leave Corumbá daily (for details, see the section on *Arrival/Departure* above). Keep in mind that the bus service is frequently cancelled during the wet season. You'll see more wildlife on the bus trip than on the train trip, although there is one obvious problem with both: you can't stop. Your bus driver will be hell-bent on reaching Campo Grande before dinner, and no amount of alligators, jabiru storks, or capybaras are going to slow him down.

There are two options, then, if you want a relatively quick road tour within the Pantanal that allows for stopping and taking pictures: either hire a car or rent one. The two car rental agencies in Corumbá are Localiza, rua América 482 (phone 231-6379) and Nobre, rua Cabral 1373 (phone 231-5566). Both will rent cars for round-trip excursions into the Pantanal on the Corumbá-Campo Grande road. Be sure, however, to read about Brazilian car rentals in Chapter 4. If you prefer to let someone else worry about the car and driving, guides can be found through Corumbatur, rua 13 de Junho 785 (phone 231-1532) or the Hotel Santa Mônica, rua Antônio Maria Coelho 345 (phone 231-3001).

If you want more than a whirlwind 'Pantanal-through-the-windshield' tour, you'll need to disembark somewhere along the railroad or highway. If you're travelling by bus, arrange before departure from Corumbá to disembark at Porto Manga (known alternatively as Porto da Manga). This is a tiny, ramshackle rivertown on the eastern bank of the Paraguai River, 61 km from Corumbá. The bus has to stop on the west side of the river and catch the ferry, resuming its journey on the other side. A single cheap hotel operates on the eastern bank, within walking distance of some fine wildlife areas along the highway. Stay here or ask to camp along the river. Early morning or late afternoon walks east from Porto Manga usually turn up hundreds of jabiru storks (known locally as tuiuíus) and basking alligators. Motorized aluminium canoes can be rented along the eastern bank for trips up the Paraguai or Taquari Rivers. Be forewarned that, leaving Porto Manga, you will have to stand up on either of the crowded buses; opt therefore for the short trip to Corumbá rather than the long one to Campo Grande.

The train makes five stops that put you off within the Pantanal proper. Running east from Corumbá, these are: Porto Esperança, Retiro Quere Ver, Carandazal, Calera, and Bodoquena. The most intriguing of these from the train — and the only one we've actually sampled — is Porto Esperança.

Porto Esperança: Piranha fishing in Paradise

We'd passed the place twice already, once the year before and once again on our way from Campo Grande to Corumbá. On this particular trip, we had planned to catch a cargo boat upriver from Corumbá. Finding boats the year before had been relatively easy; in 1986, however, we had to contend with an unusually dry 'rainy' season. Boats were few and far between, the rivers blocked by exposed sand shoals. We were told to wait.

We waited. We drank local beer on Corumbá's sleepy waterfront. We sampled the surprisingly tasty ice cream that Brazilians make from sweet corn. We bartered half-heartedly with hammock salesmen in the afternoon heat. We watched fishermen push wheelbarrows of huge river catfish toward the market. And eventually, our North American impatience got the best of us. The next day, we boarded the 'Train of Death' a second time.

No one in Corumbá could tell us if the small riverside community we'd seen from the train had a place to stay. Still, we were willing to chance it. Esperança, after all, means 'hope.' A ticket cost all of US$0.75, and we figured that for that price we could always come back to Corumbá on the evening train if things didn't pan out.

At nine that morning, we stepped off the train at Posto Agente Inocêncio. Inocêncio is nothing more than a crude station house and platform set in seasonally-flooded scrub forest above the Paraguai River. Along with a handful of Brazilians, Jayne and I waited there for a smaller train to come up the spur track from Porto Esperança.

By the time the train had coasted to a stop at the end of the track, we'd learned that lodging would be no problem; Dona Ramona ran a pensão that catered to travellers, mostly Brazilian Army personnel, and we were the only customers that day. For US$5 we bought a simple room and three meals a day.

Outside, hoofbeats signalled the arrival of a pair of local ranchers. There is no road to Porto Esperança, and these men had come overland to buy fish. Our excitement grew after a quick glance at the toothy critters in the fishmonger's basket: piranhas.

Our first intimate brush with piranhas had occurred at a waterfront bar in Corumbá a year earlier. The owner's wife specialized in *sopa de piranha*, and any doubts I might have had about the dish's authenticity vanished as soon as she served us. A single piranha lay curled there in the bowl. Both head and tail overlapped the lip of the dish, and cooking had bared the notorious set of triangular teeth. Our lunch seemed to be staring back at us with a look of piscine reproach. Jayne and I decided that if we were going to eat piranha again, the noble and just thing would be to catch the creature ourselves.

Now, a year later, our chance appeared. Would it be possible, we asked, to do some piranha fishing here in Porto Esperança?

Our hosts chuckled. Serious anglers, we were told, pit themselves against the really big tackle-busters, like the giant *pintado* catfish or the feisty, salmon-sized *dourado*. We felt humbled. Fishing for piranhas in the Pantanal was apparently akin to ordering macaroni and cheese at the Waldorf. Then again, we told ourselves, which of our friends back home would be impressed with tales of the wily *pintado*, *pacú*, and *surubim*? Trophy fish to be sure, but totally unknown to most North Americans, and not a man-eater among them. No, our reputations as adventurers clearly demanded piranhas.

There were practical considerations as well; if we managed to land a *pintado*, which is the approximate size and shape of a railroad tie, what on earth would we do with it?

Putting together a fishing expedition in a village as sleepy as Porto Esperança took the better part of four hours. But by 1300 we were cruising up the River Paraguai in a 5 m aluminium boat powered by an ancient Johnson outboard.

Roberto, the young boatman we'd hired, kept to the river's edge. We soon saw why. Here and there, sunning alligators rose from their streamside sandbars and slipped into the water.

'Jacaré', grinned Roberto. He lamented the illegal trade in alligator hides, and told us a story that was becoming familiar by now: since jacaré prey heavily on piranhas, alligator poaching has, over the years, resulted in an increasing piranha population. True or not, the quiet backwater that we were motoring through teemed with piranhas. Roberto cut the motor and we baited our hooks with live river eels (*pirambóia*) the size of licorice sticks.

The late naturalist Eull Gibbons once wrote that he didn't care to spend hours in search of some huge trophy fish; when he went fishing, he wanted to catch fish, and lots of them. Gibbons would have loved piranha fishing. We visited one tiny slough so infested with piranhas that the water surface began to boil with their activity the moment our bait touched it. Within an hour, we had the makings of a respectable *sopa de piranha*.

Our fishing done, we turned our attention to the wildlife that surrounded us. Huge jabiru storks erupted from the streamside underbrush as we puttered by. Emerald-green kingfishers watched from overhanging branches. Roberto pointed out the pill-shaped droppings which dotted the riverbank. 'Capivara', he told us with a sage nod. It wasn't until the following day that we actually spotted our first capybaras, dog-sized relatives of the domestic guinea pig.

For over-domesticated city folk like ourselves, there is an earthy, honest feeling that comes with harvesting your own food. That evening, the piranhas were served with their heads on; but this time we could look them in the eye. And there is something undeniably intriguing about dining on a creature that, given the chance, would be delighted to turn the tables.

We were up before the sun that next morning. Hiking upstream along the riverbank, we spotted our first alligator within a half kilometre of the village. A dozen more lounged below the railroad bridge, soaking in the first rays of light. We continued north along the railroad tracks, ever conscious that the 'Train of Death' was heading our way on its morning run to Campo Grande. Here and there, the elevated railroad grade became hemmed in on both sides by marshes. Before daring to cross such narrow expanses, I placed my ear against the steel tracks, listening expertly for the faint hum of an approaching train. This is one of those savvy outdoors tricks that works far better in the movies, because we ended up dashing madly for a wide spot in the grade when the train finally rounded a clump of palms directly ahead of us.

The train past, we had time to savour the landscape. Hyacinth-studded waterways surrounded us on both sides. Toucans, bitterns, hawks, finches, and spoonbills soared by from time to time. Anhingas, long-necked relatives of the cormorants, held their wings open to dry after a successful underwater fishing foray. Faint breezes rustled the purple blossoms of a score of *piúva* trees.

We returned to town that afternoon just in time to meet the afternoon train. A trio of sport fishermen from São Paulo arrived at Dona Ramona's doorstep and we soon fell into conversation. The Pantanal, they explained, was a paradise flawed in only one minor detail: it had no *infraestrutura*, no luxury hotels, no network of paved roads criss-crossing the swamps. We smiled politely and nodded, grateful for every backwater forgotten by 'progress'.

CUIABÁ

Cuiabá sits in the exact geodesic centre of South America. There are probably some metaphysical implications to this, and if you're so inclined there is a plaque marking the precise spot in the Praça Moreira Cabral downtown. For most travellers, however, Cuiabá's importance is that of the northern gateway to the Pantanal. Just a few hours from this bustling state capital begin the vast watery expanses which continue south for some 400 km.

Arrival/Departure   The bus station is located 3 km north-east of the city centre. There is direct service to and from Rio de Janeiro, São Paulo, Belo Horizonte, Campo Grande, Brasília, Rondonópolis, Poconé, Cáceres, Barão de Melgaço, and scores of smaller cities and towns. A *guarda volumes* is available for checking bags. Several city buses run from the bus station downtown, but the easiest to catch is either the number 202 (Rodo-Matriz) or the number 201 (Quarta Feira-Matriz). The end of the line for both these buses is the covered stop at the intersection of rua Joaquim Murtinho and avenida Getúlio Vargas, in the heart of downtown. This is also where you catch the return bus to the bus station. You'll find a number of hotels along avenida Getúlio Vargas and its sidestreets.

The airport (Aeroporto Marechal Cândido Rondon) lies across the river and 12 km southwest of Cuiabá proper, in the neighbouring city of Várzea Grande. There are daily flights to Belém, Rio de Janeiro, São Paulo, Campo Grande, Corumbá, Brasília, Manaus, Belo Horizonte, Porto Velho, Rio Branco, and other smaller cities. Any of four city buses will take you downtown for US$0.15: Agua Limpa, CPA-Várzea Grande, Morada da Serra, and Mapim. Catch these city buses a short

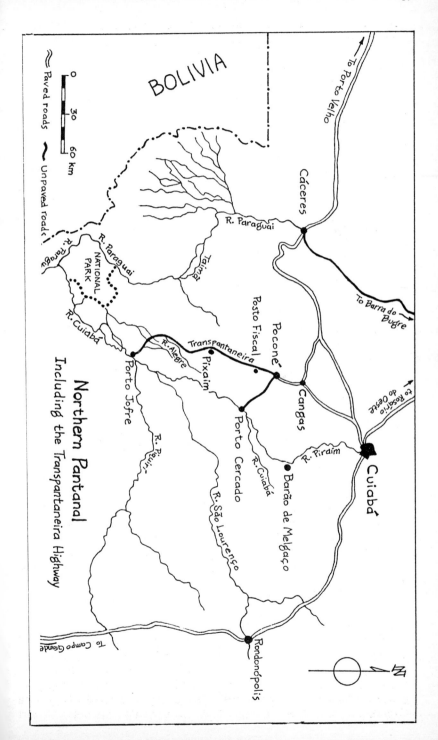

Northern Pantanal
Including the Transpantaneira Highway

walk from the airport terminal; look for a restaurant with a small playground; a covered bus stop is located on the other side. To reach the airport from downtown, wait for the Agua Limpa bus at the Drogaria Pax pharmacy, on the corner of avenida Generoso Ponce and rua Antônio Maria.

Getting around   Everywhere you'll need to go in town lies within walking distance of the centre.

Changing money   Cash can be changed on the black market at the hotel Santa Rosa Palace, avenida Getúlio Vargas 600. Ask also at the TURIMAT office (see *Information* below), and at the Selva tour office, rua Barão de Melgaço 3594. There is apparently no black market for travellers cheques in Cuiabá; cash them at the official rate on the third floor of the Banco do Brasil, rua Barão de Melgaço 915.

Information   The state-run tourist office is TURIMAT, located in the Praça da República, next to the post office in the centre of downtown (phone 322-5363). They can also arrange to have your cash changed on the black market.

Shopping   Local souvenirs — pequi liqueur, dried and lacquered piranhas and catfish, Indian artifacts, straw goods, wood carvings, and crystallized cashew fruit — can be bought at the Casa do Artesão, at the intersection of rua Senador Metelo and rua 13 de Junho, about ten blocks southwest of the city centre.

Camping and fishing gear   Look for a small store, Caça e Pesca Oliveira, avenida Generoso Ponce 186 (at the corner of avenida Generoso Ponce and rua Joaquim Murtinho in the city centre). They have a good selection of fishing lines, rods, tackle, lures, hooks, camping Gaz cartridges, backpacking stoves, rope for hammocks, and knives.

BOAT AND LAND TRIPS FROM CUIABÁ

Any environmentalist worthy of the name — myself included — has to feel more than a just a little uneasy about the rodovia Transpantaneira. A long ribbon of red-dirt highway, the Transpantaneira winds through 150 km of formerly pristine swampy plain. Mercedes diesel trucks now share the landscape with jabiru storks, alligators, capybaras, and ibises. We can wag our heads self-righteously, but the uncomfortable fact is that the Transpantaneira has also made the Pantanal far more accessible to us low-budget travellers and amateur naturalists.

The Transpantaneira was originally envisioned as a major highway connecting Cuiabá and Corumbá. Construction began in September 1973 but has been halted for at least five years as of this writing; just maintaining the existing roadway following a rainy season has proved ambitious. This is precisely the kind of project that vote-hungry Brazilian governors love to tackle, but for now at least, the Transpantaneira has bogged down scarcely half-way to Corumbá.

A fine paved highway (MT 060) runs south from Cuiabá for 98 km to the town of Poconé. TUT Transportes runs six buses each day from Cuiabá to Poconé. Buses leave the *rodoviária* in Cuiabá at 0600, 0900, 1200, 1500, 1700, and 1900. The trip to Poconé takes two hours and costs US$2. Buses leave Poconé for Cuiabá at 0600, 0900, 1200, 1500, 1730, and 1930. It is also possible to catch a bus from Poconé to Cáceres; it leaves Poconé at 1500 and drops you off at Posto 120, where you can then catch the bus going from Cuiabá to Cáceres. Poconé is not a particularly attractive town — our first sight as we stepped off the bus was of dusty streets littered with hundreds of flying cockroaches, each one the size of a golf ball. Poconé does lie at the very northern border of the Pantanal, however, and it's here that the Transpantaneira actually begins. Poconé is also where cheap, regularly-scheduled public transportation ends. If you plan to continue — and there is no sense in coming to Poconé otherwise — you'll need to hire a car, hitchike, or walk.

There is always a handful of cars for hire waiting near the tiny bus station in Poconé. During the dry season, most drivers can be coaxed into going all the way to Porto Jofre for somewhere around US$40. Be sure to bargain. Cabs will take up to four passengers, and the price remains the same regardless of whether there's one of you or four. You can try asking for Aurélio, although other cabbies are probably just as reliable. Even without the usual photo stops for alligators, capybaras, and jabiru storks, the trip will take a full four hours; plan on staying overnight in Porto Jofre. You'll be expected to pay for your driver's lodging in Porto Jofre (see below) as well as his dinner and breakfast. Arrange this before leaving Poconé. The driver will charge you for a round-trip even if you're planning to stay in Porto Jofre rather than returning with him the following day. This is only fair, since it's unlikely he'll find a paying customer in Porto Jofre for the return trip. If you're really concerned about finding the cheapest deal, walk to the main plaza in Poconé (just south and west of the bus depot), where you'll find more cars and taxis for hire, sometimes at prices lower than those near the bus station. Remember that these drivers are just that; they're not guides, and very few speak anything but Portuguese.

If you happen to get stuck in Poconé, you'll find all the accommodation cheap and simple. Try the Hotel Joana d'Arc just north of the bus depot; a number of others are located near the main square.

The Transpantaneira is one of the few places in Brazil where you can successfully thumb a ride. Here there's a steady stream of truck traffic and sympathetic drivers. Be prepared to stand in the back — there's rarely room in the cab — and in many cases to pay the driver a small fee. But besides eating dust, there is a big disadvantage to hitching a ride with truckers: you won't be able to stop to admire the wildlife. This may be no problem if you're heading to Porto Jofre to catch a boat downstream; you'll see your wildlife on the river. If, however, the trip south on the Transpantaneira will be your sole exposure to the Pantanal, think about hitching very carefully. You may be lucky, being picked up by the occasional Brazilian or foreign tourist with a car. In this case, they'll probably want to stop as often as you. Try hitching on the weekends, when other tourists and sport anglers are more likely to drive the road south.

The third option — the simplest, cheapest, and slowest — is to walk the Transpantaneira yourself. Unless you are hell-bent on getting to Porto Jofre to catch a riverboat, there is probably no reason to hike all of the Transpantaneira's 150 km. The Pantanal doesn't become any noticeably wilder as you move south, so you may want to walk just halfway. After Pixaim (km 60), in fact, there is little spectacular scenery until just before Porto Jofre itself. Camping is permitted alongside the roadway, and there are numerous wide spots that will get you away from the highway itself. The best camping spots are near rivers; not only will you have plenty of water and possibly fresh fish, but you'll be able to hang your hammock beneath any of the Transpantaneira's 126 bridges. Be sure to bring mosquito netting and a wool blanket for those cold nights in June, July, and August. Other than bridges, the Transpantaneira offers few spots from which to hang a hammock; there just aren't that many trees, and seldom will you find two of them well-placed for a hammock. For this reason, a self-standing mosquito net or tent (rather than a hammock) would be ideal.

You may want to hitch or taxi all the way to Porto Jofre, and use it as a 'base camp' for day hikes along the highway. Just 10 km north of town lies some spectacular wildlife-viewing ground.

Travelling the Transpantaneira

During the dry season, you'll come upon the first water just 10 km outside Poconé. Beyond this, at km 19, you'll reach the Posto Fiscal, a small house and barracks on the left side of the road. This is the official beginning of the Transpantaneira National Park, meaning the highway itself and a narrow band of land on either side. Although it's not absolutely required, you may want to stop here for a chat with the IBDF guard on duty. The guards can usually give you hints on what to see, where to camp, etc. A rustic *lanchonette* offers snacks and cold beer at km 28, and off to your right at km 32 you'll see the Pousada das Araras (see *Lodges* below).

Pixaim (km 60), is a major fueling stop for truckers, selling gas, diesel, and the last alcohol on the Transpantaneira. Flat tyres are almost as common as alligators along the Transpantaneira, and there's a tiny *borracharia* here to mend them. You'll also find the Pousada Pixaim, perhaps the only reasonably-priced hotel in the entire Pantanal. It's a simple wooden affair set on stilts above the Pixaim River, with ten rooms, screened windows, hot water, and ceiling fans. This place turned out to be a godsend for us one July evening when cold, gusty winds swept up from Antarctica and buffeted the Pantanal. See *Lodges* below for details.

About 10 km north of Porto Jofre, you'll enter a particularly attractive area flooded by the Rio Alegre and its numerous small tributaries.

The Transpantaneira dead-ends 150 km south of Poconé at Porto Jofre on the banks of the Cuiabá River. Nearby is the luxurious Santa Rosa Pantanal Hotel. Far more affordable, and right on the riverbank within easy hailing distance of boats travelling down to Corumbá is a small campground; there are places to cook and spotless bathrooms, all for US$1.25 per person. Sr. Nicolino, the owner, rents boats as well. Gas and diesel are available in Porto Jofre, but no alcohol.

Cargo boats

Although Cuiabá overlooks the upper reaches of its namesake river, the city is still some 110 km north of the Pantanal proper. The closest ports of call for cargo boats plying the lower Cuiabá River are Porto Jofre and Porto Cercado. Both these towns are reached via Poconé. During the dry season, cargo boats rarely operate out of these towns; indeed, the Cuiabá River is often unnavigable during this time, so plan accordingly.

Boats leave from Porto Cercado about once a day during the wet season, heading downstream for Corumbá. During the dry season — assuming that the river isn't blocked by exposed sandbars — a boat leaves about once every two weeks. Be prepared to wait; there is no schedule. In Porto Jofre, you'll have to flag the boat down from the river bank by the campground. Most of these boats are those operated by the Empresa Navegação Miguéis (see the section above on Corumbá). At this point they will have unloaded their cement and taken aboard cattle or cargo for the return trip.

CÁCERES

Cáceres has the agreeably sleepy air of all tropical river ports. Ice cream salesmen gather to chat under the mango trees in the main plaza; an occasional fisherman ambles by, balancing *pintado* catfish on a pole above his shoulders; and along the riverfront, stevedores lounge in the shade of double-decked boats being loaded for the trip downstream. Pleasant as Cáceres can be, this is the reason to come here: to catch a cargo boat bound for Corumbá on the Paraguai River.

Buses leave Cuiabá for Cáceres daily at 0630, 0930, 1240, 1430, 1800, and 2030. The fare is US$3.75 and the trip takes four hours with a single stop at Posto 120 to eat. Passengers arriving at Posto 120 from Poconé can board the bus for Cáceres here. You'll be dropped off at the open bus station in the centre of town, on the avenida 7 de Setembro. The Colibri company also runs buses back to Cuiabá daily at 0200, 0600, 0800, 0930, 1200, 1300, 1430, 1530, 1700, 1900, and 2200.

Cáceres lies along the eastern bank of the Paraguai River. It's an easy walk from the bus station to the waterfront; ask directions to the main plaza (praça Barão do Rio Branco), then head left on rua Celso Faria, which runs parallel to the river.

In the rainy season, three or four boats leave Cáceres each week, but there is no set schedule. Allow yourself several days to hunt for a boat and for the boat to be loaded. There is no need to search out the Capitania dos Portos for permission to travel; speak directly to the captains aboard the vessels. Two companies operate boats out of Cáceres: Serviço Navegação Bacia da Prata and Empresa Navegação Miguéis. Boats are 35-40 metres long and can usually accommodate 30 passengers. They run cement upriver from Corumbá and run everything downriver: furniture, soybeans, dry goods, even the occasional car. The trip downriver from Cáceres to Corumbá takes about four days in the rainy season.

In the dry season, the Paraguai River often becomes impassable near Taimã. Before you spend the time and money travelling to Cáceres, try calling the Capitania dos Portos there at (065)221-1266 for information on the river and the availability of boats. The Capitania is always a good source of general information on the upper Paraguai River. The office is located at rua Professor Rizzo 1; facing the river from the praça Barão do Rio Branco, turn right and look for a yellow pastel building.

NATIONAL PARK OF THE PANTANAL

This 135,000-hectare park, formerly the Cara Cara Biological Reserve, was set aside as a wildlife sanctuary in 1981. (Don't confuse this with the Transpantaneira National Park, which runs alongside the Transpantaneira highway joining Porto Jofre with Poconé.) It lies at the very southernmost part of Mato Grosso where the Paraguai and Cuiabá Rivers branch, midway between Corumbá and Cáceres. This is in fact the only access to the area, and you'll enter the park if you take a cargo boat from either Cáceres or Cuiabá to Corumbá. Porto Jofre on the Cuiabá River is the closest access point, 100 km upriver. The western portion of the park is dotted with lakes, oxbows, and bays. Permission to camp in the park can be had by writing the Delegacia Estadual do IBDF, avenida A, esquina rua O – CPA de Cuiabá. You'll have to provide your own transportation in (hire a boat from Porto Jofre), but check first personally with the IBDF; they may be sending a research crew into the park, and you can tag along. There are government camps within the park, but no amenities whatsoever, so you'll be on your own.

BIRDS OF THE PANTANAL

Jabiru stork   This stork (*Jabiru mycteria*) is the uncontested avian king of the Pantanal, a huge bird that has become the region's instantly-

Jaribu

recognizable trademark. One of the largest flying birds in the western hemisphere, the jabiru (*tuiuíu* in Portuguese, pronounced too-yoo-YOO) may reach 140 cm in length. Its white body feathers are offset by a naked black neck ringed at the base with a reddish collar. This featherless collar changes from pink to deep crimson when the bird is excited. Jabirus feed strictly during the daylight hours, gathering in pairs, families, or sometimes large flocks to pluck fish and frogs from the marshes. Unlike most other wading birds, which feed by sight, the jabiru feeds by touch. Periodically, it dips its huge open bill into the water and waits. When a frog, fish, or snake makes the slightest contact, the jabiru simply snaps its bill shut and swallows. This form of feeding has obvious advantages in the Pantanal, where the water is turbid and prey is plentiful. The jabiru's nest (*ninho*) is a large, sturdy structure made of sticks and placed high in the treetops. There is no trick to locating jabirus; they are extremely common throughout the Pantanal in open, swampy areas, where their size and vivid colours make them stand out like billboards. They also frequent sheltered riverbanks. I remember an afternoon's canoe trip on a small tributary of the Capivari River. A wall of reeds hemmed in the meandering waterway on both banks, and we drifted silently, the stillness punctuated only by the dip of the oars. Suddenly, a huge jabiru took flight from the riverbank

alongside us. Looking up, we could see every detail of the naked scarlet
neck, could hear the clacking of the huge bill, could even feel the rush of
air under massive wings. We had seen literally hundreds of jabirus
before, but this single and unexpected close encounter comes to mind
every time I think of the Pantanal.

Jacana   The jacana (*Jacana spinosa*) is a small, robin-sized marsh bird
sporting black feathers which fade to a gorgeous, rusty tan. This coffee-
coloured plumage gave the bird its Portuguese name, *cafezinho*. It is
only up close, however, that the jacana's real distinction becomes
apparent: its outlandishly long feet and four-inch nails. These ungainly-
looking toes allow the cafezinho to walk with confidence upon lilies and
other flimsy buoyant plants. (A common English name for these birds
— which occasionally find their way to temperate zones — is 'lily-
trotter'.)

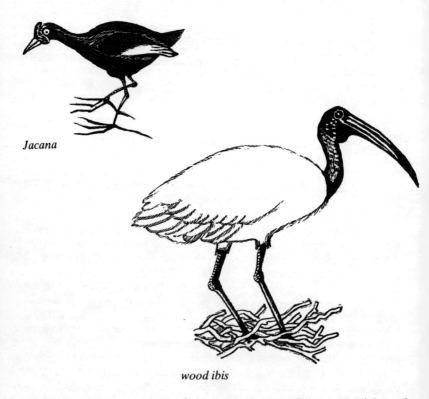

Jacana

wood ibis

Wood ibis   The wood ibis (*Mycteria americana*) is a colonial stork,
sporting a black head and neck above a completely white body. Their
colonies are impressive, sometimes exceeding tens of thousands of nests
within a small area. The nest itself, a platform of sticks built high in the
trees, is selected and defended by the male. He then sets about
attracting a mate, no mean feat for a bird that has no voice box and is

therefore mute. Males and females go through an elaborate series of courtship rituals that include head bobbing and bill gaping. The birds pair up for the breeding season, and both share in incubating the eggs. During this time, you'll often find huge nesting colonies at dead ends or oxbows in small rivers. Here, during the dry season, the storks find a ready food supply of small animals concentrated by receding waterways, including snakes, frogs, rodents, and even small birds. Like the jabiru stork, the wood ibis feeds primarily by touch rather than sight, and can snap its bill shut on a fish in 25 milliseconds, one of the fastest vertebrate reflexes. Prey is brought back to the nest and regurgitated for the young to eat. *Cabeça secas*, as they are known in Portuguese, are capable of soaring at extremely high altitudes, winding down in lazy spirals during their return to the nest.

Parakeet True parakeets (*Myiopsitta monachus*) are among the noisiest birds in the Pantanal. You'll never sleep past dawn if you pitch your hammock or tent anywhere near a parakeet nest. These are huge, ungainly tangles of sticks and twigs built in the crook of a tall tree, often a palm. We've seen these nests house upwards of twenty *periquitos*, as Brazilians call them. The occupants arrive *en masse*, a chattering chaos of small lime-green and yellow birds, darting in and out of the nest in madcap fashion. By nightfall they'll settle down, but only for a few hours. At first light — or even before — you can count on parakeets for a renewed burst of loud and manic activity.

Rhea The largest bird in the Pantanal is the rhea (*Rhea americana*, *ema* in Portuguese), which may stand as tall as 1.6 m. Rheas are closely related to ostriches, but differ from ostriches in having three toes rather than two. Rhea chicks are raised by the male, and he'll attack any and all potential intruders, including humans. Without this protection, the chicks are vulnerable to a host of predators, *caracaras* in particular. Adult rheas, on the other hand, have virtually no natural enemies. Rheas have been practically exterminated in many parts of South America because they will eat any agricultural crop. This is not a big problem in the Pantanal, where cattle ranching and natural vegetation are the rule. Consequently, rheas are a common sight, often bounding effortlessly across the open spaces in pairs or small groups.

Other birds A member of the falcon family, the **caracara** feeds primarily on carrion, and you're likely to see it alongside the road picking at the corpse of a capybara or snake. **Kingfishers** (*martim pescador* in Portuguese) nest in crevices on earthen river banks, guarding their territorial fishing grounds jealously. They'll sit motionless on a high branch, then suddenly plummet straight down and crash into the water to retrieve their prey. The **common egret** (*Casmerodius albus*, *garça branca* in Portuguese), its plumage a brilliant white, stands out easily against the Pantanal's green backdrop of vegetation. Egrets take their name from the long, lacy-white specialized feathers called aigrettes. Both males and females begin growing aigrettes just prior to

mating in the dry season, and they are among the most beautiful of all
bird feathers. Egrets, in fact, were once threatened with extinction
because of the millinery trade in aigrettes. During the mating ritual,
males will raise these feathers well off their backs, attacking any
competitors with their long beaks. You'll often see **darters** (*Anhinga
anhinga*) perched on a log, holding their wings out to dry as their close
relatives the cormorants do. Their feathers are water-permeable,
allowing them to swim low in the water, sometimes with only the head
and neck exposed. Darters hunt their food underwater, being equipped
with a bill that is serrated along the front edge, the better to hold prey.
Their long, supple necks also contain a special hinge, allowing the neck
to dart forward and impale fish or insects. Upon surfacing, the darter
shakes the prey loose, flips it into the air, and gobbles it headfirst. A bird
that you'll hear more often than see is the **curassow**, a large chicken-like
bird that lives in the forests. They are poor fliers, spending most of their
time on the ground feeding on fruits and leaves. *Mutum*, as currasows
are called in Portuguese, will also eat hard-shelled nuts, swallowing
pebbles to aid digestion.

See the *Bibliography* for a suggested field guide. In Britain, an
excellent mail order source for field guides is the Natural History Book
Service (telephone 0803 865913).

MAMMALS OF THE PANTANAL

Zebu cattle   While a beef steer can't truly be called wildlife, it is the
single animal species you'll see most often in the Pantanal. Cattle-
ranching is in fact uniquely compatible with much of the Pantanal's
wildlife; if traditional agriculture were to replace ranching, much of the
natural habitat and many of the wild animals would be destroyed. As it
is, only the capybara and marsh deer could be considered competitors
with cattle for the wild grasses, and this competition is probably
minimal.

You'll spot an occasional group of European cattle in the Pantanal,
but the white, floppy-eared and humpbacked zebu (Brahma) cattle
dominate the landscape. Originally from Asia, they've adapted to life in
South America, where they stand up well to both heat and insect pests.
There are several varieties of zebu — they breed freely with European
cattle — but Brazilians call them all *nelóre*. Nelóre mingle well with the
native wildlife of the region; you'll frequently see white egrets riding
atop a steer's back, picking off insects. Some six million nelóre inhabit
the Pantanal; stockmen also hunt down small herds of 'wild' nelóre,
runaways which have turned feral.

The meat is noticeably tougher than that of the grain-fed European
steers raised in the gaucho country of southern Brazil. Jayne and I once
spent an awkward evening at a rancher's home, trying gamely to chew
the rubbery steak proffered by our proud host.

Capybara   The name means 'master of the grasses' in the indigenous Guarani language of Brazil and Paraguay. The capybara (*Hydrochoerus hydrochaeris, capivara* in Portuguese) earns that title daily, mowing down wild grasses with its four large incisors and grinding them with a set of specialized molars. The incisors identify the capybara as a true rodent — the world's largest, in fact — rather than a pig, as early colonists regarded them. But the capybara might also be 'master of the rivers', outfitted as it is with webbed feet and the ability to stay submerged for five minutes at a time.

Capybaras, though closely related to the domestic guinea pig (cavy), weigh in at an impressive 50 kg and stand 60 cm high. A capybara's eyes, ears, and nostrils are located near the top of its head, an adaptation that allows it to see, hear, smell, and swim while mostly submerged.

Capybaras spend a good deal of the day near and in the water, and this is where you are most likely to see them. During the day, they bathe in the river until it is cool enough to begin the afternoon's grazing. (Like all rodents, they have few sweat glands, and must rely on the water to avoid a fatal case of overheating.) Grazing and napping occur at intervals throughout the late afternoon and evening. Drift in a boat downstream just before dusk, and you are likely to surprise a group of foraging capybaras on the riverbank. Their first reaction is a series of grunts, snorts, and snuffles, followed by a headlong rush for the water or, less likely, into the underbrush.

Capybara

Capybaras are social animals, living in groups of about 7-15 animals. That number swells during the dry season, when you may see as many as 50 or 100 capybaras in a single group sharing a waterhole. They observe a fairly rigid hierarchy, with a dominant male heading the group. Special male scent glands in the snout produce a sticky white substance which they use to mark territory and signal mates. The capybara's affinity for water extends to copulation, which occurs in the shallow portions of the

river. The young are totally dependent on the adults for protection from
marauding dogs, vultures, jacaré, and jaguars.

It is difficult to spend much time along the riverbanks without
encountering capybaras. Certain waterholes and beaches are especially
popular; these will be full of the distinctive webbed-foot tracks and pill-
shaped faecal pellets. Find a good vantage point nearby and wait until
the sun is high and the capybaras return to cool off.

Other mammals Unfortunately, most other mammals have been
either decimated by hunting or live secretively. You may occasionally
see **marsh deer** (*Blastocerus dichotomus*, *veado* in Portuguese), which
are listed as endangered by the U.S. government. Illegal hunting still
occurs, and some cattlemen insist that deer compete with livestock
during the rainy season when all animals are forced onto the remaining
dry ground. Diseases contracted from cattle may also be destroying the
remaining marsh deer. Only one fawn is born per year, which further
exacerbates the problem. We've only seen this species once; the deer
was apparently cooling off in a forested area during the middle of the
day when we stumbled into the clearing. Like most deer, they leave the
shelter of trees in the late afternoon to seek water; look for tracks in the
riverside mud and stake yourself out if you really want to see a marsh
deer. Consider yourself very lucky if you get a glimpse of **jaguars**,
anteaters, or **river otters**. Hunting and habitat destruction have nearly
wiped these animals out.

ALLIGATORS

I have heard these reptiles variously referred to in English as alligators,
crocodiles, and caimans. Since all caimans are members of the family
Alligatoridae, and since all alligators are members of the order
Crocodilia, you can probably take your pick without offending herpetologists. Safer yet is the Portuguese term *jacaré*. In any case, *Caiman
crocodilus yacaré* is a geographic race or subspecies of the spectacled
caiman. The spectacled caiman earned its name owing to the prominent
ridge connecting the eyesockets, and various subspecies are found
throughout most of South America. *C. crocodilus yacaré* is found only
in the Pantanal and nearby areas; it differs from the other spectacled
caiman subspecies in having several enlarged teeth in the lower jaw.
These teeth generally ride in grooves along the upper jaw but may in
some cases actually penetrate the upper jaw. I'll admit I've never got
close enough to a jacaré to appreciate this important taxonomic
difference.

Jacaré probably grow to a maximum length of about three metres,
although locals invariably have tales of much larger specimens. They eat
fish, crabs, snakes, and large aquatic snails, along with an occasional
duck, bird, capybara, deer, or smaller jacaré. Cattlemen don't regard

Alligator along the Rio Pixaim in the Pantanal

jacaré as a threat to their livestock, however, and you'll often see alligators basking peacefully within a few feet of a grazing steer. The jacaré's tail is a powerful hunting tool which can stun fish and sweep them into the mouth in a single movement.

When the rivers rise, jacaré sometimes become trapped on the huge mats of water hyacinth and aquatic grasses that break free in the floods and float downstream. Travelling this way, jacaré have drifted as far south as the Tigre Delta near Buenos Aires.

Hide poaching has taken a severe toll (see below), but as one long-time resident told us, there are still '*jacaré pra enjoar*' — alligators enough to make you sick. Indeed, it is not uncommon to come upon groups of basking jacaré piled one atop the other along riverbanks.

It is almost impossible to spend a day in the Pantanal without stumbling upon a jacaré. Nevertheless, your chances of seeing these magnificent reptiles are much better in certain locales and at certain times. Being cold-blooded, jacaré will spend the bulk of the day submerged up to the eyes, cooling off in the waterways while sun bakes the Pantanal. Just following dawn, and just prior to dusk, they'll emerge to bask along the riverbanks in an effort to warm up. For the best 'gator-viewing, then, walk the rivers or boat slowly down them during these times. Local boatmen will generally know the haul-out and basking areas preferred by jacaré. If you're wandering on your own, watch during the day for sandy riverbanks scored by tail and belly tracks; these are unmistakable. Returning to these areas prior to dusk or in the cool early-morning hours should yield plenty of jacaré. They have excellent eyesight and hearing, so remain as still as possible. Jacaré are understandably wary, and they'll slither into the water if you approach too closely for photos. If necessary, they can spend at least half an hour completely submerged. During this time, special flaps close over the ear slits and nostrils. Likewise, a throat flap slips into place allowing the jacaré to open its mouth underwater without flooding the lungs; that's important to an animal whose mouth, even closed, is never watertight.

During the cold fronts that occasionally sweep the Pantanal during June, July, and August, jacaré become difficult to spot. Since the waterways retain their heat much better than the air, jacaré will spend the bulk of the day submerged except for eyes and nostrils, often foregoing their usual basking periods.

As the morning warms up, but before the heat becomes intolerable, you'll notice basking jacaré with their mouths open, jaws gaping widely. A jacaré's mouth contains a large surface area of moist membrane; when that moisture evaporates, it cools the animal down in much the same way that sweat drying on our own skin keeps us from overheating in the sun. For this reason, you'll rarely see jacaré with their mouths agape at dusk; they'll want to conserve heat for the cool night ahead.

While the black caiman of the Amazon has been reported to attack humans on occasion, none of the spectacled caiman subspecies — which are considerably smaller — share its reputation. Let's face it, humans have lived alongside the jacaré for centuries without spinning any of the usual man-eater yarns; it's a pretty innocuous beast that can boast a record like that.

FISH AND FISHING IN THE PANTANAL

Until the more or less recent advent of wildlife-orientated travel in the area, sport fishing was the Pantanal's major draw. The lure of a huge, tackle-busting *dourado* or *pintado* still remains the primary attraction for most Brazilian visitors. The Pantanal's rivers, sloughs, and backed-dies support some 350 species of fish, and only the most adamant non-angler should go there without bringing along a spool of monofilament and a few hooks. Even if you don't plan to wet a line yourself, you'll want to know something about the local fish; 80% of the Pantanal's birds and reptiles survive on a fish diet, as do many of the human inhabitants.

Visitors interested in trophy fishing usually wind up at the lodges set aside pretty much exclusively for anglers. In addition to comfortable rooms, sport fishers are provided with bait and tackle, boats, ice, and expert guides. The *Guia Quatro Rodas* lists a number of these; see also the section above on *Lodges*.

If, on the other hand, you're like us — we're perfectly happy reeling in piranhas when nothing else is biting — you'll be able to fish easily and cheaply almost anywhere in the Pantanal.

If you plan to do quite a bit of fishing, bring your own rod and reel. A collapsible 2 m rod and spinning reel should do the trick. Five kg test monofilament line (0.30 mm) will suffice for most species, along with an assortment of hook sizes ranging from 1 to 10 and 3/0 to 9/0. Spinning lures and Rapala-type lures are also a good idea. (Be sure, however, to remove treble hooks from these lures and replace them with single hooks; treble hooks are illegal in the Pantanal.) Lures from home make excellent gifts for local fishermen — especially if they happen to catch fish. You can buy fishing tackle at specialty stores in Cuiabá and Corumbá (see the listing in those sections).

Primitive fishing gear can be made or bought for pennies. A simple fishing rod can be fashioned from any five- to seven-foot length of flexible wooden branch. Fishing tackle stores will sell you, dirt cheap, bamboo poles of varying lengths and flexibilities. A popular Brazilian rod and reel consists of nothing more than a tin can with monofilament wrapped around it; this cuts down on the fishing thrills to be had with a rod, but it does bring in the meat just as efficiently.

Finally, you can usually ask the boatman you hire to provide tackle; if he takes people fishing on a regular basis, this should be no problem. In most cases, however, you'll get the simplest of gear: tree-limb rods or tin cans.

Finding a boat

In Corumbá and Cuiabá, you'll be bombarded with offers from

professional fishing guides. Two of Corumbá's best guides are Bill Seffusatti (see the section above on *Boat Trips from Corumbá*) and Sr. Orozimbo of Pantanal Tours, rua Manoel Cavassa 61, phone 231-1559.

Putting together your own fishing trip in a tiny backwater town can be quite another matter. For one thing, you'll quickly find that the locals are reluctant to bend their schedule to yours, nor are they as impressed with *dolares* as their urban counterparts. I once spent an hour in a dirt-floored shack along the Paraguai River, patiently watching all the potential boatmen in town play snooker and drink beer; no one was particularly keen on taking us out on the river, at least not until the snooker champ was crowned. Secondly, you'll be lucky to find a single person with all the gear necessary for a boat trip; Tamires may own a boat, but it's João who has a motor, Vicente sells the only gas in town out of drums behind his house, and Raimundo is the sole outlet for live bait eels ...

My only advice is to be patient, polite, and to allow plenty of time for these things to come together. Settle the price beforehand; gasoline will be your major expense, but you'll also probably be charged per hour on the river as well as for bait. You'll cut costs considerably if you find other people to go along and share the cost; the price you pay is almost always for the boat, fuel, and guide, regardless of how many people are fishing. Most boats can handle only four anglers and a guide, however. Someone will invariably loan or rent you rustic fishing tackle if you don't have any.

Fishing licences and regulations

Licences are primarily required of trophy anglers at the fancy fishing lodges. Fishing independently in the backcountry, Jayne and I have never once been asked to produce a licence. Still, I recommend you buy one if you plan to do much fishing, and this is why: you'll provide the under-budgeted wildlife agencies with a bit of money and, far more importantly, you'll underscore the fact that foreign travellers are very much interested in resource conservation. A token gesture, to be sure, but one that will make an impression on Brazilian bureaucrats if enough travellers join in.

In Mato Grosso, licences are issued by the Instituto Brasileiro de Desenvolvimento Florestal (IBDF) located at the intersection of avenida A and rua O outside Cuiabá. In Mato Grosso do Sul, the Instituto de Preservação e Controle Ambiental (INAMB) issues licences. The easiest way to purchase a licence in either state is to visit either the Banco do Brasil or the Banco Nacional de Crédito Cooperativo branches in Campo Grande or Cuiabá. In other locales, try the city hall (*prefeitura municipal*) or ask at travel agencies and tourist bureaux.

Do not fish within 1000 metres of any dam or natural waterfall, and do not land or transport more than 30 kg of fish. Also prohibited is the use of treble hooks (*garatéias*).

The piracema

The great spawning migration of fish in the Pantanal is known as the *piracema*. Once a year, the most important game fish — pacú, dourado, curimbatá and pintado, among others — form schools and travel upstream to spawn in the smaller stream margins. Such an arduous trip costs plenty in terms of energy, and that extra energy comes from the burning of fat reserves that the fish have accumulated over the preceding year. This spawning migration generally takes place between November and February, as the rivers swell with rainfall. Commercial net fishing is prohibited during this time, but angling with sport gear is permitted. For some species, the piracema provides the best fishing.

Important fish species

Piranha   There are at least a half dozen species of true piranhas in Brazil, and only a few warrant the fierce reputation. The *piranha mafura* and the *piranha encarnada*, for instance, eat only fruits and seeds. Then there is the *piranha mucura* (the 'opposum piranha', owing to its long snout), which feeds almost exclusively on the nipped-off scales and fins of other fish. When foreigners talk piranhas, they have in mind the *piranha preta* and the *piranha caju*, two certifiably voracious carnivores.

Travellers from the northern latitudes have for years been reading adventure stories about razor-toothed fish with a taste for human flesh. It's no wonder, then, that piranhas are probably the most sought-after fish in the Pantanal and Amazon. That's fortunate, since locals claim that it's often hard to keep them off the hook. If you can't catch a piranha in Brazilian waters, we've been told, you should probably consider giving up fishing altogether.

Voracious they are, but their status as a man-eater is overblown. One afternoon Jayne and I came upon a solitary fisherman cleaning a dozen piranhas. Far more intriguing than his catch itself was the fact that he was standing knee-deep in the very same water where he'd hooked the fish only minutes before!

Piranhas, he explained, infested nearly all the local waters, yet only a few spots were actually dangerous for bathing. We later heard this same story from a number of other villagers. No one, however, could tell us why; obviously, some painful personal experimentation was involved in mapping the local swimming holes. Piranha stories tend toward wild exaggeration, but a few documented cases of attacks on humans and livestock do exist. Most locals agree that small backwaters cut off from the main rivers and streams during the dry season are dangerous due to the high concentration of piranhas and the lack of prey. Otherwise, the piranha's reputation is largely the stuff of B-grade jungle movies.

Tackle for piranha fishing is embarrassingly simple: thick monofilament line wound around a tin can or tied to a bamboo pole. Four inches of baling wire, however, must be fastened above the hook as a 'leader' to prevent the piranha's teeth from cutting the plastic line.

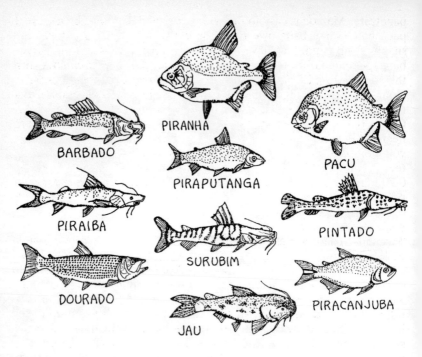

BARBADO

PIRANHA

PACU

PIRAPUTANGA

PIRAIBA

PINTADO

SURUBIM

DOURADO

PIRACANJUBA

JAU

Almost any piece of meat or fish will do for bait. We've used both strips of cooked beef and live eels. Thrash your bait about the surface for a few seconds before letting it sink. Apparently, this mimics the commotion caused by large prey falling into the water.

Piranhas put up a respectable fight even on hand-held line; on light spinning tackle they would rival the heftiest of trout. Yet the real fun begins once the creature is landed in a boat full of barefooted anglers. It's easy to believe that more piranha 'attacks' occur out of the water than in. The famous triangular cutting teeth snap pencils and plastic pens like so much balsa wood; dispatch piranhas with a sharp whack on the head if you plan to keep your toes.

Pacú The fruit-eating *pacú* looks like nothing so much as an over-grown piranha. Pacús sport two sets of teeth in the upper jaw, while piranhas have but one. I can't recommend this test with live fish. Biologists now suspect that pacú and other fish which eat whole fruits and seeds contribute to seed dispersal, and therefore affect the distribution of vegetation along waterways just as birds do on land. The Pantanal hosts a number of species of pacú, some of which reach 12 to 15 kg. The minimum legal size at this writing is 40 cm. Best fishing occurs between October and March, with February especially good. The pacú is generally an herbivore, and the most popular bait is manioc root that has been boiled or roasted just long enough to allow a hook to

penetrate. Manioc is easy to buy and store, and may thus be the ideal
pacú bait. Some baits owe their success to the pacú's proclivity for
snapping up fruits that have fallen from trees overhanging the river
bank; *genipapo* fruit, figs, a small wild orange known as *laranjinha*, and
the so-called *melancia do pacú* are all fruit baits, especially popular
along the River Paraguai and its tributaries. Fruit and vegetable baits
reportedly don't work well in some waters, however; on the Taquari and
Coxim rivers, for example, the preferred baits include chunks of beef
heart or filets cut from other fish such as the *curimbatá*. Whichever bait
you choose, it must be very firm or you'll lose it to the pacú's strong
teeth. Number 5/0 or 6/0 hooks are ideal, with 20 kg test (0.60 or
0.70 mm) monofilament line. Spinning reels, baitcasting reels, bamboo
poles, and tin cans all work for pacú. Look for spots along the river with
overhanging fruit trees which supply pacu with natural food. To keep
your chummed bait from going downstream too quickly, try to find a
place where the stream widens and forms back-eddies. Chum with
manioc chunks or corn kernels before fishing — ideally, a day before.

Catfish   Some of the most highly-prized gamefish in the Pantanal are
whiskered: *pintado*, *surubim*, *jaú*, *piraíba* and *barbado* are all shovel-
nosed catfish, and the first two form the mainstay of all fish restaurants
in the Pantanal. Pintado and surubim (the former striped and the latter
spotted) can weigh up to 90 kg, but generally run from 2 to 15 kg. The
minimum legal size is 80 cm. Best fishing occurs from September
through March, and these species — like all catfish — feed primarily in
the hours from dusk to daylight. You'll need a fishing rod (preferably
2 m long and fairly stiff) and a reel if you tie into a pintado of any size;
sticks and cans won't do. The bait must be live — eels such as *pirambóia*
or small fish such as *lambarí* are ideal. The pintado is a cautious fish; the
slightest movements on your part or the smell of petrol transferred from
hands to bait may be enough to spook these giant catfish. If you're really
set on catching a pintado, you would be wise to hire a guide. The jaú is a
more cylindrically-shaped catfish than the pintado and surubim, but
may reach the same monstrous size and is caught in much the same way.
Fishing for jaú is good the year round, and the minimum legal size is
90 cm. The barbado is the smallest (rarely larger than 8 kg) of the edible
catfish. It also happens to be the easiest to catch without a guide and is
every bit as delicious as its heftier brethren. As Jayne can testify, you
can haul barbado inshore with the most primitive of equipment — a tin
can wrapped with 0.40 mm monofilament is more than adequate. While
live bait helps, it's by no means necessary — any chunk of fish flesh will
work. Ask locals for advice on the best locale; you may be invited, as we
were, to join villagers for an evening of barbado fishing. Once again,
wait for dusk, when the barbado leaves its hiding places to forage.

Dourado   As its name implies, the *dourado* is a golden yellow-orange,
the handsomest fish in the Pantanal. Looking much like a salmon, the
dourado is excellent table fare and without a doubt the most sought-

after freshwater game fish in South America. The minimum legal size in the Pantanal is 55 cm, but dourado can weigh up to 30 kg. Fishing is best from August through December. Unlike the catfish, dourado prefer well-oxygenated, swift-running water, and feed during the day. Use a 24 kg test (0.70 mm) monofilament line and hook sizes from 5/0 to 9/0, baiting them with live fish or eels. Artificial lures such as Rapalas also work well for dourado.

LODGES

Jayne and I used to be more than a little sceptical of the safari lodge concept. We were, after all, ruggedly independent backcountry types, swashbuckling adventurers determined to see everything on our own and at the cheapest possible price. With a collective condescending shrug, we passed off such lodges as dude ranches, country clubs. Finally, we swallowed our travel snobbery long enough to visit a lodge outside Corumbá and had, naturally enough, a splendid time. Instead of a swank Club Med atmosphere, we found a funky, functioning cattle ranch catering to small groups of wildlife lovers (including some repentant travel snobs not unlike ourselves). The fishing and birdwatching were spectacular, the price reasonable.

Such lodges are springing up throughout the Pantanal. Many are working cattle ranches moonlighting in tourism. Others are sport fishing lodges, eager to please the growing number of travellers more interested in photographing egrets than landing trophy catfish. Their big advantage is convenience; you can be whisked by plane, boat, or truck directly to the lodge, see abundant wildlife, and return to the city with a minimum of time wasted. So, while somewhat structured, such lodges are ideal for travellers on a tight schedule. Food is generally excellent, with huge portions of local fish. Reservations can be made well in advance through travel agencies in Campo Grande, Corumbá, Cuiabá, even Rio and São Paulo. You can opt to handle everything yourself, but the state tourist boards (MSTUR in Mato Grosso do Sul and TURIMAT in Mato Grosso) will gladly call the lodges for you and make reservations as well. Make certain exactly what you are paying for; many side trips to bird nesting areas and fishing spots cost extra. Transportation to and from the lodge is often tacked on as an extra. You may be able to reduce this expense by finding other guests and sharing the ride. In some cases, public transportation at least part of the way is available. This fact may not always be mentioned by travel agents, so check with locals. Don't be afraid to bargain, especially during the off-season. A sampling of lodges:

Pousada do Pantanal (Fazenda Santa Clara)   120 km from Corumbá near the highway to Campo Grande. Ten simple rooms with private bathrooms, cold showers, and electricity until 2200 when they shut down the generator. The food is excellent and the portions enormous. All meals are included in the cost of lodging, around US$25 per person per night. Horses, horse-drawn buggies, canoes, and powerboats are available for excursions. These generally cost extra. Phone (067)231-5797 in Corumbá or (011) 284-4877 for reservations. You can also deal through Hermann at the Bar El Pacu on Corumbá's waterfront. During the off-season you can bargain the price down almost fifty percent. Transportation by truck to the ranch is extra (and expensive), but you can cut this substantially by taking the Corumbá-Campo Grande bus and disembarking at the access road (all the bus drivers know it); arrange to be picked up there. The place is loosely structured, surrounded by wildlife, and is highly recommended.

Pousada das Araras 132 km from Cuiabá, 30 km south of Poconé on the Transpantaneira highway. Comfortable rooms with private bathrooms, hot showers. You can arrange transportation with the lodge, take a taxi or hitch from Poconé. All meals are included with lodging, about US$30 per person per night. Excursions by boat cost extra, but there is plenty to be seen on foot. Phone (065)721-1170 in Poconé for reservations.

Pousada Pixaim 162 km from Cuiabá, 60 km south of Poconé on the Transpantaneira. Ten simple, rustic rooms with private baths, hot showers. All meals are huge, tasty, and included in the lodging price of US$15 per person per night (half that with breakfast alone). This is a frequent stop for truckers. Boat trips on the Pixaim River cost US$7.50 per hour, for up to four people. Phone Fátima Ourives at (065)322-8961 in Cuiabá for reservations. You can either hitch from Poconé or Miguel the owner will pick you up there, charging only for gasoline.

Santa Rosa Pantanal 148 km south of Poconé, near Porto Jofre at the southern terminus of the Transpantaneira. As the Pantanal goes, this is a fairly swank tourist complex, with a swimming pool, bar, 10 rooms and 24 bungalows, all with private baths, hot showers, and heat. Horses and boats are available at extra cost for fishing and wildlife-viewing. Excellent regional meals are included in the lodging cost, about US$40 per person per day. Phone (065)321-5514 in Cuiabá for reservations. The Selva travel agency in Cuiabá, rua Barão de Melgaço 3594 can also make arrangements.

WILL THE PANTANAL SURVIVE?

Environmentally speaking, the Pantanal's future is on much more solid footing than the Amazonian rain forest. The huge cattle ranches that dominate the area lie on naturally open and fertile grasslands, not the thin jungle soil being cleared daily in northern Brazil. Ironically, as long as beef production remains lucrative, much habitat will undoubtedly remain in its present, relatively pristine state. But whether or not there will be wildlife to fill that habitat is still uncertain. Poaching, commercial fishing, and mining all pose serious threats to the Pantanal's future.

Poaching has taken a severe toll in the Pantanal, and no single species has been more devastated than the alligator (*Caiman crocodilus yacaré*). Valued for its hide, the jacaré has for decades been pursued by *coureiros* (leather hunters) from both Brazil and nearby Bolivia. Each year, they butcher an estimated one to two million alligators in the Pantanal. The economic crisis in Brazil has only worsened the problem; one local resident admitted to us that a ranch hand could make more in a single night of alligator poaching than his entire monthly salary. The poachers — perhaps as many as 5000 in the Pantanal — hunt primarily at night, using flashlights and lanterns to spot the reflective eyes of their sluggish prey. It is not uncommon for a single *coureiro* to shoot 200 jacaré in a single night. Poachers flay only two small strips of leathery hide from the jacaré's flanks and leave the rest, including the tail meat, to rot.

While alligators lead the list of poaching targets, the *coureiros* regularly shoot a number of other species for their pelts or feathers: river otters, blue macaws, pacas (another oversized rodent), and monkeys. Jaguars, which poachers hunt with the aid of trained dogs, are now extremely rare within the Pantanal.

It's true that the Brazilian government has made recent strides in coming to grips with the poaching problem. Army troops, for instance, are now combining jungle-combat training with anti-poaching patrols. Yet the problem is not likely to go away, and may actually get worse if Brazil's economy continues to stagnate. A staggeringly huge chunk of real estate, the Pantanal is almost impossible to effectively patrol. A dozen IBDF agents have responsibility for all 230,000 square kilometres. And poachers, like the drug cartels, are becoming increasingly sophisticated; some now use radios to warn their cohorts of an approaching patrol. Eliminating the demand for these goods — the market is primarily European — seems far more likely to succeed than on-site surveillance. Strict import controls and certification of farm-origin furs and hides will help stem the flow of these animal goods; this is one of the few areas where non-Brazilians can truly effect change.

Mechanized mining, concentrated near Poconé and Nossa Senhora do Livramento in Mato Grosso, is permanently scarring huge tracts of land. The resulting runoff clogs streams and smothers fish eggs for miles. Meanwhile, the mining industry burns some 40 tons of mercury each year in Mato Grosso alone. This toxic metal ends up a permanent and deadly part of the Pantanal's earth and water supply.

Commercial fishing goes on largely unrestricted. Fishing with illegal nets and traps, even during the *piraçema* (spawning migration), is flagrantly commonplace.

Finally, chemical spills are no longer unheard of in the Pantanal. Just before one of our visits, hundreds of thousands of fish were washed ashore near Miranda in the wake of a massive fertilizer spill.

There are no environmental groups devoted strictly to preserving the Pantanal. Wildlife Conservation International (a branch of the New York Zoological Society, Bronx, New York 10460 USA), however, has been involved in a great deal of research in the region and deserves your support. Likewise, take every opportunity while in Brazil to talk to the state tourist-agency personnel; let them know that you are there to observe wildlife in a relatively undisturbed state, and that you'll spend money to do so. Tell them — and anyone else who'll listen — that what the Pantanal needs isn't fancy hotels but more protection. And urge your own politicians to ban the sale of non-farmed alligator hides and animal furs.

Collared peccary

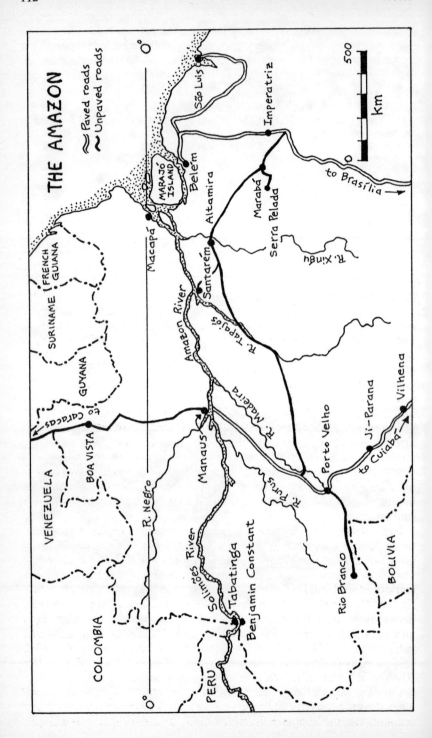

Chapter 6

The Amazon

Amazônia — the great river, its tributaries, and rain forest — spans portions of nine South American countries. But Brazil's share is by far the largest, and it claims almost half the entire country.

Sadly, first-time visitors to the world's mightiest rain forest often come away mildly disappointed. You'll find that the few remaining Indian tribes are accessible only to legitimate anthropologists. You won't see boa constrictors draped from every tree branch, and monkeys don't swing from every vine; the truth is, they never did. But free yourself of these expectations, and your trip to Amazônia will prove rewarding. You'll witness *caboclos*, mixed-race descendants of the original Indians, living in stilt houses along the river; you'll meet gold prospectors and manioc farmers; you'll watch freshwater dolphins play in the wake of your cargo boat; you'll camp in a lush green kingdom containing over one-fifth of the world's plant species; with patience, you'll see some of the region's elusive wildlife — especially if you strap a headlamp on and poke around at night; and finally, you'll witness first-hand the shameful and short-sighted exploitation that is destroying the rain forest.

Exploitation is hardly new to Amazônia. Indeed, the first Europeans to set foot in Amazônia did so in a frenzy of greed. Gonzalo Pizarro, governor of Quito and Francisco's lesser-known half brother, set out in 1541 with an army of conquistadores to find and plunder El Dorado's lost city of gold and La Canela, the Land of Cinnamon. By the time they reached the jungle, however, the expedition had already soured and run dangerously short of rations. Pizarro dispatched Francisco de Orellana and some sixty of his men to search for food. After a month and a half rafting down the Napa River, Orellana finally reached, on February 11, 1542, a body of water so immense that he called it 'El Rio Mar' — the River Sea. It was, of course, the mainstem Amazon.

Orellana soon abandoned the idea of returning to Pizarro's party even after the discovery of food at a well-stocked Indian village. Some accounts cite the impossibility of travelling upstream against the Napo;

others blame the lure of El Dorado. In any case, Orellana and his men continued downriver. Along the way, probably close to the Nhamundá River delta, their chronicler reported fierce battles with a race of tall women warriors not unlike the Amazons of Greek myth. Orellana reached the Atlantic on August 26, 1542, sailed northwest to the island of Cubagua off the Venezuelan coast, and eventually returned to Spain. King Carlos V apparently forgave Orellana his desertion of Pizarro's group, for in early 1544 he rewarded the conquistador with an appointment as governor of the Amazon region. The next year Orellana returned on an ill-fated expedition that ended with his death along the mighty river he had discovered.

By the late 1500's, Spain was calling back its conquistadores, reluctantly abandoning the search for the mythical riches of El Dorado. But their Portuguese counterparts, the *bandeirantes*, continued the quest in earnest. Tough, merciless freebooters from the São Paulo region, the *bandeirantes* penetrated Amazônia as far as the Andes by the middle of the next century. Gold remained elusive, but the *bandeirantes* returned from the jungles with equally precious booty: Amerindian slaves. Portuguese Jesuits had already established missions in Amazônia, where they armed and protected the local Indians from *bandeirante* attacks. Yet the Jesuits' intervention only prolonged the inevitable, and their entire order was eventually ousted by the Crown.

By the middle of the 18th Century, both Jesuits and *bandeirantes* had retreated from the Amazon basin. Their presence had permanently bolstered Portuguese claims to the area, but Amazônia again became, for all intents and purposes, the sole domain of Indians and wildlife.

This period of slumber lasted until the rubber boom of the late 19th Century when, for a short but wildly decadent time, Manaus found itself the world's only source of rubber (see the section on Manaus).

In 1967, geologists discovered the world's largest deposit of high-grade iron ore in the state of Pará. Copper, manganese, and bauxite were found nearby, along with a concentrated gold deposit which was kept secret for ten years. Once discovered, Serra Pelada became a human anthill, a vast pit swarming with over 30,000 *garimpeiros* (prospectors) who, by 1986, had extracted more than 30 million kilograms of gold. Large-scale development in Amazônia really began in 1969, with the enactment of Brazil's National Integration Programme, aimed at building roads and settling the basin with drought-stricken *nordestinos*. The centrepiece of the programme was the Trans-Amazon Highway. Mining and agriculture, still important, have recently taken a back seat to cattle ranching, which currently comprises the biggest threat to the remaining rain forest.

The present inhabitants of backcountry Amazônia call themselves *caboclos*. Theoretically they comprise a mix of Amerindian and Portuguese blood, but virtually anyone living in the hinterlands is considered a *caboclo*. Most of the boatmen or jungle guides you hire in Amazônia will be *caboclos*, and they are renowned for their knowledge of river and forest life.

How to get there Gateway cities along the Amazon river itself are Belém, some 100 km from the mouth, and Manaus, 1600 km upriver. Both are served by Varig/Cruzeiro do Sul flights from all major Brazilian cities as well as several international flights (see the sections below for details).

Getting around Some major highways now cut through Amazônia, but overland transportation remains difficult and, at times, impossible. Buses travelling BR-319 between Manaus and Porto Velho take at least 22 hours during the driest months (July through September). The bus must cross six tributaries of the Amazon via ferry, any or all of which may be broken down or backed up with waiting truck traffic. The 'paved' road is terrible for all but 200 km of the total 900 km (the stretch between Porto Velho and Humaitá), and officials sometimes close the highway altogether during the rainy season. The rodovia Trans-amazônica (BR-230, the Trans-Amazon highway) remains completely unpaved, and buses do not attempt to travel it during the rainy season. Even during the dry months, we've heard that the bus trip between Santarém and Belém along the Transamazônica is a nightmare, taking at best two days and often many more. There is only one other major overland arterial within Amazônia, an unpaved highway between Manaus and Boa Vista, 760 km to the north; the journey takes 18 hours by bus.

As the preceding paragraph suggests, boats and aeroplanes still provide the most practical transportation throughout Amazônia. Everything from tiny cargo boats to ocean liners ply the mainstem Amazon from its mouth (near Belém) to Iquitos, Peru. Virtually all cargo boats take paying passengers along as a matter of course. The trip from Belém to Manaus (or at least to Santarém) is a must for every backcountry traveller wishing to know the river. Smaller cargo boats make trips up and down most other navigable tributaries. Especially on the tributaries, river travel is slow and not too dependable for those on a tight schedule. Aeroplanes fly everywhere in Amazônia, but all that convenience and dependability gets expensive. If you can't find a scheduled flight going where you want to, try one of the numerous charter airlines located at every city airport; since they specialize in flying *garimpeiros* (gold prospectors) into the bush, these air taxis can be very pricey.

When to go Amazônia is one of the wettest places on earth. The rainy season north of the Equator runs from April through August, while the region south of the Equator — and this includes the areas described in this book — receives heaviest rainfall from December to June. Inhabitants often refer to this rainy season as *o inverno*, the 'winter.' But don't think of the rainy season as one continual downpour. At one forest camp we visited north of Manaus, an astounding 56.8 mm of rain fell on May 21; the next day, not a single drop was recorded. Toward the end of the rainy season, in May or June, the Amazon River and its

tributaries typically crest and flood. To avoid the floods, the rains, and
the worst of the mosquitoes which accompany all this water, plan to visit
during one of the 'dry' months: July to November. Plan on getting wet
regardless. In addition to the frequent violent downpours that occur
even during the dry months, humidity is always around 80%. Temperatures run just a bit higher during the dry months, ranging from 24° to 33°.

Fortunately, Brazilian holidays and vacations won't have much effect
on your travel plans in this area. If Brazilians visit Amazônia at all, it's to
shop in Manaus' duty free shops or to take touristy day trips to the
'meeting of the waters.'

Vital statistics   The Amazon River is the second-longest river in the
world, after the Nile, and of its 6,437 km course, fully half runs through
Brazil. Ten of its 1,100 major tributaries are longer than the Rhine, and
seven run for more than 1,500 km. In terms of volume it is the world's
largest river; each minute it sends 12.9 million litres of water into the
Atlantic, a flow 13 times greater than that of the Mississippi River.
Scientists estimate that 20-25% of all the water that runs off the earth's
surface is carried by the Amazon. This discharge is so great that it turns
the ocean water brackish for more than 150 km offshore. At its mouth,
the river spans more than 400 km, and there are spots between Belém
and Manaus where the river widens to over 5 km. At some points the
river reaches depths of 90 metres, and deep-draft ocean-going vessels
regularly navigate all the way to Iquitos, over 3,000 km upriver.

Amazing as it seems, all this water once flowed in the opposite
direction. About 180 million years ago, when South America and Africa
were still a single land mass, the Amazon and Niger Rivers were one and
the same, a waterway running westerly to the Atlantic. The same
pattern continued as the South American continent separated 65 million
years ago. Geologists speculate that this ancient river system came to a
standstill several million years ago when the Andes began heaving up,
and sediment layers miles deep in the area lend confidence to their
hypothesis. Gradually, the water trapped in this huge inland sea began
to work its way to the Atlantic, and the Amazon River was born.

Brazilian Amazônia comprises the states of Pará, Amazonas, Rondônia, and Acre, as well as the territories of Amapá and Roraíma.
Contrary to popular belief, not all this land is covered with forest. Yet it
is the rain forest that draws people, and this chapter deals exclusively
with the river and true *mata* (jungle) surrounding it. The three basic
forest types found here include the *várzea*, the *igapó*, and the *terra
firme*. The *várzea* refers to land that is seasonally flooded. Much of what
you'll see from a cargo boat heading up the mainstem Amazon is *várzea*,
although it makes up only about 2% of the entire basin. *Igapós* comprise
the permanently flooded areas, filled with floating lilies and elevated
root systems. Most of Amazônia, however, consists of *terra firme*, the
upland rain forest. The suggestions below allow you to see some of each
forest type.

Suggestions for a trip in Amazônia My ideal trip would start with a journey by cargo boat up the mainstem Amazon River, from Belém to either Santarém or Manaus. You won't see but a fringe of the rain forest, and you'll be lucky if you sight a toucan in the distance. You will, however, get a first-hand appreciation of the river itself, the sheer immensity of it. Nothing you have read or seen in magazines, books, or television can quite prepare you for that experience. And, travelling by cargo boat, you'll get a feeling for the ebb and flow of commerce within Amazônia. Finally, you'll get glimpses of *caboclo* life along the forest edge and meet residents of the region first hand; boat travel affords lots of time for conversation.

Following this overview of the Amazon River, I'd recommend a trip by small guide boat into the *igapós*, small watery channels well off the main tributaries that remain permanently flooded. Winding through the forest, these watery channels provide the classic cinematic image of 'The Jungle,' and they're usually narrow enough for effective wildlife viewing.

The third and final part of an ideal Amazon trip should include camping and exploring on foot within the rain forest itself, the so-called *mata fechada* (closed forest) or *terra firme*. You might want to include this along with a visit to the *igapós*, or as a separate trip altogether. Arrange to spend several nights — the rain forest is at its most fascinating after dark. And as a sobering final note to your journey, arrange to see a portion of the forest that was but is no longer — a cattle ranch or plantation. Unfortunately, you won't have to go very far out of your way to see the rain forest denuded.

Both the *igapó* and the upland forest (*terra firme*) are most easily seen via Manaus. You'll find detailed advice on this kind of three-part trip in the following sections.

BELÉM

On our first visit to Belém, we met an elderly Welshman who was re-visiting the ports he'd savoured most during a lifetime in the Merchant Marine. Belém somehow manages to exude that kind of funky, tropical charm although neither we nor the Welshman could figure out precisely why; the city is mostly a sprawl of skyscrapers and shantytowns housing nearly a million people. Perhaps Belém's elusive appeal owes to its constant reminders that a vast and wild place, maybe the vastest and wildest place left on earth, lies just around the bend upriver. Whether worming your way through the Ver-O-Peso market or strolling past street corner ice-cream vendors, you'll be confronted by the myriad products of the rain forest — everything from medicinal herbs like *jambú* and weird fruits such as *bacurí* to the huge *pirarucú* fish, whose scales are sold as fingernail files.

Belém serves as the departure point for cargo and passenger boats ascending the Amazon.

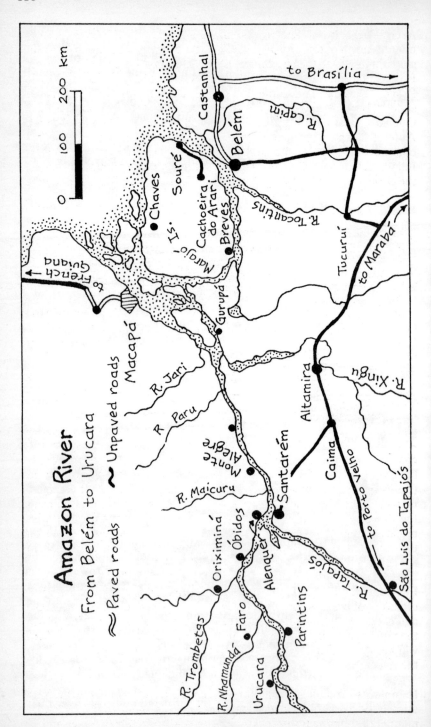

Amazon River
From Belém to Urucara

~ Paved roads
~ Unpaved roads

Arrival/Departure The international airport, Val de Cans, lies 15 minutes north of town by taxi; just outside the terminal a cheap local bus stops on its way to the city centre. Daily flights go to and from Fortaleza, Rio de Janeiro, São Paulo, Santarém, Recife, Manaus, São Luis, Rio Branco, Macapá, and numerous smaller cities in Pará and Amazonas states. There are extremely crowded weekly flights to Cayenne (French Guiana), Paramaribo (Suriname), as well as a weekly flight to Miami. At least seven companies running small aircraft throughout Amazônia operate out of a second airport, Júlio César, on avenida Senador Lemos, telephone 233-3868. The bus station is a long 5 km walk west of the city centre; dodge traffic across avenida Almirante Barroso and take any bus marked Aeroclube into town. Daily buses run to Fortaleza, Recife, Salvador, Santarém, São Luís, São Paulo, Rio, Teresina, and João Pessoa, in addition to hundreds of smaller towns in Pará.

Getting around Within walking distance of the city centre lie most of the cheap hotels, three of the principal boat docks, the Ver-O-Peso market, the natural history museum, and the money-changers. You'll find the cheap hotels concentrated close to the docks and just off the centre's main drag (avenida Presidente Vargas) in either direction; rua Gaspar Viana, travessa da Indústria, avenida 15 de Novembro, and rua Frutuoso Guimarães are good streets to investigate. The only other places you're likely to visit are the more distant city docks; see *Boat Trips* on the next page.

Changing money Belém has no *casas de câmbio*, but cash and cheques can be readily changed on the black market at a number of the cheap and funky 'gringo' hotels. It eases the process somewhat if you're actually booked into the hotel, but it isn't absolutely necessary. We've changed both travellers cheques and cash at the Hotel Vitória Régia, travessa Frutuoso Guimarães 260, and cash at the Perfumaría Orion (that's right, a perfume shop!), nearby on the same street. If you have no luck in the cheap hotel district, order a beer at the Bar do Parque in the Praça República, where you're sure to meet other travellers with money-changing advice. As a last resort, change travellers cheques on the official market at Banco do Brasil, avenida Presidente Vargas 248 in the centre.

Information PARATUR, the state tourist agency, operates a new office out of Praça Kennedy at the artesans' market near the waterfront, and occasionally staffs booths at the bus station and airport. Check also the municipal tourist office at avenida Nazaré 231. None of these offices will help you much if you want to travel cheaply and independently on the river.

Hammocks You'll need a good hammock (*rede*) whether travelling upriver on cargo/passenger boats or camping in the rain forest. A number of shops near the docks, along avenidas Castilhos Franca and 15 de Novembro, sell hammocks for about US$8, cheap mosquito nets (*mosquiteiros*), and rope to sling the whole affair. See the section on *Camping* in Chapter 4. You won't need a mosquito net if you're just travelling the mainstem Amazon by cargo boat.

BOAT TRIPS FROM BELÉM

Upriver to Manaus or Santarém

This is the classic trip, and one that I recommend every backcountry traveller take as a starter course on Amazônia. As I've mentioned before, don't expect to be mobbed by wildlife, nor to see anything more than the fringing wall of the rain forest. The rationale for this trip should be to experience the river itself; until you've seen the mainstem Amazon first-hand, the superlatives don't mean much.

You could, of course, make the trip downriver from Manaus or Santarém to Belém. Coming downstream, however, the boats keep to the centre of the channel to take advantage of the current, and consequently you'll see more water and less rain forest.

Finding a boat   You have a choice of two types of boats: the government-run ENASA boats, or the countless smaller cargo boats which take passengers as space allows. Fares are almost identical. The cargo boats, however — particularly those going downriver — put you in close quarters with the rich produce of Amazônia: Brazil nuts, hardwoods, bananas, dried fish, manioc meal, and a multitude of jungle fruits which even most Brazilians don't recognize.

ENASA runs a large diesel ferry once a week to Manaus, stopping along the way at Monte Alegre, Santarém, Óbidos, and Parintins. The boat carries about 600 passengers as well as cars and cargo, leaving the dock at 2200 every Wednesday. The full trip to Manaus takes five days, the boat arriving on Tuesday morning; to Santarém, it's a two-day trip with arrival on Saturday. You'll pay US$40 for hammock space (*classe popular*), with three meals a day provided; a bar aboard sells beer and

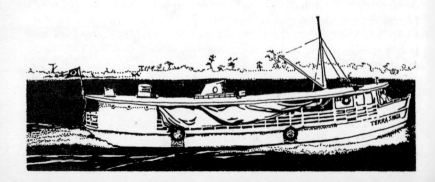

cold sodas. Confirm these sailing times, buy tickets, and catch the boat at the ENASA dock on avenida Castilhos França, right next to Ver-O-Peso marketplace (telephone 223-3011, extension (*ramal*) 34). Bring your passport when buying a ticket, since you may be required to show it. Schedules and information on this and other ENASA boats are also available at the main ENASA office, avenida Presidente Vargas 41, telephone 223-3011 (you can't actually purchase tickets here, though). ENASA also runs two new tourist-class catamarans to Manaus once a month. The journey takes six days, the boats carry 140 passengers in air-conditioned cabins, and the fare is US$550 per person.

We've never actually taken the ENASA boats. Frankly, they look far too huge and far too crowded, and plenty of reliable sources have confirmed this first-hand. The food, they say, is edible but scanty, thefts of baggage are common, and you stand in long lines for both food and bathrooms. There are only three advantages to the ENASA boats: they leave on schedule, they arrive on schedule, and it's supremely easy to buy a ticket. I've never met a traveller who said they'd take ENASA a second time, so these can't be very compelling advantages.

You'll have a far more relaxing and enjoyable trip — and at no additional cost — if you just spend a little extra time arranging passage on a small cargo vessel. These run anywhere from 10 metres to 30 metres in length and generally carry only two dozen or so passengers. Thus, you're rarely standing in line; everyone eats together family style and you quickly become friends rather than competitors for space and food. Whenever you feel like it you can stroll up to sun on the top deck or chat with the captain in the pilothouse. Drawing less water, these cargo boats heave closer to shoreline going upriver, and make stops in the smaller river outposts.

Be aware that the small cargo boats almost never go all the way to Manaus; you'll generally have to disembark in Santarém and arrange for another cargo boat to take you to Manaus.

Small cargo boats leave from several docks throughout the city, but two of the closest and most reliable are Portos 9 and 10 CDP. Go to the guard post at avenida Marechal Hermes and travessa Quintino Bocaiuva. Tell the guard you're looking for a boat going upriver; he'll let you pass and may be able to tell you which boats are being loaded for departure. If you have no luck here, try the Porto das Lanchas (Armazén 9), at the end of avenida Castilhos França next to Ver-O-Peso market; or try the Porto das Balsas, avenida Bernardo Sayão (catch the Cremação bus from the centre and ask the driver to put you off at the docks).

When you've located a boat going to Santarém, ask for the captain. Assuming that he takes passengers — most of them do — he'll quote you a price which should be fairly close to ENASA's *classe popular* fare; you can try to bargain, but fares are pretty standard for this sort of thing. Most boats also offer a few private cabins sleeping two, but these cost double the standard fare besides being stuffy and cramped; I can't recommend them except for those who absolutely must sleep in a bed.

Sometimes these cabins boast air-conditioning, which doesn't seem much of an advantage — after all, you won't want to be cooped up in a cabin during the day, and things get plenty chilly at night on their own.

Generally the boats take several days to load, and delays of one to three days are common. Stop by at least once each day to see how the loading is progressing, and plan to move aboard early on the day of departure — otherwise you'll be crowded into a corner or worse. (We once travelled next to a fellow who was stuck sleeping on top of a car being shipped upriver!) To reserve your spot, just sling your hammock and let the captain and crew know you've arrived. The cargo boats almost always leave Belém after dark, allowing the trickiest and narrowest portions of the river to be navigated during daylight.

If you want to save on hotel bills, ask the captain if you can sling your hammock immediately upon buying passage, sleeping aboard at no additional cost while the loading takes place. They usually don't refuse, although you'll have to put up with a lot of noise and lights throughout the night. Also, you won't be provided with meals or showers until the boat actually sails.

What to bring   In addition to your hammock, bring plenty of rope to sling it with — at least three metres. It gets unbelievably cold at night on the river, so bring a cotton sheet and wool blanket, as well as several layers of clothing. T-shirts, shorts or loose nylon pants, and rubber thongs will do for the daytime. Bring your own towel for showering. Check to be sure that plates and cutlery are provided (they usually are). We bring several plastic litre bottles of mineral water, fresh fruit, and snack items to supplement the meals aboard. Some but not all boats carry canisters of safe drinking water. Keep insect repellent handy and don't forget your malaria pills; despite what you may have read, mosquitoes can and do light aboard these boats, and we've been swarmed instantly by clouds of them as our boat moved along shore while navigating an especially tricky section of river. Carry a small flashlight to find your way around the boat after dark. Binoculars are a must. If you want acceptable shots of life along the river, bring along a telephoto lens. Finally, don't forget some reading matter, playing cards, a Portuguese dictionary, and some personal photos from back home; everyone gets bored on the river, and after a few days even the shyest *brasileiro* will be eager to spill his or her life story and to hear yours.

I recommend keeping your passport, money, cheques, and plane tickets on your person at all times — in a concealed pouch — even though I've never heard of thieves operating on these small boats. Your backpack or bags can be safely stored on the deck beneath your hammock. If you're returning to Belém anytime within a month, consider leaving extra gear with your hotel there (see *Stashing Gear* in Chapter 4).

Life on board   Living space can be cramped. At the beginning of the trip, hammocks are strung so closely that they touch. Passengers and cargo leave the boat at stops along the way, however, and rarely does the boat fill up again. You'll have to thread your way around cargo, which is stacked on all decks. Upriver cargo tends to be uninteresting manufactured goods being shipped to the hinterlands: spools of wire and rope, machinery, canned goods, concrete, finished lumber, even automobiles.

Most boats offer a simple shower which draws on river water.

Food on the cargo boats is simple but filling. Breakfast usually consists of white bread, margarine, and coffee. Lunch and dinner are hot meals, with rice, noodles, beans, chicken or beef, and the ever-present *farinha* (manioc flour) to sprinkle over all. Sometimes turtle or even alligator may be substituted if it's available. Since most of the boats will be carrying two dozen passengers, meals are taken in two shifts. Your fellow passengers will usually wake you rather than allow you to miss a meal, and you should do the same for them if they're napping. Meals break the monotony of the trip, and they're often the day's major social event and topic for endless hours of conversation. We travelled upriver once with a wizened old gent who insisted that chicken was '*carne fraca*' ('weak meat'), a steady diet of which would surely sap our strength before we reached Santarém; beef was invigorating meat, except for the tripe served one day which drew several hilarious hours of abuse. Unless the food is downright inedible, however, I don't recommend complaining. On riverboats, as in the army, it never hurts to lavish some praise on the cook. Many boats will sell you cold sodas and beer if they have a refrigerator.

You'll meet all sorts of people on such a boat trip: wrinkled *caboclo* grandmothers (plenty of women ride the cargo boats, by the way), gold-seekers from the fields of Serra Pelada, students on vacation, *nordestinos* fleeing a drought, and a sprinkling of fellow foreigners seeing the Amazon. Amazônia attracts migrants from throughout the country, so you may find yourself, as we did one evening, passing around a gourd of hot *chimarrão* — a stimulating herb tea — with *gauchos* from the far south of Brazil. After the evening meal passengers typically get together to chat, play cards, dominoes, or *palitas*, a simple game played with toothpicks of varying length. Well after nightfall, the crew unrolls canvas tarps along the sides of the boats to keep chilly winds out.

The Amazon funnels into narrow channels at various points along the way, and this is where you'll get your best view of the jungle wall. This is the edge of the *várzea*, the seasonally flooded forest of Amazônia. During the rainy season, areas more than 150 km across become flooded, and some regions — the *igapó* — remain flooded year round. The first narrow channel on the Belém-Manaus run begins just 200 km upriver, at the southwestern corner of Marajó Island; this stretch, often covered at night by the cargo boats, runs over 100 km, opening into a wider channel near Gurupá. You'll pass through others during daylight, and cargo boats get extremely close to shore when manoeuvering around the numerous *taboleiros* (sand bars). Keep a watch for toucans and macaws flying just above the forest canopy, and be prepared for mosquito attacks when the boat cruises close to the jungle's edge.

Except for the occasional glimpse of bird life, what you'll mostly see along the shore will be the stilt-houses of the local *caboclos*. Called *palafitas*, these homes appear to be comfortably perched well above the muddy waters of the Amazon, but we've been told that unusually high floodwaters will swamp them. These simple shacks made of tree limbs and palm-fronds stand directly at the river's edge, and entire families flock to the doors when a cargo boat passes. Sometimes your boat will be met by locals in a dugout canoe offering fish for sale. We've seen *caboclo* children less than eight years old expertly paddling canoes across bow wakes. You'll also see local fishermen (*mariscadores*) working out of dugout canoes, some outfitted with sails. A popular fishing technique for the *pirarucú* involves harpooning the giant fish with a buoy tethered to the harpoon tip; the fishermen follow the buoy, waiting for the *pirarucú* to tire so that they can haul it aboard. A second method of fishing relies on simple traps made of sticks plunged into the river bottom, and you'll often see these fence-like affairs when your boat approaches the shore.

Finally, you'll watch boat traffic come and go on what amounts to the only working 'highway' in Amazônia. Easily the most beautiful boats are the graceful white cargo boats fitted with a forward mast and sail. These you'll see mostly in the very lower reaches of the river close to Belém.

Other Boat Trips from Belém

Marajó Island can be reached by ENASA boats as well as smaller cargo vessels. ENASA departs for Souré, the principal town on the island, on the following schedule: Wednesdays and Fridays at 2000, Saturdays at 1400. Return boats leave Souré Thursdays and Sundays at 1700, with an additional return boat leaving Sunday at 2400. The trip takes six hours one-way and costs US$3. SENAVA runs a boat once a week to Macapá which stops at Breves, along the southwestern tip of the island (check with their office at avenida Castilhos França 234 for schedule). A boat leaves twice a month from the Porto das Lanchas next to the Ver-O-Peso market for Breves, and another leaves on an irregular basis to Cachoeira do Arari (a smaller town on the island) from the Porto do Sal docks in the Cidade Velha. Marajó Island isn't actually rain forest — the eastern half is seasonally-flooded savannah — but it's famous for its buffalo ranches and bird life.

MANAUS

Manaus overruns the northern bank of the Rio Negro, just above the point where its dark blue waters meet — but resist mixing — with the dirty yellow water of the Rio Solimões (the mainstem Amazon).

Rubber put Manaus on the map and, for about 20 years following the invention of the car tyre, the rubber barons basked in almost unimaginable wealth. They built with Italian marble, sent their clothes to be laundered in Europe, heard Pavlova sing in the lavish Opera House, and installed electricity throughout the city before Asian rubber plantations eventually ran them out of business. Now a relatively modern city of 630,000 people, Manaus attracts Brazilian tourists shopping for duty-free foreign-brand goods in the Zona Franca (Free Trade Zone) established in 1967. Yet the city still relies heavily on the abundant produce of the rain forest for its existence. And, within a few hours of the city, you can still sling your hammock in jungle that's straight out of Conrad.

Arrival/Departure   Eduardo Gomes International Airport is 14 km from the centre, and a taxi will cost you US$8.00. For about US$0.10, you can catch the city bus marked Aeroporto International-608, which departs from a covered stop to the right of the airport as you're leaving the terminal; it drops you off at the Praça da Matriz next to the cathedral, on rua Tamandaré. Daily flights to Rio, São Paulo, all capital cities in the north, north-east, and centre-west of Brazil, as well as Parintins, Santarém, Tabatinga, Altamira, Borba, Carauarí, Guajará-Mirim, Manicoré, Itaituba, Maués, São Gabriel, and Trombetas. International flights include Miami, Mexico City, Iquitos, Panama City, Bogotá, Caracas, and Santa Cruz del la Sierra, Bolivia. Because of the Free Zone, customs runs at a turtle's pace and the airport often becomes a madhouse; arrive there early for check-in. The bus terminal lies 8 km out of town, and runs daily buses only to Boa Vista, Porto Velho, Humaitá, and Itacoatiara. River boats run to literally hundreds of destinations in Amazônia; these are discussed below.

Getting around   There's not much to see in Manaus, and what there is – the marketplace, docks, and opera house — all lie within easy walking distance of the hotels. The cheapest hotels and eateries are located on and around avenida Joaquim Nabuco in the centre.

Hammocks, maps, and camping supplies   If you haven't already bought a hammock (*rede*), stroll around the intersection of ruas Miranda Leão and Rocha dos Santos, just a block from the municipal marketplace in the centre; you'll find most of the good hammock stores here. Don't forget to buy a mosquito net (*mosquiteiro*) while you're at it — a good one with fine mesh will cost you US$7.00. Casa dos Mapas, on rua Saldanha Marinho 773 in the centre, sells radar maps of Amazônia (scale 1:250,000) for US$9.00 each, and has large-scale quadrangle maps of the area (scale 1:100,000) for US$13.00 each. O Elefante Esportivo, 169 rua dos Barés next to the municipal marketplace, has a good selection of fishing, hunting, and camping gear.

Changing money   Many people in Manaus will tell you that only Banco do Brasil (rua Guilherme Moreira 315 in the centre) changes travellers

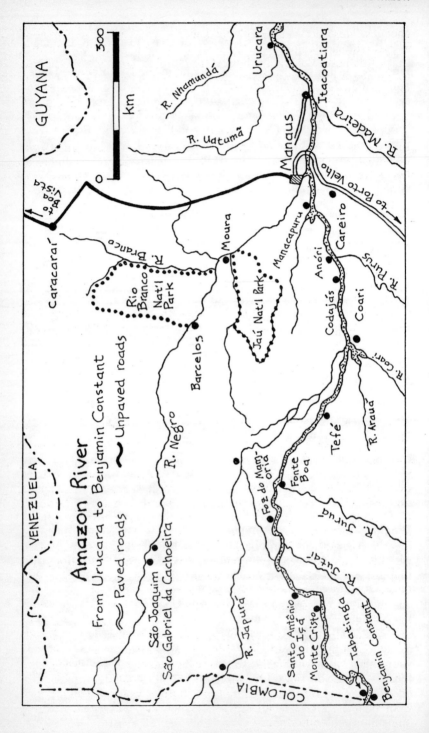

cheques. This isn't so, although black market rates aren't quite as good as in Rio or São Paulo. We've had success changing cheques at Selvatur, praça Adalberto Vale (at the base of the Hotel Amazonas). Cash is easy to change on the parallel market at a number of places, including Selvatur, and Luciatur, rua Guilherme Moreira 281. If you must change cheques at Banco do Brasil, note that they open for foreign exchange only between 0900 and 1200.

Information   Emantur, the local tourism bureau, staffs an office some way north of the centre (rua Tarumã 329, open Monday through Friday from 0700 to 1900 and Saturday until 1300, phone 234-5503), as well as booths at the airport and at the floating docks. For rain forest and river travel, you're better off getting tips from local boatmen and the folks at INPA.

TRIPS INTO THE IGAPÓ

The *igapó* is the permanently-flooded swamp forest of Amazônia. Cargo boats don't penetrate the *igapós*, nor can you reach them by land, so you're pretty much consigned to hiring a local boatman to take you. Few people actually live in these permanent swamps and consequently there is no cheap local transportation. You'll find the small motorized canoes running such trips scattered amongst the bigger cargo boats along the Escadaria dos Remédios docks near the municipal market. Other guides operate out of the Porto Flutuante, the floating docks jutting out in front of the Customs House.

   Guides will generally approach you as soon as you stroll out onto the docks. Some will automatically offer you the names and hotel addresses of recent customers; ask for such references if they're not offered. Most travellers opt for either a day trip or two days and a night. Nights are spent camping in the *terra firme*, and if you don't plan a separate overnight trip in the rain forest, go for the overnight here rather than the simple day trip. Prices vary tremendously, but most guides want about US$60-80 per person per day for the overnight trips (food included) and about US$40 for the day trips. Be sure to bargain. Gasoline is one of the biggest expenses, so many guides charge the same price regardless of whether you go alone or with one or two other travellers during trips that last a single day; overnight trips are generally priced per person. Guides can easily arrange food and hammocks for overnights, but you're better off bringing your own and trying to shave this amount off the asking price.

   If you'd rather not go shopping for a *barqueiro* (boatman) yourself, ask at Luciatur, rua Guilherme Moreira 281. Make sure that most of your time is spent touring the *igapó* by canoe, not tramping through rain forest — that you can do far more cheaply without the services of a *barqueiro*. For overnights, bring food, bottled water, a hammock, a wool blanket, and a headlamp for night walks. For all trips, bring binoculars and bottled water.

RIVER DOLPHINS

Spend a few days on the river and sooner or later your afternoon slumber will be interrupted by cries of '*bôto!*' from the upper decks.

The *bôto* (*Inia geoffrensis*) is actually one of two species of river dolphins seen in the Amazon, the other being the *tucuxi* (*Sotalia fluviatilis*). With their prominent 'foreheads', long beaklike jaws, small dorsal fins, and tiny eyes, these ancient toothed whales bear scant resemblance to their more recently-evolved saltwater relatives. Large eyes are just so much extra baggage for river dolphins living in a silted, muddy environment; those of the *bôto* and, to a lesser extent the *tucuxi*, have degenerated over millenia to the point where they can only distinguish day from night. River dolphins find their food — mostly bottom-dwelling fish and shrimp — by echolocation.

Both species are grey on the upper body and pale pink or even white on the belly, but the *bôto* has a more prominently bulging forehead, a longer beak, and a more developed dorsal fin. River dolphins won't dazzle you with their acrobatics — they prefer to roll on the surface rather than leap — but like marine dolphins they enjoy an occasional frolic in a boat wake, sometimes 'escorting' the cargo boats for several kilometres. Early morning and late afternoon are the best times to watch for river dolphins.

Soon after the first *bôto* sighting, your fellow boat passengers — those from Amazônia at least — will undoubtedly fill you in on some of the legend which surrounds these gentle mammals. The *bôto* symbolizes sexual potency throughout the Amazon, and locals say that the male dolphin frequently takes the shape of a human to seduce women, especially virgins. Sometimes the *bôto* masquerades as a husband in order to sleep with an unsuspecting but otherwise loyal wife; a number of inconvenient pregnancies have undoubtedly been explained handily with this story. Women travellers should know that the *bôto* is so fond of menstruating humans that he will reportedly tip over their canoes in order to work his seductive magic on them.

Not surprisingly, a number of sexual charms and potions are made from *bôto* parts. The dried and grated left eye and penis of a dolphin form a powerful aphrodisiac. A man who places the grated left eye in a woman's food is guaranteed to win her affections. Dried and powdered dolphin penis mixed with a local herb may be rubbed on a man's penis to create a large and long-lasting erection.

River dolphin meat is oily and tasteless, so fishermen rarely go out of their way to catch *bôto*. Nevertheless, dolphins frequently find their way into nets used for fish. Dam construction also threatens river dolphin populations in Amazônia.

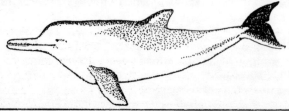

OTHER BOAT TRIPS FROM MANAUS

There's no reason to pay a *barqueiro* to see the 'meeting of the waters'; the Careiro ferry crosses the river throughout the day delivering cars, buses, and trucks to the other side, where BR-319 heads south to Porto Velho. Take the bus marked Ceasa from the Cathedral in the centre.

Double-decker cargo/passenger boats ply the mainstem Amazon and its larger nearby tributaries (the Purus, Madeira, Juruá, and Negro) on a daily basis. It's much easier to find a boat here than in Belém; they all leave either from the Escadaria dos Remédios docks by the municipal market or from the Porto Flutuante near the Customs House, and most display their destination and sailing time on huge placards. Boats upstream to Tabatinga near the Colombian border take five days to a week (roughly US$40), with another three days or so to Iquitos, Peru (about US$10). Boats headed up the Rio Madeira to Porto Velho take five days and charge around US$30. Regular boats travel up the Rio Negro as far as Barcelos (2 days, about US$10), from where you can catch smaller *motores* all the way to São Gabriel da Cachoeira (nine days, around US$50). All these prices include food. As in Belém, most boats leave the dock at around 1800.

While the Purus, Madeira, and Negro are all tributaries of the Amazon, don't get the impression that you'll be brushing against lianas as you motor through narrow, braided channels — all three are larger than the Mississippi River. Wildlife viewing is only marginally better on these tributaries than on the mainstem Amazon between Belém and Manaus. Still, if you speak some Portuguese you'll be able to use towns like Barcelos as 'base camps' from which to explore the smaller tributaries; guides are cheaper than in Manaus, although gas costs more.

WORLD WIDE FUND FOR NATURE (WWF) CAMPS

WWF provides one of the most educational and certainly the cheapest rain forest experience at their research camps north of Manaus. These camps are located within four huge privately-owned *fazendas* (ranches) in the upland forest known as *terra firme*. WWF welcomes visitors to most of these camps, where they can spend up to three days in the rain forest observing Brazilian and foreign biologists at work.

For the past eight years, WWF has been involved in a joint research project with INPA (Brazil's National Institute of Amazon Research) called the Minimum Critical Size of Ecosystems Project (MCSEP). Headed by WWF's Dr. Thomas Lovejoy and INPA's Dr. Herbert O.R. Schubart, the project's goal is to understand what happens when developers turn rain forest into ranches, leaving only isolated patches of undisturbed wilderness.

Brazilian law forbids an owner from razing more than half of his rain forest land, but a very obvious loophole makes the law less than effective; the owner merely sells his undeveloped half to a second party, who is then free to develop half of *his* parcel, selling the undeveloped half to a third party, and so on.

The question that WWF and INPA hope to answer then, is: Just how small an isolated parcel of rain forest can ranchers leave and still maintain its integrity in terms of plant and animal life? In addition to answering basic biological questions, the project also hopes to raise the environmental consciousness of the Brazilian public, and to train a dedicated cadre of Brazilian scientists who will become effective defenders of the forest.

To visit one of the camps, you should be a member of WWF. See the section below on *The Disappearing Rain Forest* for addresses of WWF and other effective forest conservation organizations. You should also write to the WWF in Manaus (rua 11, Casa 29, Parque Tropical, Parque Dez, Manaus, CEP 69000) giving at least two weeks notice before planning to visit a camp. After determining if there is space in the camps, WWF will require non-Brazilians to get authorization from INPA to visit. Authorization forms are available at either WWF's office in Manaus or their U.S. headquarters (1250 24th St. NW, Washington, D.C., 20037, phone (202)293-4800). Completed forms should be received by the Manaus office at least one week before your visit so that they can get the proper government signatures. It's also possible to get the authorization signed directly at INPA (Dept. de Ecología, INPA, estrada do V-8, Manaus). If your schedule doesn't allow all this pre-planning, give WWF a call anyway (236-5568 or 236-8155 in Manaus) and they can probably *dar um jeitinho* ('find a way') around all the red tape. Most of the folks at the Manaus office speak English.

To reach the WWF office from the centre, take the Parque 10/Chapada Cachoerinha bus from the big covered stop at the corner of avenida 7 de Setembro and avenida Getúlio Vargas. The office is located very near the end of this long bus route; get off near Patty's restaurant, or at the end of the line just past it, and look for rua 11, Casa 29 (it's an unassuming residential street).

WWF furnishes camp visitors with transportation, food (three meals a day), hammocks, mosquito nets, and wool blankets, all for about US$8 per day. Obviously, they're not making a profit on this; their hope is that visitors will spread the word about rain forest conservation, and consequently Brazilian journalists and filmmakers have priority in the unlikely event that the camps become full. Most visitors tend to be foreigners, and there's no requirement that you be a biologist or student. Your visit will, however, have to be timed with the schedules of either camp workers or biologists so that you can ride in with them. Allow yourself a few days in Manaus to accommodate this scheduling and be flexible.

Bring along only a small backpack with the absolute essentials: insect repellent, long-sleeved shirt, t-shirt, socks, towel, soap, flashlight, head-mounted spotlight for nature walks at night, knife, compass, binoculars, camera, tripod, film, plastic water bottles, and malaria pills.

INDIANS

Brazil's remaining 150,000 or so Indians live within five parks (the largest and best-known being Xingu Park in Mato Grosso) and a scattering of isolated villages. Unless you are a bona fide anthropologist, FUNAI (the National Indian Foundation) will not permit you to visit Amerindian reservations. It's a wise policy, one designed to insulate the tribes from both disease and cultural dilution. Lately, however, in the wake of some bad publicity which has tarnished the agency's image, FUNAI's protective attitude seems motivated more by self-interest. But the tribes still have the last say, and some Indian leaders realize the political value of visits by influential foreigners; British rock star Sting recently flew in to a Kayapo village over FUNAI's protests.

Those of us with less political clout will have to content ourselves with reading about the tribes (see the *Bibliography*), or visiting one of the pathetic 'Indian villages' on the tourist circuit.

If you'd like to try arranging a visit, or simply want information, write: Fundação Nacional do Índio, Assessoria de Comunicação Social, SIA Trecho 04, Lote 750, Brasília DF, CEP 71200.

All the camps have open-air but rain-proof shelters. There are pit toilets and bathing streams nearby. Meat is kept fresh on ice, and water from the local streams is purified by ceramic filters in camp. All camps stock freeze-dried snake antivenom. You'll be provided with a hammock and wool blanket at WWF headquarters in Manaus before you leave.

Exploring Camp 41

We visited one of the larger and more remote WWF camps, called Km 41, located about four hours north of Manaus via BR-174 and a series of dirt roads which wind through the forest. WWF's driver coaxed a battered but serviceable Toyota Bandeirante — Brazil's version of the Land Cruiser -- over roads slippery as grease with last night's rain, and within three hours we'd arrived at the Fazenda Esteio adjoining the reserve. The plan is to study these reserves first in their virgin state, and again after the *fazendas* have whittled away at their borders and isolated them from the adjacent forest. One of the researchers studying this particular bit of virgin forest called Km 41 had accompanied us from Manaus: Heraldo Vasconcelos, a Brazilian ant biologist. As we waited in the shade of a ranch house, Heraldo explained that he was documenting the relationship of a particular ant species called *Pheidole minutula* and the plant within which it makes its home. Other scientists are busy studying monkeys, bats, soil invertebrates, carrion beetles, frogs, snakes, termites, and butterflies. Soon, researchers hope to have an overall picture of the way this jungle works, and the minimum sized-borders needed to maintain it.

After dropping off supplies at the *fazenda*, we continued on red-mud roads another hour to Km 41. Jayne, Heraldo, and I bid our driver farewell and tramped down a forest trail to the camp clearing, some 20 minutes into the forest. Raimundo and Alberto, two *caboclo* camp workers greeted us and helped stow the week's supplies. The camp itself consisted of a covered cook house and two tin-roofed sheds for hanging hammocks. Blue morpho butterflies flitted about in the clearing as Jayne and I unpacked our gear and prepared to explore.

Camp 41's 'boundaries' take in 625 hectares of rain forest, but except for the muddy road we'd arrived by, the nearest cleared land lies about 10 km away through virgin jungle. Some or all of this will eventually be cleared by the *fazenda* owners, leaving Camp 41 an isolated chunk of forest. Similar WWF camps include Gavião, Dimona, Florestal, Agroman, and Cabo Frio. The latter is a 1,000 hectare reserve located on a neighbouring *fazenda*, and along with Camp 41 the one best suited for visitors. WWF also maintains 10 isolated reserves completely surrounded by deforested land, but visitors won't be too keen on seeing these camps for obvious reasons.

To aid in mapping research results, Camp 41 has been criss-crossed with a series of foot trails, marked every 100 m with a small tag fastened to a tree. Unless you stray outside the camp boundaries, you are far less likely to get lost here than in downtown Salvador. Even after the trails peter out, walking remains relatively easy; Hollywood has fostered the myth of the 'impenetrable jungle', but the truth is that mature upland rain forests rarely become choked with plants at the ground level.

Jayne and I poked through the forest that day, binoculars at the ready. Every few steps we paused in silence, searching the canopy above for capuchin monkeys and bearded sakis. The rain forest doesn't parade its wildlife about as television would have us believe, and what we saw mostly were fleeting glimpses of furred tails which we had to assume were connected to monkeys. Heraldo later identified most of these monkeys based on the noises we'd heard, and we soon came to appreciate his wisdom in choosing to study ants rather than primates. He told us that Edson Frazão, a primate ecologist with INPA, sometimes went weeks at a stretch without seeing a single bearded saki. 'I only have to step out of my hammock in the morning,' bragged Heraldo, 'and I'm surrounded by my work!'

Ants were indeed everywhere. Heraldo pointed out that if you were to trap each and every vertebrate in this forest — all the monkeys, birds, snakes, lizards, frogs, and peccaries — their total weight wouldn't come anywhere close to that of the ants. Fascinating as our fellow primates can be, they don't affect the environment nearly so much as the Lilliputian armies swarming at our feet. Consequently, most WWF rain forest research centres on the 'lowly' invertebrates.

One of the species most common at Camp 41 and throughout Amazônia is the leaf-cutter ant (*sauva*). Living in highly-structured communities with over a million workers, the leaf-cutters practise an amazing form of 'agriculture'. Hordes of specialized worker ants climb high into the forest canopy, each ant carrying back to the colony a single leaf. Specialized 'police' ants from the colony direct traffic along this highway, while the largest members of the colony — the so-called soldiers — stand ready to defend the workers from all disturbances, even those created by nosy biologists. Back at the nest, workers shred the leaves and fertilize them with a drop of excrement. This compost heap is then injected with spores of a particular species of fungus carried by the queen. Eventually, this fungus crop produces food for the colony. Leaf-cutters eat nothing else.

Equally fascinating — but for far different reasons — are the *toucandeiro* ants. A black ant about 3 cm long, the *toucandeiro* packs a wallop with its venomous sting, producing what has been described as 'almost supernatural pain.' Certain local tribes use the *toucandeiro* in a particularly gruesome coming-of-age ritual for young men: live ants are collected and carefully fitted into a corset-like affair made of tree fibres. Only the working end of the ant — the head and mandibles — protrude on the inside of this 'garment,' and a single corset may hold hundreds of squirming *toucandeiros*. Young male initiates wear this corset, tightly cinched around the torso, and their ability to withstand the ants' venomous bites signals their arrival at manhood. We've heard this story enough times and from enough people of all social strata in Amazônia to give it some credence. If, like me, you have a perverse desire to meet *toucandeiros* first-hand, stroll the forest at night and look for a hole about 4 cm in diameter at the base of a tree. Scrape or tap such trees, and within seconds you'll be greeted by *toucandeiros* swarming to its defense. Why these nectar-feeders feel the need to defend a mature forest tree is still a mystery.

Close relatives of the ants, termites (*cupim*) also populate much of the Amazonian rain forest. Their nests, like massive brown goitres, festoon many of the trees at Camp 41. A network of small tunnels criss-cross the tree leading to the nest, and their trails on the forest floor are no less impressive. We found termites gluing particles of earth and leaf litter together with a sticky secretion, building in the course of a single night a covered highway at least five metres long next to our camp. Knock this tiny tunnel down, and workers immediately scurry about to rebuild it. (I am ashamed to admit that we actually timed this process on numerous occasions.) Amazonian termites come in a variety of forms, and once during a night walk we came upon a species which advertised its presence with a series of faint clicking noises. They swarmed next to our feet, either beating their oversized heads against the earth or, more likely, gnashing their mandibles in termite fury. To complement the clicking, they also exuded an odd, sweetish perfume. And when all this failed to send us scurrying, they climbed over our sandals and used those oversized mandibles on our bare feet.

Back at camp, we washed off in a small *igarapé* that had been dammed up to create a bathing pool. Fish no longer than a fingernail nipped harmlessly at my legs for the first few minutes. As night fell, bats wheeled and turned in the air above the clearing, and we listened to a lilting 'bird' song which, as Raimundo patiently explained, came not from a bird but a frog. But the forest noises were soon drowned out by a raging argument on how best to cook dinner. Two workers from the *fazenda* had hiked into camp, and with Raimundo, Roberto, and Heraldo, they debated the proper recipe for *caldeirada de peixe*, a sort of Amazonian bouillabaisse. Raimundo prevailed, and set about cooking over a propane camp stove.

At one point during dinner a flying bug the size of a golf ball landed in my stew, buzzed angrily for a few seconds, and flew off into the forest. A few minutes later the same bug — or one just like it — was back, buzzing around our propane lantern. Raimundo and Roberto jumped up and swatted excitedly at the thing, crying 'O picado deste bichinho queima!' — 'This critter's bite burns!' Raimundo is the kind of tough jungle stoic that you can picture cauterizing a severed limb in the campfire, so we took his warning seriously. But the burning bugs never returned, and we were able to sleep that night without benefit of mosquito nets.

The next day saw Raimundo and Alberto up early. They donned canvas jungle boots, buttoned up their collars and sleeves against insects, and filled two plastic ziplock bags with cold spaghetti noodles for lunch. They planned to head north, out of the reserve if necessary, to locate a band of capuchin monkeys for an INPA biologist who would be arriving in a few days. Jayne and I continued our own less-demanding brand of exploration. We watched toucans near the clearing, and startled a couple of curassows (*inambú*) — plump, grouse-like birds — along one of the paths. At a number of spots on the forest floor we found odd, phallic mud towers, all of which turned out to be hollow. Heraldo later explained that these were temporary incubation shelters built by juvenile cicadas. When the insects within matured and grew wings, they would break out the top of their mud towers and join the adult cicada community.

After three days, our trip to Camp 41 ended on a sobering but thoroughly appropriate note. On the way out our truck stopped at a recently-cleared *fazenda*. A handful of white zebu steers grazed among the burned stumps of what had once been majestic tropical hardwoods. Heraldo confirmed our suspicions: these were all the cattle this patch of impoverished jungle soil was likely to support. Our righteous anger evaporated instantly when we met the *caboclo* couple that owned the small ranch. They were pinning their hopes for a better life on this patch of razed land, and all I could feel for them was sorrow. A well-heeled *gringo* has no place lecturing these people. Only a Brazilian can convincingly explain to other Brazilians the value of this great forest, and perhaps education on the local scale will turn out to be the true and lasting value of WWF's project here.

Night walks in the rain forest

Spend the whole day in your hammock if you must, but make sure you see the forest at night. Much of the wildlife activity takes place high in the forest canopy during the daylight hours, frustrating all but the most patient observers and straining even the toughest necks. After dark, on the other hand, the canopy slumbers while the forest floor surges to life. What's more, nocturnal animals are by and large a more sluggish, easily observed lot than their diurnal brethren. And besides the opportunity it provides for watching animals, night transforms the forest into a magical and eerie place.

It's entirely normal to feel nervous traipsing around after dark in a jungle setting. But the rewards are so great, the experience so unlike that of the daytime forest, that you'll find yourself counting the hours till darkness, bounding out of your hammock, and grabbing your head-lamp. Remember, you are undoubtedly far safer here than on the streets of your own city at night. The only fear with any rational basis, in fact, is the fear of getting lost; and that much you can easily prevent by always carrying a spare light and batteries, marking your path as you go (see *Getting lost* below).

Don't start your walk right after dusk. Waiting until about 2000 will give nocturnal animals a chance to ease from their hiding places and take over the forest. Take along a standard flashlight as a backup, but for your primary light you'll want a headlamp (see *Equipment* in Chapter 2 for specific suggestions). Bring your camera if you've got a flash; you'll be able to get amazingly close to many nocturnal animals without disturbing them.

Choose a path you've taken during the day, or follow the path of a small creek. Walk as slowly as you possibly can, sweeping the area around you with your headlamp. Don't forget the creek itself; a number of fish are nocturnal, and you stand a good chance of spotting a *traíra* or a huge cichlid cruising the shallows. Familiar creek banks that you've walked before suddenly glow with luminescent fungi. It's normal to search the ground for animals, but budding herpetologists shouldn't overlook small trees and branches just above eye level. Here you may find numerous tree-dwelling frogs, as well as arboreal snakes such as boa constrictors. Much of the best night-viewing, in fact, centres on twigs and branches at or just below eye level. Lots of the larger insects — mantids, moths with bright red eyes, and stick insects — can be seen here.

Watch for eyeshine. Reflective eyes of every colour and size really do peer from the forest at night — it's one of the few cinematic jungle clichés that actually holds water. Nocturnal animal eyes have been outfitted with a reflective lens called the tapetum which bounces dim nighttime images off the retina. It is this tiny mirror which allows nocturnal animals to forage so effectively in what appears to be 'total' darkness; it also creates the eerie glow of jungle eyes reflected by your headlamp. A headlamp, in fact, allows you to see animal eyeshine much better than a hand-held light (which, since it isn't aligned with your line of sight, often fails to reflect directly off the tiny tapetum).

After about 2300, nocturnal animal activity tapers off for reasons not well understood, and there is a marked period of inactivity from midnight until an hour or two before dawn. This pre-dawn period provides another excellent opportunity to view nocturnal animals. As dawn approaches, these animals retreat once again to their burrows, under rocks, logs, or vegetation.

Night walks work best when the moon is waning or the sky is overcast. Moonlight filtering down into the forest keeps many animals 'indoors'. Rainy nights provide excellent — if inconvenient — opportunities for wildlife viewing.

The section on *Animals of the Rain Forest* discusses some of the wildlife you're likely to encounter during night walks.

Finally, don't forget occasionally to turn off your headlamp and savour the forest in near-total darkness for a few minutes.

Getting lost

Hollywood myths aside, the Amazonian jungle is not a risky place to wander about for short periods. There are plenty of troublesome animals, but almost none that are actually dangerous. Hostile tribes — as well as non-hostile tribes — have been pushed to the brink of extinction. There are no extremes of weather, and lots of shade and water. So even if the worst happens and you find yourself lost, take heart; the Amazon rain forest is a rather benign place, particularly when compared to the mountains and forests lots of us like to hike through at home.

To avoid getting lost in the first place, mark your path. You can do this simply by cutting underbrush every few metres and putting notches in tree trunks. A more elaborate system requires a roll or two of plastic flagging tape, preferably international orange or red. Simply pull off a 20 cm strip and tie it to some nearby vegetation at eye level; do this every ten metres or so. These gaudy trail markers will eventually weather and degrade — some animals will even eat them — but try to remove as many as possible on your return. Always carry a compass and know how to use it. Streams often provide a sure 'path' to follow through the forest, but beware when they fork.

PLANT LIFE OF THE RAIN FOREST

Even before Europeans arrived in Brazil, Amerindian tribes had discovered the great paradox of the rain forest: when the trees and underbrush were cleared for farming, the soil produced only one or two years worth of crops before giving out completely. How could the greatest forest on earth grow from this poorest and most infertile of soils?

The forest, as it turns out, doesn't depend much on soil. In fact, 'soil' as we know it hardly exists in the Amazon. Kick the ground and you'll find an extremely thin layer of topsoil, with virtually none of the humus and leaf litter we might expect from our own temperate lands. In a

---

WHITE RIVERS, BLACK RIVERS

Locals distinguish between two types of river water in Amazônia, and when you arrange for a trip into the rain forest it's important to know the difference. The so-called 'black' rivers (*rios da agua preta*) run tea-coloured from tannic acid or nearly black from humic acid, and support little aquatic life. These rivers, such as the Rio Negro and its tributaries, drain ancient rock formations which have been leached of nutrients by tropical downpours for millenia. While fishing is poor in such waters, don't get the idea that the forest surrounding them is barren. 'White' rivers, on the other hand (*rios da agua barrenta*), drain from the Andes, carrying suspended silt which imparts a yellow or muddy colour to them. Such white-water rivers as the Solimões and the Madeira and its tributaries are rich in aquatic life; unfortunately, this includes mosquitoes and other biting bugs.

---

sense, the rain forest vegetation is its own 'soil' — virtually all the nutrients of the Amazon are tied up in the trees, plants, and vines themselves. These are constantly and quickly recycled, bypassing the soil stage. And when that vegetation is cut, burned, and washed away, those nutrients are lost forever.

This notion takes some getting used to, especially for those of us from temperate lands where soils are the great reservoirs of nutrients. How is it, for instance, that nutrients can bypass the soil stage? Look at that chunk of rain forest land you've turned over with your boot for the answer. Fine white filaments of fungi called mycorrhizae form a complicated web just below the topsoil. This mycorrhizal network quickly sops up decomposing nutrients and feeds them back to the forest via a whole series of shallow, intertwining rootlets. Aiding this process is the tropical heat, the humidity, and the action of microbes, ants, and termites, all of which speed the breakdown. Unlike our own temperate forests, there is no build-up of nutrients; what isn't reabsorbed quickly is washed away by the constant rains. It is a rapid recycling system that works admirably — so long as things aren't disrupted.

Nowhere else on earth has plant life reached such levels of diversity. The Amazon basin boasts more than twenty times the tree species found in Europe — and that includes only the species thus far discovered. Unlike trees in our temperate forests, rain forest trees rarely grow in stands of the same species; this is an adaptation to the poor soil, preventing groups of trees with identical nutrient requirements from depleting the earth around them. This also makes logging difficult and wasteful — loggers must sometimes cut down ten trees to reach a species with marketable wood. Most of the large trees you'll see in the forest support themselves on thin topsoil with flange-like buttress roots.

Plant life in the forest involves a manic competition for sun. To this end, creepers and lianas (the first soft, the second woody) wind their way up to the canopy, where they provide convenient 'highways' for monkeys and other arboreal animals. A number of plants — the epiphytes, or 'air plants' — have simplified matters by cutting all contact with the earth, growing in moist crooks and hollows high in the trees.

Palms dominate the *igapó* and even much of the *terra firme* forest. A number of these have evolved long, needle-like spines encircling their stems, so watch what you grab for support.

Probably the signature plant of Amazônia is the giant water lily *Vitória Régia*. You'll see these in the *igapó*, where they grow to 1.80 m in diameter. Their huge flowers (30 cm in diameter) last only three days, and the plants themselves are scarce during the rainy season. These lilies sport a set of spines on their undersides, presumably for protection.

ANIMALS OF THE RAIN FOREST

No single habitat on earth contains as many animal species as does the Amazonian rain forest. And unlike our our own temperate forests, which contain large numbers of relatively few species, the rain forest is home to a bewildering array of species, none of which exist in particularly great numbers in any one area. As one rain forest biologist puts it, 'common species are rare and rare species are common'. The following section is therefore intended to highlight just a few of the more interesting and/or easily seen animals in Amazônia.

Spiders and insects   Tiny green or blue eyes reflected in your headlamp at night often indicate a spider nearby. Tarantulas (a number of species exist, often referred to as *caranguejeiros* by locals) are primarily nocturnal, preying on small insects near their burrows. You can locate these burrows at the base of trees, and they may be as wide as 15 cm. Tarantulas can often be enticed out of their den — they live singly — by scraping a small stick near the entrance. This trick doesn't work during the daytime. I've been told by an INPA biologist that tarantulas attack only objects weighing less than 30 g — someone has actually tested this — so that placing your finger near the den will elicit no response. You can be sure I would have tried this, except that we had no scale in camp for accurately weighing fingers.

Ants and especially termites perform one of the most important tasks in the forest: reducing fallen vegetable matter into humus. Several of the more interesting species are discussed above in *Exploring Camp 41*.

Frogs and reptiles   It's not surprising to find plenty of frogs inhabiting one of the wettest places on earth. Still, the variety of frogs in Amazônia is astounding. The WWF reserves north of Manaus, for example, contain 42 frog species in less than 13,000 hectares of land, while the entire North American continent boasts only 81 frog species. Most of the rain forest frogs are nocturnal, and you'll find them everywhere, especially on wet evenings: on tree branches, under leaves, in streams, in hollowed out trees. Some croak in the familiar fashion, but others 'bark', and still others trill like a bird. Most frogs will leap or climb to safety as you approach; and the ones that don't flee have protection of another kind from the predators they normally face. *Phyllomedusa*, for example, is a bright green, fist-sized frog which stands out in the forest like a neon sign. It allows itself to be plucked off a branch and will wander complacently up your arm and around your shoulders until replaced on a tree. *Phyllomedusa's* complacency is well-warranted; its mucus coating contains a poison which potential predators have come to associate with the frog's neon-green colouration. I paid only a slight price for handling *Phyllomedusa*: a mild rash on my hands and wrists which itched for a few hours.

Phyllomedusa frog

Besides *Phyllomedusa*, a number of frogs have developed toxic defences to make up for their obvious lack of shell, claws, teeth, and speed. Perhaps best known are the 'poison-arrow' frogs of the genus *Dendrobates*. Their bright yellow, blue, red, or orange colouration has evolved as advertisement rather than camouflage, and their toxic secretions can enter and kill through simple cuts in the skin. In 1985, *Dendrobates* figured in a Brazilian news story which blended science, 'witch doctors', presidential politics, and Indian land rights. Famed Brazilian hummingbird biologist Dr. Augusto Ruschii became seriously ill, and after numerous and inconclusive medical tests he called in Amerindian chief and political activist Raoni, along with Raoni's *pajé* ('witch doctor') to diagnose the problem. Raoni announced that Ruschii's liver was failing due to his handling of *Dendrobates* specimens years before in Amazônia. According to Raoni, Ruschii had actually taken on the appearance of his amphibian tormentors. He would cure the beloved scientist, but he called on President José Sarney to pay for the cure by guaranteeing a boundary around certain Amerindian lands.

Ruschii (who was in his eighties), died after an extended illness despite Raoni's cure.

Although Amazônia is rich in snake species, populations aren't huge, and you may spend a great deal of time searching before you actually find a snake. Most species are nocturnal, so night walks provide the best opportunity for amateur herpetologists. Look not only on the ground but in trees (a great many rain forest species never touch ground) and even in streams and temporary ponds. Remember that very few species are venomous, although many will bite if you attempt to handle them. The one you're most likely to see on night walks in Amazônia — indeed anywhere in the South American forest — is the fer-de-lance, *Bothrops atrox*. Fer-de-lances (called *jararacas* or *jararacussus* locally) often congregate near recent tree falls, feeding on the wide variety of smaller animals found there. Like all pit vipers — a group which includes rattlesnakes — fer-de-lances possess a tiny heat-sensing pit below their eyes which allows them to detect and strike at body warmth even in total darkness. You'd be wise to stay out of striking distance, although I have inched to within 30 cm of a lethargic specimen. I'd seen this particular animal on a low-lying tree branch, and the next day retraced my steps; not surprisingly, it was gone. That night, however, I returned with Jayne, and the same fer-de-lance (or one just like it) had draped itself over the exact same branch, practically begging to be photographed.

The black alligator (*jacaré uassus*), now nearly wiped out, was one of South America's largest reptiles. On the other end of the size spectrum — and apparently still thriving — are the the so-called 'dwarf alligators.' We stayed briefly at one jungle camp with an Australian researcher with INPA who for years has been radio-collaring and tracking the *jacaré coroa* (*Paleosuchus trigonatus*) deep in the forest. Until Bill Magnusson's work began, even Indians and local hunters weren't aware that

Fer-de-lance

the *jacaré coroa* rambled so extensively throughout the forest, often more than 100 m from the nearest creek. They invariably make their nest beside a termite hill, allowing the rotting vegetation to warm the eggs. Spurned by hunters because of its unmarketable leather, the *jacaré coroa* seems to be far more abundant than anyone guessed a few years ago.

Fish   The Amazon and its tributaries play home to more species of fish than are found in the Atlantic Ocean. Fishing for the game species is best from September through November, before the rivers swell. You'll find many Amazonian species, including piranhas, *pacú*, and catfish discussed in Chapter 5, along with fishing tips that work equally well in the Amazon. Interestingly, one of the more highly-prized catfish in the Pantanal, the *jaú*, is despised as a trash fish throughout much of Amazônia. A variety of other delicious species, however, are pretty much limited to Amazonian rivers: the gorgeously-coloured cichlid called the *tucunaré*, the *curimatã*, the *acari-bosó*, *cará-açu*, *jaraqui*, and my own favourite the *tambaqui*. Most spectacular of the basin's fish is the *pirarucú*, at 115 kg the world's largest freshwater fish.

Besides the much-maligned piranha, the Amazon and its tributaries contain several other fish that deserve caution. *Candirus* have by now eclipsed piranhas in the field of gruesome fish lore; they comprise a family of mostly tiny parasitic catfish which enjoy swimming up swimmers' urethras, anuses, vaginas, and nostrils, lodging themselves painfully with a pair of sharp pectoral spines. Although we've never been warned to stay out of the water on account of them, I wouldn't bathe nude in the Amazon. On several occasions we've been told by locals that the waters were swarming with *arraias* — freshwater stingrays. Supposedly these won't sink their barb into your ankle if you shuffle your feet along the bottom, as opposed to stomping on top of the animal.

Mammals   People generally think of monkeys, tapirs, peccaries, otters, and jaguars as the dominant rain forest mammals. Yet none of these animal groups outweigh the **bats** in terms of sheer biomass. This becomes more apparent at dusk, when more than 100 known species take to the air. While most rain forest bats eat insects, as do our familiar temperate-zone species, Amazônia has a few surprises: some species hunt birds and lizards, another prefers frogs, still others eat fruit, and there are even species that sip nectar from flowers, pollinating them as would a bee. Brazil possesses true vampire bats (*Desmodus*), but they are found primarily near cattle or horses, and rarely in the rain forest itself.

One nocturnal mammal you're sure to see — particularly if you're camped near a stream — is the **spiny rat** *Proechimys*. Spiny rats spend their day in burrows or under logs, creeping about the underbrush at night in search of food. Indeed, they creep in a curious cat-like fashion that's quite unlike anything I've ever seen in temperate zone mice or rats. Spiny rats don't grow much longer than 5 cm, yet they are closely related to the giant capybara.

At least thirty six species of **monkeys** live in Amazônia. Active during the day and extremely wary, many species will be difficult to see simply because they live in the forest canopy. Most of our own monkey sightings have been but fleeting glimpses, such as the characteristic twitching black tail of the *macaco prego*. Unless you are more patient than us, you will hear far more monkeys than you will ever actually see. And the monkey heard most easily in the rain forest is unquestionably the howler, or *guaríba*. Two of the six howler monkey species — the red howler and the black howler — inhabit the areas near Manaus. The 'howl' of these animals is one of the rain forest's most unforgettable experiences, a thundering roar which shakes most travellers out of their hammocks during the first night. Howlers usually live in troops of 10-20 individuals, but a single dominant male does most of the troop's howling. An enlarged bone in the howler's throat serves as a sounding box for the call, which can be heard for over 3 km through dense forest. You'll hear the roar throughout the night, but especially at dawn. Howlers howl to warn other troops of their presence. While troops don't actually claim a particular part of the forest — they roam over areas as large as 75 hectares — they don't like other troops getting too close. The 'cascading' quality to the roars results when the call of one male is answered by another troop's male, and then another, even more distant male. Despite the howler's strident roar, it is a gentle creature which eats leaves and fruits. Although Brazilian law prohibits commercial export of howlers, they are threatened with habitat destruction as jungle is cleared for ranches and farms.

The only mammal that I've heard *caboclos* mention with anything resembling fear is the **collared peccary** (*porco da mata*). Peccaries are pig-like animals which feed largely on roots, seeds, insects, and fruits, but they can turn nasty if threatened. Since herds generally run from 15 to 50 animals strong, it's not a good idea to give peccaries the idea they're being cornered. Peccaries feed almost exclusively during the daytime. Like most large rain forest mammals, they've always been hunted for their meat; it is habitat destruction rather than hunting that threatens peccaries.

Unfortunately, you will probably see more dead **armadillos** (*tatús*) than live ones; they are the most common road-kill in Amazônia. Almost entirely nocturnal, the nine-banded armadillo trots about the forest, sniffing for its steady diet of larval and adult insects. Armadillos dig their burrows near streambanks, padding the insides with soft carpets of forest vegetation. *Caboclos* have long prized the white, succulent meat of the armadillo, but this is one amimal that can probably withstand not only hunting pressure but some habitat loss.

Nine-banded armadillo

THE DISAPPEARING RAIN FOREST

By now everyone realizes that the Brazilian rain forest is being methodically chopped and burned down for cattle and farm land. Unlike our own temperate forest soils, which have been subjected to the mineral-enriching activities of glaciers and mountain-building fairly recently on the geological timescale, rain forest soils are ancient. Pounded by tropical downpours for over 200 million years, jungle soils have become thin and nutrient-poor. Clearing and burning destroys the mycorrhizal fungi-and-root network which normally recycles nutrients so effectively (see *Plant Life of the Rain Forest*). After a few seasons, the nutrients released by burning slash have been washed away, the earth turned hard as a concrete parking lot. Farmers must move on and clear another plot after just two years; ranchers get about eight to ten years out of their pastureland before abandoning it.

Amerindian tribes have successfully practised this slash-and-burn agriculture for centuries, so why the outcry from environmental groups? The important difference, of course, is scale. A tribe cannot possibly clear more than a hectare or two of land every couple of years. Such tiny tracts of lands regenerate naturally over about 20 years when left fallow; seeds from neighbouring trees easily reach the cleared area, and the mycorrhizal network again infiltrates the tract. Fallow time is perhaps irrelevant, since the tribe isn't likely to return and clear this land again anyway.

Modern agribusiness plays the game on a far larger (and far more destructive) scale. Most *fazendas* span hundreds of thousands of hectares. Reseeding and re-establishment of the mycorrhizal network cannot possibly occur except at the margins of such an expanse. Besides, the flood of Brazilians into Amazônia limits the amount of time a farm or pasture can lie fallow. Despite this poor outlook, investors continue clearing, in large part due to government incentives which reward even money-losing operations.

Mining, logging, and hydroelectric dams also take their toll on the forest. The scale of the Grande Carajás Project, which includes all three enterprises along with cattle ranching and agribusiness, is almost beyond comprehension; 895,000 square kilometres, or 10% of the entire country, developed for US$70 billion. The Project began in the mid-1970's with a surprisingly enlightened plan that included deforestation of only a tiny percentage of the total concession. Mismanagement, corruption, and chaotic development by hordes of immigrants has undermined the Project, however.

The rain forest remained largely untouched until 1969, when Brazil inaugurated its National Integration Programme, aimed at settling the area and turning a profit with cattle ranching. Following the completion of the Transamazon Highway, wealthy ranchers and thousands of *nordestinos* from the Drought Polygon began pouring into the area. The Smithsonian Institution estimated in 1988 that about 0.33% of the Amazonian rain forest is being destroyed each year. Obviously, some areas have been harder hit than others, notably the state of Rondônia, where experts believe 20% of the forest has already been cleared. Just how much of the entire forest is gone and how much is left remains open to debate: In April 1989, ex-President Sarney claimed that a mere 5% of the nation's rain forest had been destroyed, based on satellite photos. The *New York Times*, however, estimated that 3% had been taken down as far back as 1977.

Why should we worry if Brazil decides to level its forests? There are plenty of practical considerations, but the one we used to hear a decade ago — that our oxygen would disappear along with the forests — has been largely debunked. A mature rain forest consumes almost as much oxygen as it produces, and most scientists now agree that phytoplankton in the oceans is responsible for our oxygen supply.

Concern today centres instead on potential climactic changes caused by the destruction of the forest. Carbon dioxide released into the atmosphere by burning fossil fuels is already credited with global warming and rising sea levels; rain forest slash burning on the current scale may magnify the problem. And since the forest creates about half its own rainfall, the potential exists for massive droughts when the trees have been taken down.

A huge bank of genetic diversity will also disappear with the rain forest. If the modern-day agricultural strains of corn, tomatoes, potatoes, sweet potatoes, and manioc are to thrive in the face of diseases and pests, they will need an occasional genetic shot in the arm from their wild ancestors, which originated in the Latin American rain forests. The WWF estimates that fully one-quarter of the drugs prescribed in the

United States contain plant ingredients from tropical rain forests, and Amazônia accounts for the lion's share.

Those of us who love wild places have other, less tangible reasons for wanting the great forest saved. But only economic incentives are likely to sway a government staggering under the burden of a US$109 billion debt. If Brazil can be convinced that the living forest is worth more in cash dollars than pastureland, there may be hope for Amazônia.

Such hope glimmered briefly in Acre, where a poor rubber tapper named Francisco Mendes Filho had organized his fellow *seringueiros* to protect the forest where they traditionally made their living. 'Chico' Mendes proposed the idea of 'extractive reserves', large tracts of jungle set aside in their virgin state, where the forest's bounty of rubber, Brazil nuts, fruits, and valuable plants could be harvested without destroying the source. Mendes organized blockades to prevent illegal razing of the forest, and successfully persuaded the Inter-American Development Bank to suspend funding for the paving of BR-364 between Rondônia and Acre. Mendes was not only a Brazilian but a native Amazonian; the Brazilian government could no longer complain that it was being unfairly badgered by smug First World environmentalists. As Mendes put it, 'We became ecologists without even knowing the word'. But his efforts had angered powerful ranching interests. On December 22, 1988, Chico Mendes was gunned down outside his home in Acre. Already, Japanese investors are renewing efforts to pave BR-364 all the way to Peru.

Prodded by international outrage at Mendes' murder and the wholesale destruction of the rain forest, ex-President Sarney outlined in April 1989 a plan to protect Amazônia. '*Nossa Natureza*' ('Our Nature') includes 17 presidential decrees and seven bills to be sent to Congress. These include ending incentives for cattle ranching, controlling the sale of toxic mercury (used by miners to extract gold), and creation of a special forest police. How effective these measures will be remains to be seen.

WHAT YOU CAN DO TO HELP

Those of us who live in developed countries can't get overly smug on the topic of rain forest destruction. The United States, for example, is responsible for the bulk of the carbon dioxide being added to the earth's atmosphere, while nations like Switzerland continue to log off their remaining forests at an astonishing rate. If we hope to convince Brazil of our sincerity, we must take an active role in cleaning up our own back yards. If you're not already a member of a local environmental group in your own country, join now and press for stiffer controls on auto emissions, air standards, and logging.

One of the most promising tactics in protecting the forests is the so-called debt-for-nature swaps. Forgiving a portion of Brazil's foreign debt in return for either total protection or rational development of certain forest tracts is now being discussed by creditor nations; such schemes have already worked in Bolivia and Costa Rica. Urge your local politicians to support these measures.

Consider joining at least one of the following organisations, all of which work to save rain forests in Brazil and throughout the world:

United States

World Wide Fund for Nature (WWF), 1250 24th St. NW, Washington, D.C. 20037.

Rainforest Action Network, 300 Broadway, Suite 28, San Francisco, CA 94133.

The Basic Foundation, P.O. Box 47012, St. Petersburg, FL 33743.

Rainforest Alliance, 295 Madison Avenue, Suite 1804, New York, NY 10017.

· Fundacão Pro Natureza (FUNATURA), Latin American Program, 1785 Massachusetts Ave. NW, Washington, D.C. 20036.

Environmental Defense Fund, 257 Park Avenue S., New York, NY 10010.

Conservation International, 1015 18th St. NW, Suite 1002, Washington, D.C. 20036.

Great Britain

World Wide Fund for Nature (WWF), Weyside Park, Godalming, Surrey GU7 1XR.

Living Earth, 37 Bedford Square, London WC1B 3EG.

Friends of the Earth, 26-28 Underwood St, London N1 7JQ.

The South American Explorers Club

For travellers needing information on backpacking, mountaineering, white-water rafting, and travel off the beaten track.

The $25 membership fee covers use of the club in Lima and Quito and the informative quarterly magazine *The South American Explorer*. Members travelling to Brazil have access to *Trip Reports*, written by members, to aid them in their explorations.

THE HAMBURGER – RAIN FOREST EQUATION

Since beef production is the rationale behind much 'development' in Amazônia, it makes sense to ask a simple question: Just how much beef does the world stand to gain from the deal, and what will it cost? Christopher Uhl, a visiting biologist from Pennsylvania State University, did some basic cost-benefit calculations in a recent issue of Belém's daily newspaper *O Liberal*. Uhl estimates that a single hectare of virgin Amazonian jungle contains close to 800,000 kilograms of plant and animal matter. Once cleared, how much food can we expect this chunk of land to produce? A steer grazing this single hectare is expected to put on about 50 kilograms of weight per year, or some 400 kilos in an average eight-year life span. Subtracting hide, bones, and other non-edible parts of the steer, we end up with approximately 200 kilos of beef, enough to produce 1,600 hamburgers.

I happen to enjoy a good burger, and this would strike me as a reasonable trade-off if we could continue fattening steers on this hectare of former jungle land. But it doesn't work that way in Amazônia. By the end of eight years, this hectare of thin, nutrient-poor soil will be as dead as the steer that grazed it; our stack of burgers is a one-time transaction. Thus, 800,000 kilos of living jungle have been effectively converted into just 1,600 hamburgers — or about half a ton of jungle per burger. Considering the loss in terms of area — 10,000 square metres per hectare divided by 1,600 hamburgers — we discover that each burger represents 6.25 square metres of rain forest. As Uhl puts it, 'that's almost the size of a small kitchen!'

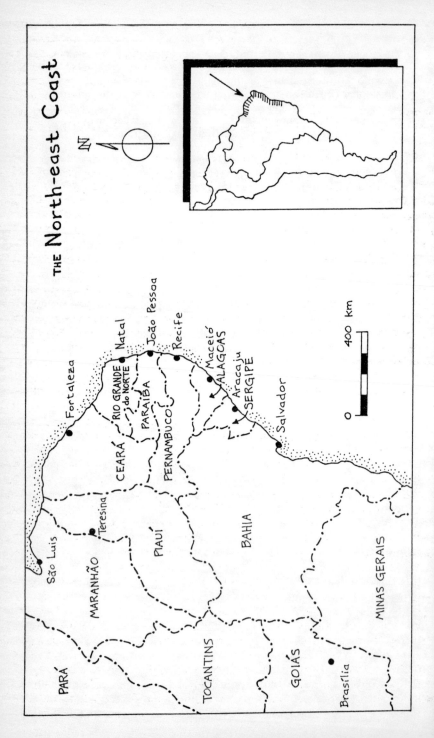

THE North-east Coast

Chapter 7

The North-East Coast

As far as most of the world is concerned, there are exactly two Brazilian beaches: Copacabana and Ipanema. And I wouldn't suggest that Rio's famed twin beaches don't have their charms: miles of sugar-white sand jam-packed with Brazilians at play — eating, drinking, making music, playing soccer, flirting, gossiping and even, occasionally, swimming.

Yet there is another kind of Brazilian beach — not too surprising in a country that boasts over 7,000 km of Atlantic waterfront. This beach is fringed not with skyscapers but with slender coconut palms. Here, the big entertainment involves the afternoon arrival of the *jangadas*, primitive fishing boats powered by the wind. And the only traffic you'll have to avoid on this beach will be the occasional donkey-drawn cart.

Welcome to the north-east coast, a largely-undeveloped stretch of shoreline with beaches so spectacular that even *cariocas* sometimes search them out. Northeastern Brazil encompasses nearly 20% of the entire country, including the states of Bahia, Sergipe, Alagoas, Pernambuco, Paraíba, Rio Grande do Norte, Ceará, Piauí, and Maranhão. Much of the interior is dry scrub desert, sparsely-populated badlands known as the *sertão*. While the narrow coastal strip has attracted all the north-east's major cities — among them Salvador da Bahia, once the nation's capital — it also includes hundreds of kilometres of pristine beaches punctuated with rustic fishing villages.

North-eastern Brazil can boast a richer human and historical fabric than any other portion of the country. It was here that Portuguese navigator Pedro Cabral first landed in April 1500, near present-day Porto Seguro, Bahia. And it was here that colonists from the Azores introduced the colony's first 'boom' crop, sugar cane. Over the next three centuries, Portuguese slavers delivered between 3 and 15 million Africans to work the plantations. No one today can be sure of the number, because Brazil destroyed all records of the slave trade in 1891.

Regardless of the correct number, the vast majority of slaves landed in the north-east, which remains to this day the most distinctly African region of Brazil. Catholicism and African deities mingled here to form *candomblé*, the equivalent of Haiti's *vodoun* ('voodoo') and Cuba's *santería*. Music, dance, even the rich and spicy food of coastal Bahia reflect the region's African heritage. That influence fades as you move north, toward Rio Grande do Norte and Ceará, being replaced by a mixture of Amerindian and European elements. Here you'll often come across beige-skinned Brazilians with frizzy hair and green eyes, living reminders of the short-lived French and Dutch occupations in the 17th Century.

North-eastern Brazil remains the most impoverished region in the country. Even in the best of years, inhabitants of the *sertão* find it hard to scrape a meagre existence from its parched soil; when periodic droughts strike, the hardy *sertanejos* migrate by the thousands to crowded shantytowns in the coastal cities or industrial centres in the south. Such migrations are the stuff of legend in Brazil, inspiring songs, films, and novels, but they are by no means a thing of the past; in Alagoas, we've seen buses stop along the highway to accommodate whole families of drought-stricken *sertanejos* dragging aboard everything they own. Despite these hardships — or perhaps because of them — *sertanejos* are Brazil's friendliest people.

Sugar cane remains a major crop along the coast, although much of it nowadays goes into the making of fuel alcohol for cars. Not all cane alcohol finds its way into gas tanks, however; Brazil's most popular brands of *cachaça* (sugar cane rum) come from the north-east. Cacao, corn, and cotton exports also fuel the regional economy. The *sertão* is primarily cattle and goat country. The north-east also produces Brazil's finest crafts, including gorgeous lacework, clay figures, woodcarvings, hammocks and embroidery.

How to get there   Gateway cities for the north-east coast include eight of the state capitals: Salvador, Aracaju, Maceió, Recife, João Pessoa, Natal, Fortaleza, and São Luis. (Teresina in Piauí lies well inland.) Varig, Cruzeiro do Sul, and Vasp all run daily flights from Rio and São Paulo. From Belém, there are direct flights to Recife, Fortaleza, and São Luís. Buses run daily to all the gateway cities from Rio and São Paulo; from Belém, you'll find direct buses to all the gateway cities except Aracaju, Maceió, and Natal.

Getting around   Buses will get you within striking distance of most of the beaches in the north-east; in some cases, you can simply step off the bus in a tiny fishing town within minutes of the water. Most of the time, however, you'll either have to walk or rely on more sporadic local transport to reach the truly pristine beaches.

Even when the road runs out and formal transportation ends, you can be sure there's some way to get to the beach. Local fishing villages, after all, need to get their fish to market and to receive supplies. So in many cases, you can hop a ride with the supply truck or jeep as it passes through town. Popular forms of transport include *Kombis* (Volkswagen vans) and *bugres* (four-wheel drive vehicles with balloon tyres, especially suited for dune- and beach driving). *Pau de araras* — large supply trucks that also hold up to 60 paying passengers — still ply many kilometres of coastline on a daily basis. The *pau de arara* (literally, 'the parrot's perch') enjoys the same legendary status in Brazil that the Conestoga wagon does in North America — ride one if you get the chance. Finally, in the really remote spots (or those where shifting sand renders roads useless), you may have to hire a local to walk you from some inland point to the beach.

Walking the coast is supremely easy except when you run up against rivers and high tides. The former rarely present major problems, since fishing villages tend to spring up around a river mouth, and boats are easily hired for the crossing. In some cases, there are small ferries that run on what passes for a schedule in the *nordeste*.

Tides are a different matter. Be very alert to the tide level, since many of the beaches in the north-east are fringed with steep sandstone cliffs that can't be scaled. In this situation, take careful note as you hike of escape routes that will take you up to the ridge tops. You'll sometimes find beaches that are blocked by headlands which jut out into the water; some, but not all, are passable at low tide. Never attempt to pass such headlands during a flooding tide. When in doubt, look for a way to climb the headland rather than risk being trapped by the tide.

Drinking water can be scarce along the beach. Coastline fringed with steep sandstone cliffs often contains small springs issuing from the bank, but be sure to ask locals if it's potable; such springs are used strictly for washing clothes in many cases. The only fresh water you're likely to find along coastline backed by sand dunes is river water, and this is likely to be polluted. Freshwater lagoons sometimes occur between the dunes; once again, check with the locals before drinking. Fishing villages almost always rely on wells for their drinking water, and you can often fill a canteen from the local hand pump. Frequently, well water will contain small amounts of salt water, and we've even run into faecally polluted well water before. (See the section on *Water sterilisation* in Chapter 3 for advice on disinfecting.) In short, you should bring as much water as you possibly can when hiking deserted and semi-deserted coastline. Coconut 'milk' is an excellent substitute; coconuts are available almost anywhere you find a fisherman's hut along the beach, and they are much safer than well water. Coconut 'milk' is an almost perfect electrolyte, so it's excellent if you have diarrhoea. Ask for the coconuts to be opened, and insist on paying for them.

Note When you're asking directions, be aware that backcountry residents in this part of Brazil invariably use *leguas* (leagues) rather than kilometres as a measure of distance. One *legua* equals 6 km. Another cautionary note: the locals here customarily travel enormous distances daily just to sell fish, buy coconuts, or wash laundry. Consequently, when you ask for directions, try to get as specific a distance estimate as you can squeeze from your source. '*Pertinho*' (extremely close by) often translates into an eight-hour trek!

When to go   In terms of weather, virtually any month is splendid in the north-east. Heaviest rainfall occurs from March through July, but rarely will you be rained out for more than a day or two in a row; more often than not, all the day's rain will be dropped in a single downpour of short duration. Temperature varies little year-round, averaging 28° and virtually never dropping below 20°.

If at all possible, let the Brazilian vacation schedule determine when you go rather than weather. Avoid January and February, the first week of March in those years when Carnaval spills over, and July, when vacationing Brazilians from the south invade the north-east in droves.

A caution   Unlike the Pantanal and Amazônia, which are seldom visited by Brazilian tourists, the north-east coast draws more and more people every year. Many a peaceful fishing village or deserted stretch of beach has been 'discovered' and completely transformed within the space of a few years; witness Arembepe in Bahia and Canoa Quebrada in Ceará. These places are still pleasant enough, but they no longer meet my admittedly vague definition of 'backcountry'. Therefore, be fore-warned that information contained in this chapter concerning specific beaches may well be outdated six months from publication. Remember that the north-east boasts 3,000 km of shoreline and literally thousands of named beaches and fishing villages; what Canoa Quebrada was fifteen years ago exists today elsewhere. You'll find here a starter course featuring the states of Ceará, Rio Grande do Norte, Alagoas, and Bahia.

What then qualifies a fishing hamlet as 'backcountry?' I suggest the simple test developed by our Cearense friend Wellington Franklin: ask the locals if someone can fix you a cheeseburger (*X-burger*, pronounced shees-BUR-gee). If no one can produce a cheeseburger, you've landed in bona fide backcountry; if they don't know what a cheeseburger *is*, stay put, because you've stumbled into Eden.

AFRO-BRAZILIAN RELIGIONS

Uprooted from their homes in Angola, the Congo, Guinea, Mozambi-que, Dahomey, the Sudan, and all over West Africa, black slaves were landed by the millions in north-eastern Brazil. Many of them had been wealthy tribal leaders before being sold into slavery; some even had slaves of their own. But when the Portuguese loaded them aboard the ships, they left behind everything. Everything, that is, except their *orixás*.

Ethnologists have identified at least sixty separate *orixás*, or deities, which made the trip from West Africa to Brazil. Heading the list are Oxalá, the chief spirit; Iemanjá, the goddess of the sea; Xangô, the thunder god; and Oxóssi, god of the hunt.

Umbandistas (practitioners of Umbanda) gather on a beach in Ceará beneath an effigy of Iemanjá, Goddess of the Sea.

Once in Brazil, the slaves mingled with Tupi Indians and ended up borrowing a number of their local forest gods, making them *orixás* as well. Always ready to accept new spiritual allies wherever they found them, blacks enlisted the Tupi spirit Japetequara (the Alligator) and Tapinaré (the Jaguar). Some of the tribes sold into slavery had been Muslims, and an element of Mohammedanism crept in as well. Before long, the slaves were celebrating a distinctively new kind of religion.

To appease their Portuguese masters — who had summarily banned the worship of African deities — slaves simply merged their traditional *orixás* and the new Catholic saints. Iemanjá, with her white gowns of sea-foam, became the Blessed Virgin. Xangô, the spirit of wilderness, was now St. John the Baptist. Omulu, the spirit of disease, merged easily with St. Lazarus. And Ogun the warrior god became St. George the Dragonslayer.

This spiritual gumbo of African, Catholic, Amerindian and Muslim elements simmered for a few decades before spilling throughout Brazil. In Bahia (where the purest, most African form is practised), this hybrid religion is known as Candomblé; in Recife you'll hear it referred to as Xangó; and in Rio, the original term, now much abused, was Macumba. Umbanda is a less orthodox form, nowadays extremely widespread throughout the north-east and Brazil as a whole. Crossing all racial and economic barriers, Umbanda is practised not only by manioc farmers in Pitombeiras but also by Fortaleza office clerks. This new yet ancient form of worship has augmented rather than replaced Catholicism; many Brazilians attend the spirit tents on Saturday night and go to Mass on Sunday.

Long before we attended our first full-blown Umbanda ceremony in the north-east, Jayne and I stumbled upon — quite literally — an offering to the *orixás*. There it was, at the intersection of two dirt paths in the backcountry: a paper plate filled with dried corn kernels, cooked beans, and manioc flour. A candle sat upright in the centre of the plate, its base supported by the beans, and an empty bottle of cane rum lay alongside. We later learned that such offerings are typically placed at crossroads, being meant in this case for the messenger spirit Exu. Actually, there is not one Exu, but rather a series of Exus, each with different traits, powers, and appetites. Most Exus appreciate offerings of rum, tobacco, or meat; we've seen cigars and *cachaça* placed alongside a pair of sacrificed chickens. Since some of the Exus tend toward mischief (there is one which is said to destroy happy marriages, another which promotes venereal disease), it was easy for Christian observers to confuse Exu with the Devil. The many Exus, however, all serve as messengers between worshippers and the gods; as such, they are invoked at the beginning of virtually all rituals, even the most benign.

And, sensationalism notwithstanding, the Afro-Brazilian religions concern themselves almost exclusively with good works. Quimbanda — officially outlawed in Brazil — is the single splinter sect which deals in black magic. Animal sacrifice plays a part in all the Afro-Brazilian religions, but the killing itself is done in private by the priest and a few assistants, well before the public ceremonies held in the evening.

One of the most impressive and easily-witnessed Umbanda rites along the north-east coast is the Festival of Iemanjá, goddess of the sea. Ceará honors Iemanjá on August 15th, with the largest celebration in Fortaleza. The faithful from some 200 local *terreiros* (churches) arrive by bus at noon, each *terreiro* claiming its own particular piece of beach at the Praia do Futuro (take a bus of the same name from the centre).

Terreiro members beat drums, chant, and parade likenesses of Iemanjá about the beach. Iemanjá favours long, flowing white-and-blue robes, and worshippers usually follow suit. Priests (*pai-de-santos*) and their female counterparts (*mãe-de-santos*) enter into inspired religious trances, dancing spasmodically, spittle dribbling from their mouths, eyes rolled up so that only the whites show. We once watched a transfixed *mãe-de-santo* repeatedly cut herself with a fish knife, but self-mutilation is rare. Usually, *terreiro* members are on hand to steady and protect those who enter into trances.

Visitors (foreigners included) may enter the circle of worshippers to *pegar um passo* (enter into a brief trance) at the hand of the *pai-de-santo*. As drummers beat a frantic rhythm, the priest takes the initiate's hand and twirls her or him in circles, puffing clouds of cigar smoke and chanting all the while. Church members stand ready to catch the initiates if they stumble during trance. The entire *passo* lasts only a few minutes.

Though deeply spiritual, Umbanda has an openly carnal element as well, and a great deal of drinking (usually cane rum) and smoking (cigars and long-stemmed pipes) goes on. Many of the *pai-de-santos* and their assistants (*filho-de-santos*) are homosexuals or bisexuals; indeed, many of the *orixás* themselves are sexually ambiguous. Iemanjá, a fancier of carnal pleasures herself, adores jewelry, perfume, roses, champagne and *cachaça*; these are loaded upon tiny wooden rafts and pushed to sea at dusk, then overturned. In smaller celebrations, worshippers simply throw these offerings into the surf.

Authentic Candomblé rites can best be seen in Bahia. The state tourist bureau in Salvador, BAHIATURSA (telephone 241-4333), offers lists of the many local *terreiros* which allow visitors. These operate daily on a year-round basis, except during Lent (the forty days following Ash Wednesday and Carnaval), when no public rites are performed. Dress conservatively (no shorts of any kind). Men and women will be expected to sit on opposite sides of the *terreiro*. These are not 'shows,' and no real *terreiro* allows cameras or tape recorders. In the suburban and rural areas of the north-east, visitors may be grudgingly accepted to private rites. These generally occur just once or twice a week, and your only chance of seeing one is through a Brazilian friend with contacts.

JANGADAS

No other single image conjures up the north-east coast as does the *jangada*. Jangadas are crude wooden fishing rafts rigged with a single cotton sail, and you cannot possibly wander this part of the coast without seeing scores of them. Typically, the entire fleet of a small coastal hamlet will sail off in the morning, returning one by one in the afternoon with their catch. During these short trips, the fleet may split up, each raft fishing a separate area. Sometimes, however, depending on the season, the fleet will stay at sea for as many as five consecutive days. During these longer trips, the boats stay within sight of each other, returning to the village *en masse*.

The typical crew of two to five *jangadeiros* per boat carry no compasses or sextants despite the fact that they sail well beyond sight of land even on the day trips. Instead, they rely on an intimate knowledge of winds and tides to bring them back their own tiny speck of coastline. It's a feat that takes on heroic proportions once you've actually sailed on a jangada. Launching a jangada in heavy surf requires both strength and split-second timing; the raft is rolled out to the water on two logs, the crew boards, and then a shore crew waits for a light set of waves to begin the final push. We've seen jangadas pitch-pole back onto the beach more than once.

With about a half metre of freeboard, waves continually wash the deck even in the calmest of seas. There are no bunks; on the overnight trips, jangadeiros must curl up on a wooden deck never more than two metres wide. The only covered space is reserved for the catch and some meagre rations. At regular intervals, the jangadeiro must douse the cotton sail with buckets of water so that it holds the wind.

All of this is mere existence at sea — the business of fishing requires a whole separate set of skills. Depending on the season, jangadeiros may use either hook-and-line or nylon nets, and the catch is often a mixed bag of grouper, mackerel, skates, sharks, and eels. Once they're beyond sight of land, jangadeiros have only their depth-sounding leadlines and fisherman's sixth sense to locate the fishing grounds. I'm an ex-commercial fisherman myself, and I've asked jangadeiros to describe this process in detail. They can't possibly regard me as a competitor — I can't clear the breakwater without LORAN, radar, and a full set of nautical charts; still, I get the kind of response you might expect from a chef asked to divulge his recipe for shrimp bisque.

The high point of the afternoon in most coastal hamlets is the arrival of the jangadas. Women, children, and old men — in short, the only members of the village that aren't active jangadeiros — crowd around the boats as the catch is pitched ashore. If the fishing has been good, the surplus is up for grabs, and if you're bold you can join in the bargaining. I'd keep this to a minimum — never outbid the locals if they want the fish.

Similarly, I recommend against paying for unsolicited jangada rides in the truly remote coastal villages. By all means go for a jangada ride, but do so in Maceió or Recife or Canoa Quebrada; the experience will be the same, and you won't be undermining a fishing economy with tourist dollars, turning jangadeiros into sightseeing guides.

Jagandas

FORTALEZA

A sprawling city of 1.3 million people and capital of Ceará state, Fortaleza provides access to what Jayne and I consider the finest beaches in all of Brazil. Apparently we aren't alone; the national edition of Playboy featured no less than six nearby beaches on its list of the 'Twenty Most Afrodisiacal Beaches of Brazil.' Ceará's coast is noted for its towering sand dunes, and one story has it that the state's name itself is a bastardization of 'Sahara.'

Arrival/Departure   Pinto Martins airport lies 6 km south of the city centre. Daily flights go to Rio, São Paulo, Belém, Salvador, Recife, Manaus, Natal, João Pessoa, and Natal. City buses run from just outside the terminal to Praça José de Alencar, located in the centre near all of Fortaleza's cheapest hotels. The spacious new bus station is about 4 km south of town. Buses run daily to hundreds of small towns in the state, as well as Belém, Rio, São Paulo, and all state capitals in the north-east. To get to the centre, catch any city bus headed for Praça José de Alencar; a number of buses make the return trip from the Praça.

Getting around   Unfortunately, the city centre — with all the cheap hotels, the state tourist bureau, and the crafts market — lies some distance from Iracema beach. Though too polluted for swimming, Iracema becomes especially lively at night, and here you'll find the better hotels and restaurants. From the centre, catch buses marked Serviluz or Caça e Pesca. Fortaleza's buses get impossibly crowded even by Brazilian standards.

Changing money   Curiously, Fortaleza has never had *casas de câmbio*. Ask first at the EMCETUR office downtown in the converted jail; they'll often put you in contact with a money-changer. Then try your own hotel or the craft shops surrounding EMCETUR. Once you locate a *cambista* you shouldn't have trouble changing travellers cheques.

Information   EMCETUR, Ceará's state tourist authority, staffs offices at the airport, bus terminal, and a fairly large one at the converted jail that's now a tourist centre; this takes up a whole city block at rua Senador Pompeu and avenida Dr. João Moreira. You can buy a good state map here, but they're a bit skimpy with advice on the remote beaches. You might ask here for free-lance guide Wellington Franklin; despite the name, he's pure Brazilian and pure Cearense, always ready to lead foreigners well off the beaten path and into the 'real Brazil.' Young as he is, Wellington's already something of a local treasure, brimming with the lore and fact of Ceará. He speaks excellent French and German, he's working on English, and his sense of humour manages to transcend all linguistic barriers.

Hammocks and other local crafts   Fortaleza inspires even non-shoppers like us to shop. Typically Cearense crafts include fine lacework, leather goods, clay figurines, and coloured-sand artwork. Everywhere you'll see ceramic likenesses of Padre Cícero, a backcountry cleric and religious fanatic disavowed by the Vatican but revered by *nordestinos*. But first stop for backcountry travellers should be a hammock (*rede*) shop. Fortaleza vies with Manaus as the best place in Brazil to buy hammocks, and many hammock factories sell their own products out front; ask for a tour of the factory as long as you're browsing. Try the Central de Artesanato, avenida Santos Dumont 1500 (in the Aldeota district), the Centro de Turismo, rua Senador Pompeu 350 (surrounding EMCETUR in the centre), and the Mercado Central, rua General Bezerril 14 (nearby in the centre, and generally the cheapest). In the evenings, you'll find hammocks and all the Cearense crafts at makeshift stalls along Iracema beach (avenida Presidente Kennedy). See the section on *Camping* in Chapter 4 for more on hammocks. Mosquito nets (*mosquiteiros*) aren't as easily purchased here as in the Amazon.

BEACH TRIPS FROM FORTALEZA

South of Fortaleza

Unpolluted white-sand beaches begin just 32 km south of Fortaleza, near Aquiráz. Prainha, Iguapé, Caponga, Barra Nova, Morro Branco, and Uruaú are all relatively small coastal villages accessible by public bus from the Fortaleza terminal. *Jangadas* return daily with their catch, and you can join the locals as they barter for fresh hammerhead shark, skate, and mackerel. Tiny beachfront shacks (*barracas*) roofed with palm leaves serve beer, fried fish, manioc meal, rice and beans. Gorgeous as these beaches can be, they lie so close to Fortaleza that residents of the big city flock to them in droves, especially on weekends. Prainha and Morro Branco get most of the crowds. None of these beaches therefore qualify as particularly remote, although backpackers will find deserted stretches just beyond the villages. Unfortunately, a series of rivers makes a complete traverse of this coastal stretch impossible (see the map).

The more isolated shoreline begins south of Aracati. An inland town of 60,000 people, Aracati is accessible via four daily buses (0700, 1145, 1400, and 1700) from the main terminal in Fortaleza. The trip takes about 3 hours. Getting off the bus, you'll be besieged by *kombi* and *bugre* drivers offering rides to Canôa Quebrada, 11 km to the east. Canoa inherited Arembepe's reputation as Brazil's 'in' beach town, and while there is still no electricity or running water, the once-idyllic fishing hamlet hasn't really qualified as 'remote' since about 1982. Drugs, venereal diseases, crime — including at least one rape — and terminal hipness long ago scratched Canoa from our list. I mention it here mainly because you will be steered there frequently by well-meaning Brazilians who still regard it as primitive.

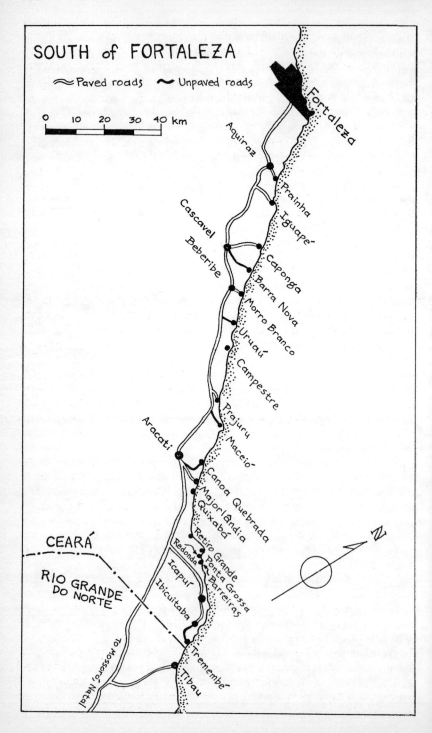

SOUTH of FORTALEZA

≈ Paved roads   ∼ Unpaved roads

0   10   20   30   40 km

Fortaleza

Aquiraz

Prainha

Iguapé

Cascavel

Caponga

Beberibe

Barra Nova

Morro Branco

Uruaú

Campestre

Prajuru

Aracati

Maceió

Canoa Quebrada

Majorlândia

Quixabá

Retiro Grande

Redonda

Ponta Grossa

Icapuí

Barreiras

Ibicuitaba

CEARÁ

RIO GRANDE
DO NORTE

To Mossoró (Natal)

Tremembé

Tibau

N

Canoa's beach itself, however, flanked by massive white sand dunes, is still fabulous, and provides a starting point for backpacking trips to the south. From Canoa, you can hike south along the coastline all the way to the state border, crossing into Rio Grande do Norte and arriving at the town of Tibau. Only just before Tibau will you run into an unfordable river, and it's served by a makeshift ferry.

About 70 km separates Canoa Quebrada from Tibau. Only three spots along this stretch are accessed by decent roads, so the coast is largely deserted, punctuated here and there by truly primitive fishing settlements and some breathtaking scenery. Sadly, the unobstructed shoreline also tempts jeep and *bugre* drivers to make the trip, occasionally spoiling a quiet day of hiking. This is most likely to happen on weekends and Brazilian holidays, and even then only at low tide. Most of the time, you'll encounter only donkey-drawn carts hauling firewood and fish.

Hiking down the coast, you'll first hit Majorlândia, just 7 km south of Canoa. Majorlândia is a fishing town and popular beach resort, quite crowded on weekends. If you want to skip this 7 km stretch, take the bus to Aracati from Fortaleza (see above), then hire a jeep to take you to directly to Majorlândia, 12 km east, continuing on foot from there. About 3 km south of Majorlândia lies Quixabá, much smaller than its neighbour to the north, but still with electricity and simple overnight accommodation. Sandstone cliffs and deserted beaches occupy the next 15 km to Retiro Grande, 6 km from the highway and served by a dirt road. The cliffs are a vivid orange-red, spattered as if by paint with white, purple and brown splotches. Now and then you'll meet women, clothing piled high in pans balanced on their heads, going to wash in freshwater springs. Goats bleat from the cliffside. Here the coast turns slightly north-east, toward the tiny fishing village of Ponta Grossa, which lies another 6 km from Retiro Grande.

We stopped here late one afternoon and bought yellow coconuts from the villagers for US$0.15. Sipping the cool, watery milk, Jayne felt a curious kinship with the local fisherfolk; like her, at least half the villagers sported blond hair, a legacy of 17th Century Dutch invaders. They seemed unnacountably shy by Brazilian standards, but we lingered anyway, taking in the bucolic setting. Draped on crude wooden frames lay a handful of nylon fishing nets, the village's single concession to the 20th Century. Even the anchors for the half-dozen or so *jangadas* were rustic, hand-made affairs: stones encircled by saplings, then lashed with reeds.

Just beyond Ponta Grossa lies Redonda, a much larger fishing village with electricity and served by a dirt road from Icapuí, incidentally, is widely reputed to have Ceará's most beautiful women). A bus runs daily to Redonda from Icapuí, which in turn is served by three daily buses from Fortaleza. A third way to reach Redonda involves catching the so-called "Misto", an hilariously claptrap cross between bus and *pau-de-arara*. On a daily basis, the 'Misto' leaves the inland city of Mossoró in Rio Grande do Norte, heads to Tibau on the coast, then plies the beach north to Redonda. After that, it heads back to Icapuí and the coastal highway. Not surprisingly, the schedule is highly variable.

Ask around and you'll find cheap, simple lodging in Redonda. We stayed at Fátima and Assis' place, hanging our hammocks in the back room over the snooker tables. The snooker room/dormitory doubles as a dance hall on Sunday afternoon, when couples shuffle around the cement floor to *forró* music. Redonda has no running water, but virtually every home has a well for bathing.

Redonda's *jangada* fleet numbers about eighty, plus a couple of motorboats. We arrived during lobster season, and Dona Fátima apologized profusely that she could serve us no fish; we had to settle for lobster or go hungry.

South from Redonda you'll pass the beaches of Picos and Barreiras. Our thirst got the better of us in Praia dos Picos, and we stopped at one of a half dozen huts for coconut water. The owner turned out to be a lobster fisherman, prematurely wrinkled from years of salt spray and sunshine on the *jangadas*. Two of his three children had blond hair. He scurried inside to provide us with wooden benches and sent one of his sons shimmying up the nearest tree for coconuts. Rather than allow us to drink and eat directly from the husk, he insisted on bringing glasses and spoons for his distinguished guests. Such hospitality is typical not only of Ceará, but of hinterlands throughout the north-east.

Continuing south, past Icapuí and Ibicuitaba (both served by a road, but some distance inland from the beach itself), the inshore bluffs and sandstone formations gradually disappear. The last settlement you'll find in Ceará is Tremembé, some 8 or 9 km from Ibicuitaba and within sight of Tibau, Rio Grande do Norte. Tremembé has electricity and gets a few weekenders, but remains a fairly placid fishing town. Some of the lobster fishing here is done by divers. Using helmets and surface-supplied air, they'll spend spend four or five days at sea before returning with their catch. Freshwater fish abound in the nearby rivers but, as is typical in north-east beach towns, the residents absolutely refuse to eat them.

Just before reaching Tibau you'll have to cross a small river; there's a ferry of sorts operating during the day.

North of Fortaleza

The first decent beach starts 35 km north of the city after about a one hour bus ride: Cumbuco. Not surprisingly, Cumbuco draws a lot of people on the weekends, but the beach is deserted beyond the point to the north for some 10 km.

Paracuru lies 101 km northwest of Fortaleza; several direct buses run there daily, taking about two hours. This town of 30,000 boasts electricity, running water, several cheap hotels, rustic *barracas* on the beach, and a good fish restaurant (O Ronco do Mar, 'Snore of the Sea').

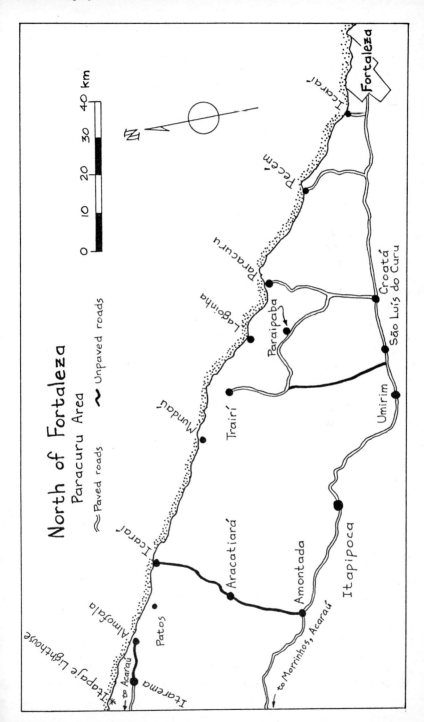

North of Fortaleza
Paracuru Area

≈ Paved roads   ∿ Unpaved roads

A real sleeper of a town when we first visited in 1984, Paracuru is now grooming itself as the Carnaval party headquarters of Ceará. Nevertheless, the beaches just east and northwest remain largely deserted most of the year. They are wide and open, flanked by low-lying dunes but without the characteristic sandstone bluffs commonly found south of Fortaleza. The wooden structures just offshore are *armadilhas*, crude but efficient fish traps tended daily by the locals. You can hike for hours east of town; 18 km northwest lies Lagoinha, reportedly a gorgeous beach but perhaps not accessible on foot due to rivers.

From Paracuru to Acaraú, a distance of some 130 km, the coast is seldom visited, though accessible by bus from Fortaleza via the towns of Trairí, Icaraí, Acaraú, and Itarema. We've personally travelled to only one area along this stretch — Almofala — but if it's at all typical, connoisseurs of the off-beat have much to explore.

Almofala lies at the very end of a dirt road, 180 km northwest of Fortaleza. The asphalt runs out at Itarema, 10 km away and the last point on most maps of the area. A direct bus from Fortaleza goes once a day all the way to Almofala, however. The village is partially ringed by sand dunes, although they are somewhat less spectacular than those surrounding Jericoaquara or Canoa Quebrada. For fifty years, the town church lay mostly buried by shifting sands until the winds — or Providence — uncovered it again in the 1940's. Coconut palms and mango trees ring the village as well; mangoes are so plentiful that the locals actually feed them to their pigs. Inland, much of the terrain has been planted with *carnaúba* palms, which produce the world's finest car polishing wax.

Almofala has no running water, no hotels, and no restaurants, but lodging in a local fisherman's home runs about US$2 with two meals a day (provide your own hammock). Huts down by the beach can be rented long-term. We were the only outsiders in the village except for a fellow boarder in 'our' house, an itinerant projectionist who travelled the backlands showing 16 mm films on whatever reasonably flat surface he could find. A whitewashed garden wall served as movie screen in this particular case. That night the whole town turned out for a Chinese martial-arts film, badly subtitled in Portuguese — the subtitles themselves were only partially visible. No one complained, however, and the projectionist had to explain what should have been obvious to us from the start: the villagers were, without exception, illiterate.

The beach south of Almofala remains absolutely deserted for 11 km; there you'll find a freshwater lagoon surrounded by dunes and the tiny lobster-fishing community of Patos. The coast north of Almofala is even more remote, with the Itapajé lighthouse at 17 km the only structure evident.

Until very recently, Jericoaquara lay claim to being Ceará's — and perhaps Brazil's — most spectacularly secluded beach. Even in 1984, when we first visited, Jericoaquara had already acquired a certain mystique among off-the-beaten-track types. Jeri's saving grace was that it lay *so far* off the beaten track that very few people did anything but talk about it.

We landed there the first time via public bus from Fortaleza's main terminal, leaving at 0800 and arriving at the town of Cruz eight hours later. After much lingering, we caught the twice-weekly *pau-de-arara* to Mangue Seco, a four-hour ride over dusty dirt roads. Mangue Seco is nothing more than a collection of huts some twenty minutes on foot from the beach. By then it was pitch black, so we hired two young boys to lead us down a forest path to the Atlantic. They pointed to a dim light in the eastern distance — the mast light of a lobster boat anchored off Jeri — and we were on our own. After an 11 km beach hike, we tramped into town.

Our second trip involved a six-hour bus ride from Fortaleza to Gijoca, some 10 km southeast of Jeri. We spurned the offers of young villagers who will guide visitors over the dunes for US$3. They ride a burro for the four-hour hike while you walk behind. Instead, we bought plastic bottles of mineral water and headed north on our own. Rain had come to the north-east after a five-year drought, and between the dunes we sometimes found placid freshwater lagoons ringed by palm trees — the classic cinematic oasis.

Only twice did we meet people. It didn't take us long to realize that getting directions in the dune country of northwestern Ceará was an altogether different type of proposition than asking a Fortaleza banker the whereabouts of the city post office. For one thing, the locals here used *leguas* rather than kilometres; they spoke with a pleasant but virtually indecipherable accent; they used a slight jerk of the head to indicate either that the village was just over the next dune, or that it was a day's journey; and finally, they knew Jericoaquara by a different name: 'Serrote'. But the setting sun proved a reliable compass, and we trudged into Jeri just as the last light faded.

At last report, these two routes will still land you in Jericoaquara. Lately, however, the way has been made easier — much *too* easy, some would say — by 4-wheel drive vehicles leaving Gijoca each afternoon. There are even traction mini-vans making the trip directly from Fortaleza.

Why all the fuss? Well, while Jeri may no longer quite qualify as a 'hideaway', it remains idyllic and post-card gorgeous. Jeri itself is nothing more than few dirt paths and simple houses, but it is nestled at the base of massive white sand dunes that roll inland as far as you can see. Palm trees flank the village, and there are places where the dunes have literally buried them up to their tops. Just east of town, the women of Jeri comb the rocks at low tide, collecting sea salt that has dried in tiny natural pockets. Village children pluck an occasional spiny lobster from out of the crevices at the water's edge. Here the dunes give way to sandstone cliffs reminiscent of Ceará's more southerly coast. Climbing to the top of this headland — as you must when the tide comes in — you pass gnarled clumps of cacti rooted in rust-colored earth. Photos are

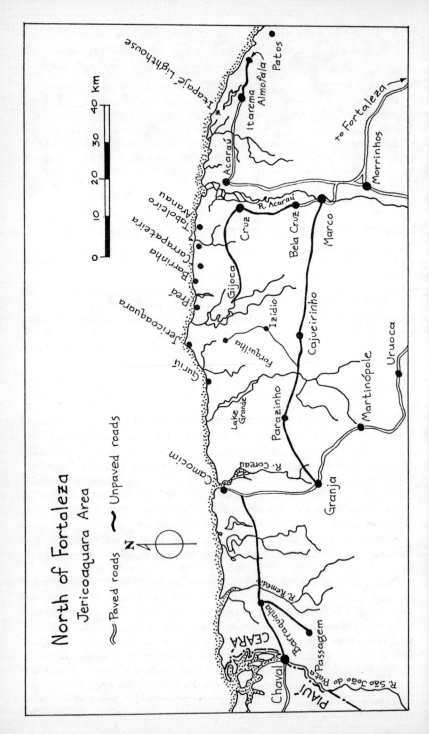

North of Fortaleza
Jericoaquara Area

≋ Paved roads ～ Unpaved roads

N

Irapajé Lighthouse
Patos
Almofala
Itarema
Acaraú
Taboleiro
Ipanau
Carapateira
Barrinha
Preá
Jericoaquara
Gurin
Cruz
R. Acaraú
Bela Cruz
Marco
Morrinhos
to Fortaleza
Gijoca
Izidio
Forquilha
Cajueirinho
Uruoca
Martinópole
Lake Grande
Parazinho
Camocim
R. Coreaú
Granja
R. Remedios
Barroquinha
Passagem
R. São João do Rato
Chaval
CEARÁ
PIAUÍ

FOOD AND DRINK IN THE NORTH-EAST BACKCOUNTRY

The food and drink served in remote fishing villages isn't one of those travel experiences you'll get nostalgic about back home. In Jericoaquara, we always dreaded Sundays; that meant the fishermen didn't fish, which meant that we would be eating chicken. The only reason we could see for slaughtering these pathetically scrawny and diseased birds might have been to put them out of their misery.

Nevertheless, much of the food you'll eat is particular to this portion of Brazil, and there are pleasant as well as unpleasant surprises. You'll often start the day off with *tapioca* cakes instead of bread; this is a granular form of manioc starch baked into rounds with coconut milk. Fish dishes include mackerel (*cavala*), hammerhead shark (*tubarão martelo*), and skate (*arraia*). Stingray stew (*ensopada de arraia*) can be particularly tasty. *Nordestinos*, like all Brazilians, love sweets; in the backcountry you'll get *cocada*, a chewy macaroon-like concoction of shredded coconut and sugar. For real sugar-holics there's always *rapadura*, a hardened cake of raw cane broth that's been boiled down to its sugary essence. *Cachaça* is, of course, the national drink, but here you'll often take it with cashew fruit syrup (*mel de cajú*).

---

obligatory at the Pedra Furada, a natural stone archway located on the beach just 2 km east of Jeri.

West of town, the beach is broader and the headlands are replaced by low-lying dunes all the way to Mangue Seco. About 1 km from Jeri lies a cluster of palms that make for perfect hammock camping.

Jeri currently has no formal lodging; either go in with other travellers as we did and rent a mud hut, or buy hammock space in any of three dozen fishermen's houses. Hammocks can be rented as well. Likewise, you'll find no cafés; local women such as Dona Marina fix simple meals for next to nothing. There is cold beer despite the lack of electricity (Jeri's residents long ago discovered propane refrigerators). Camillo's bar and general store down by the beach became our favourite watering hole. When we last saw Camillo — in fact, *whenever* we saw him — he was lying on his back upon the bar, head propped on a burlap sack of sugar, groaning at the prospect of fetching anyone a beer.

When it came time for bathing, a growing pack of local children followed us to the town pump, watching silently as we took a modest bucket shower in our swim suits.

Pigs, chickens, goats, and donkeys roamed the beaches, dirt streets, and, on occasion, even the houses of Jericoaquara. One evening in our mud house I woke to the sound of hooves, and spent the next half hour learning that donkeys apparently do not have a reverse gear that will take them back down a hallway. In another north-east coastal village, I found myself trapped in a bathroom, trying to push open the door against a 150-kilo hog that had wandered inside the house to feed on spilled corn. Wherever pigs are found along the north-east coast, you'll find them wallowing and feeding on the beach. This prompted a Swiss traveller to tell a Brazilian friend of ours that 'here in Brazil, even the pigs have the right to sun and the beach. Meanwhile, we Swiss have neither one nor the other.'

NATAL

Like most capital cities in the north-east, Natal is likable but not memorable. A city of 400,000 people, it provides access to about 380 km of coastline in Rio Grande do Norte state. Natal doesn't attract the same crowds of vacationing Brazilians that cities such as Fortaleza and Salvador do; consequently, its dune-flanked beaches and fishing villages remain relatively pristine. The locals are friendly even by north-eastern standards, and some of the older folk speak rudimentary English; the Americans established a large air base here during World War II from which to attack German strongholds in Africa.

Arrival/Departure   The new bus station lies 6 km from the centre, in the Cidade da Esperança neighbourhood. Walk outside and catch the bus marked Via Tirol to get downtown. Buses run daily to and from Fortaleza (9 hrs), Salvador (22 hrs), Recife (5 hrs), Rio de Janeiro, São Paulo, Aracaju, João Pessoa, and hundreds of towns in Rio Grande do Sul. An older bus terminal near the centre serves more local destinations (see below). The airport, Internacional Augusto Severo, is located 15 km from town in the Eduardo Gomes district. Daily flights serve all the cities mentioned above plus Belém and minus Aracaju.

Getting around   You'll find most cheap lodging in the centre (known as the Cidade Alta); from there, everything but the new bus terminal is within walking distance. Natal itself doesn't offer much to see, and the city beaches are rocky and dismal.

Changing money   If there exists a place to change travellers cheques on the *paralelo*, we've never found it in two extended trips to Natal. Cash might be easier; ask at hotels, travel agencies, and the Centro de Turismo. The Banco do Brasil in the Cidade Alta changes cheques at the official rate.

Information   The Centro de Turismo is yet another converted prison, this one located on a hill overlooking the Praia do Meio, at the end of rua Aderbal de Figueiredo. Here you'll get second-hand (though fairly reliable) tips on remote beaches in Rio Grande do Sul. Natal's cheapest place to stay is right next door: A Casa dos Estudantes, men's and women's 'student' dorms.

BEACH TRIPS FROM NATAL

Everyone raves about Genipabu and its gigantic *duna*. Just 30 km north of Natal, it's unquestionably pretty but no longer pristine. You can

reach Genipabu by direct bus from the old bus terminal at Praça
Augusto Severo; it's next to the train depot in the Ribeira district,
within walking distance of the centre. A far nicer route involves a bus
ride across the Potengi River to Redinha (these buses also leave from
old bus terminal). Redinha is a funky beach used mostly by locals. From
here, start walking north — it's about 8 km to Genipabu — along a
more-or-less undeveloped shoreline.

Not surprisingly, the truly deserted coastline of Rio Grande do Norte
lies much further afield from Natal. Baía Formosa is a medium-sized
fishing town providing access to some 20 km of stunningly beautiful
beach, extending all the way south to the border with Paraíba state. You
can reach Baía Formosa on either of two direct daily buses (one at 0730
and the other at 1530) from Natal's new terminal. The bus takes three
hours, dropping you off on the hill above the harbour. If you're not
planning to camp, your best bet is to bring a hammock and rent a local
fisherman's cottage; the owner of the single *pensão* in town (the
Miramar) charges outrageously for a dungeon of a room facing the sea.
Ask at the simple café across the street from the Miramar regarding
house rental.

The bay itself blocks much hiking to the north. Walking south, you'll
pass a few huts before landing on totally unspoiled beach which extends
to Paraíba. The waves are just big enough to *pegar jacaré* (body surf),
and a rippling series of tall sand dunes provides escape from the
occasional wind. Bring plenty of fresh water — we never saw any, nor
did we run into a single person on this shoreline. Despite the direct bus
to Baía Formosa, tourism has for the moment passed the place by.

Similarly deserted stretches of shoreline lie just to the north, in the
vicinity of Tibau do Sul and Barra do Cunhaú. To reach Pipa, probably
the most scenic and unspoiled of the villages giving access to this
coastline, you can take any of the morning buses leaving Natal's new bus
terminal for Goianinha or Cunhaú; even the interstate buses going to
João Pessoa and Recife can drop you off. In all cases, tell the driver
you're going to Pipa and ask to be dropped off along the highway; the
stop itself is near Goianinha. A daily afternoon bus leaves from this
collection of houses along the highway for Pipa (about a two-hour trip
over a terrible dirt roadway).

Pipa itself consists of about thirty simple houses, all perched on a bluff
overlooking the beach. There are no hotels or pensions — rent a
fisherman's house and sling your hammock. One fellow in town sells
vegetables, and there are two tiny stores where you can buy other food
items. A single café provides meals. Pipa is a fishing village, but like
Baía Formosa, its fishermen don't sail the jangadas typical of the north-
east. The tides are spectacular here, exposing immense stretches of
beach during the ebb, and virtually eliminating it during the flood.
Instead of sand dunes, you'll find impressive reddish-orange cliffs
flanking the beach. Hiking is good in both directions, but carry lots of
water; there are no settlements or springs nearby. To leave Pipa, catch

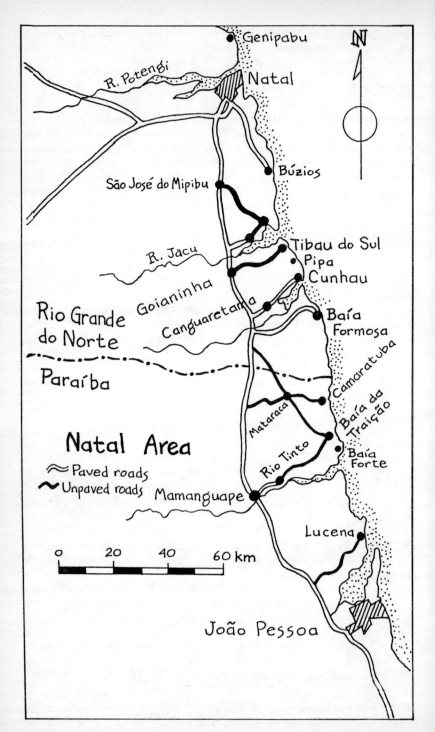

Genipabu

R. Potengi

Natal

N

Búzios

São José do Mipibu

Tibau do Sul

R. Jacu

Pipa

Goianinha

Cunhau

Canguaretama

Baía
Formosa

Rio Grande
do Norte

Camaratuba

Paraíba

Baía da
Traição

Natal Area

Mataraca

≈ Paved roads
Unpaved roads

Rio Tinto

Baía
Forte

Mamanguape

0   20   40   60 km

Lucena

João Pessoa

the daily bus at 0500 for the highway (BR-101). Here you can flag down any number of buses going north to Natal or south to Recife.

MACEIÓ

Maceió is a pleasant, not particularly interesting port city of 400,000. Vacationing Brazilians flock to the Praia da Pajuçara, a beach just 3 km north of the centre that's famous as a *piscina natural*. Lined by a distant coral reef, Pajuçara turns into a vast, shallow pool at low tide, filled with scores of tourist-laden *jangadas*. A mere 45 km to the north, however, independent travellers will begin to find the same 'natural swimming pools' in a far more tranquil setting.

Arrival/Departure   The bus station is located a good 5 km from the city centre and hotels. Daily buses run to Salvador, Recife, Rio de Janeiro, São Paulo, João Pessoa, Aracaju, Penedo, and numerous other small cities and towns. EMATUR, the state tourist agency, staffs an extremely helpful information booth here; they'll tell you current prices for all the local hotels, from flophouse to four-star, and make reservations. Catch the Serraría Mercado bus (US$0.20) for the lengthy trip to the centre. The airport lies 20 km from the centre; catch the Rio do Largo bus, which runs downtown along the rua João Pessoa. There are daily flights to all the cities listed above except Penedo.

Getting around   You'll only need to take the bus if you plan to visit Maceió's popular local beaches (the two nearest the centre, Praia da Avenida and Sobral, are polluted). To Pajuçara Beach, hop any number of local buses (such as Ponta da Terra) along the avenida Duque de Caxias. Garça Torta Beach further north is accessible on the Fátima bus. For bodysurfing, try Praia do Francês to the south; catch one of the frequent *kombis* (passenger vans) on the highway near Praia do Sobral (there's also a bus to Marechal Deodoro and Praia do Francês from the bus station).

Changing money   The black market doesn't thrive here; your best bet is trying all the local travel agencies; sometimes they're buying travellers cheques, sometimes not.

Information   The bus station booth is most helpful, but TURIMAT also staffs (on an irregular basis) an information booth in the centre at the Calçadão do Comércio.

BEACH TRIPS FROM MACEIÓ

With so many beaches nearby, most vacationing Brazilians stay within 20 km of town. Of the populated beaches, our favourite is Praia do

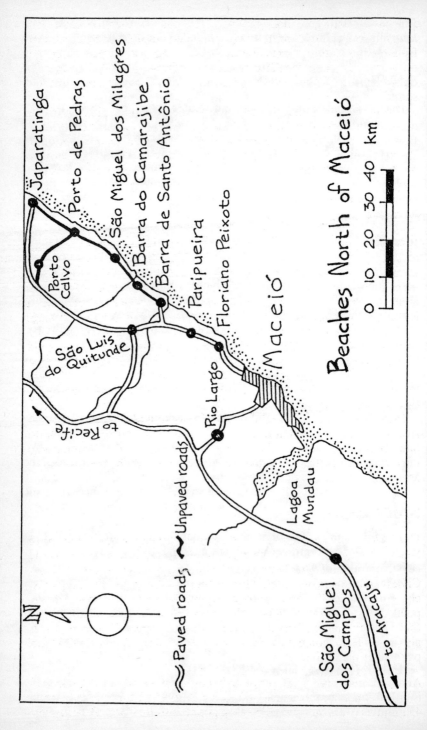

Beaches North of Maceió

Francês — with great bodysurfing — 22 km south of the centre via *kombi* from Praia do Sobral, or via scheduled bus to Marechal Deodoro from the bus station. Garça Torta, 14 km to the north, is especially fun on weekends; take the Fátima bus from downtown. At *barracas* at either beach, try the *agulhas fritas*, tiny fried fish with an elongated snout.

But for a truly idyllic stretch of deserted coastline, plan on hiking north from Barra de Santo Antônio, located 45 km north of Maceió. Buses run daily from the city terminal to Barra de Santo Antônio. Plenty of small boats are available here, most of them taking visitors to nearby Ilha da Croa. Hire one instead to take you across the Santo Antônio River; just on the other side you'll find a smaller village, fringed by coconut palms and absolutely the last outpost of civilization for the next two days of walking. Once on the beach, simply head north toward a second, much smaller fishing town, Barra do Camarajibe. Bring along plenty of fresh water; you'll find only one *fonte* (spring) after you leave Barra de Santo Antônio and it's located just south of Barra do Camarajibe, where there's plenty of water anyway. Local maps put Antônio and Barra do Camarajibe 13 km apart, but that's along the dirt road to Porto de Pedras; along the undulating coastline, it is considerably longer, demanding about two days of leisurely hiking.

The coast between Antônio and Barra do Camarajibe consists of a series of spectacular, crescent-shaped bays separated by headlands and bluffs to the east. Not a single human dwelling stands here, probably owing to the lack of fresh water. One of the beaches along this stretch is known locally as Carro Quebrado (Broken Car), presumably because of the rugged terrain.

Once in Barra do Camarajibe, you'll have to find a boat to cross the river if you plan to continue along the coast. This stretch of beach, to São Miguel dos Milagres and thence to Porto de Pedras, is reportedly uncluttered and attractive. Buses run daily from Porto de Pedras back to Maceió.

SALVADOR

Until 1763, Salvador reigned as Brazil's capital city. Today it vies with São Paulo as the cultural capital of the country, and with Rio as the centre of tourism. Salvador boasts the best musicians (Caetano Veloso, Gilberto Gil, Gal Costa, and Moraes Moreira among others), the most churches (reputedly one for each day of the year), the most famous poets and authors (among them Jorge Amado), the richest and spiciest food, and the most vibrantly African influence of any Brazilian city. It also provides a home base from which to explore Bahia's 880 km of palm-strewn coastline.

Arrival/Departure   I still refuse to believe that Salvador's bus terminal is only 5 km from the centre; the Rodoviária-Sé local bus takes at least 45 minutes of tortuous winding to negotiate this distance. Other buses, equally slow, run to Campo Grande, Terminal da Barroquinha, and Avenida da França. Except for the Sé bus, you'll still be let off some distance from the cheap hotel district in the upper city near the Pelourinho. Splurge and take a cab if you've got baggage. Daily buses go to and from all state capitals in the north-east, plus Belém, Rio de Janeiro (27 hrs), and São Paulo. Dois de Julho International Airport lies 28 km from the centre, and runs daily flights to all state capitals as well as flights to Miami, Frankfurt, Lisbon, Madrid, Paris, and Asunción, Paraguay. An air-conditioned bus goes to Praça da Sé in the centre.

Getting around   The centre is divided into two sections: the Cidade Baixa (lower city), where most businesses are located, and the Cidade Alta (upper city), the older part of town containing the major historical sites and cheap hotels. A century-old elevator joins the two 'cities'. Everything in the upper city is within reasonable walking distance, but the bus system for all other parts of the city can be confusing. Ask at BAHIATURSA for help.

Changing money   Especially in the Praça da Sé neighbourhood, you'll be approached by men on the street offering to change money at some unspecified location. With plenty of other options, why chance it? Try Casa de Câmbio Salomão Feinstein, actually a business furniture store on the avenida Estados Unidos 379 (telephone 242-0837). They've cashed both travellers cheques and cash on the *paralelo*. There are others as well, mostly in the lower city; ask at BAHIATURSA.

Information   BAHIATURSA, the state tourist agency, has a central office within the Palácio Rio Branco in the upper city near rua Chile (open 0800-1830). They also staff booths at the bus terminal (0900-2100), and airport (0900-2230). Excellent information on local lodging, money changing, and transportation; the central office has a message board.

BEACH TRIPS FROM SALVADOR

Salvador's popularity with both Brazilian and European travellers means that remote coastline in the state of Bahia is getting tougher and tougher to find. Fortunately, if you avoid the holiday seasons and hike past the villages where visitors stay congregated, you'll still find plenty of the 'real' Brazil.

Morro de São Paulo, like Ceará's Jericoaquara, has finally been 'discovered.' Soon it may turn into another Canoa Quebrada, but its stunning beaches, clear water, and tranquil (as yet) fishing village still make Morro de São Paulo a deserving destination. It also has the distinction of an island setting, but it's one that you pay for dearly; virtually everything but fish must be shipped from the mainland so that food is extremely expensive. Stock up before leaving Salvador.

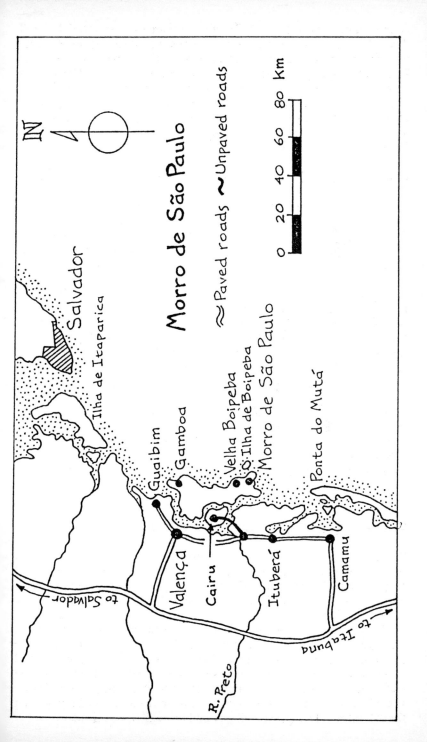

From Salvador, take one of the many daily buses to Valença. Because the buses drive all the way around the Baía de Todos os Santos, it's a 272 km, 5-hour journey. If you're successful in hitching a ride with a private motorist, you'll go via Itaparica Island, a much more direct route. Plan on spending the night in Valença due to the ferry schedule.

The single ferry to Morro de São Paulo leaves the docks on rua Madureira at 1230 (Monday-Friday) and at 0700 on Sundays. The fare is US$0.50, the trip takes about 2 hours, and the two-tiered ferry holds approximately 40 people. There are other, smaller craft bound for the island of Tinharé and Morro de São Paulo which follow no set schedule but will charge more. Check the ferry schedule with BAHIATURSA in Salvador; additional ferries run in the summer, but the island is besieged during that time with visitors.

The ferry stops first at the village of Gamboa, surrounded by mangroves, picking up and discharging passengers, then continues on to Morro de São Paulo. The entrance is dominated by the huge stone portal of the fort and prison constructed here in 1630. Continue up the steep hill to the village itself and a 19th Century lighthouse.

The village consists of but a single 'street.' You'll find lodging in a number of simple pensions or else rent a house from the locals; they use beds rather than hammocks here. Camping is possible along the beach on the eastern side of the island. Even with sea breezes, the place can be insufferably hot, but if you leave your shutters open, be prepared for guests; huge swarms of bats fill the night skies around Morro de São Paulo.

One of the draws here is the crystal-clear water, an anomaly along most of Brazil's coast. Virtually all of the eastern side of the island, extending 35 km, contains white-sand beach.

Two final reminders: avoid Morro de São Paulo during Brazilian holidays, and bring as much of your own food as possible.

Trancoso, some 743 km south of Salvador, is Bahia's Canoa Quebrada, minus the huge sand dunes. But as in Canoa, a short hike down the beach will soon put you far from the hip crowd and into some gorgeous scenery.

To reach Trancoso, take any of the buses to Eunápolis, from where you'll hop one of the frequent buses to Porto Seguro. The whole trip takes about 12 hours. Porto Seguro is a tourist mecca, with literally scores of hotels and *pousadas*. The next day, walk to the southern end of town and catch the tiny ferry-barge across the Buranhém River (US$0.15), from where an ancient bus makes three runs a day to Trancoso (0700, 1000, and 1400), 22 km south on a dirt road. The road is narrow, deeply rutted, steep in spots, and impassable during heavy rains. When we last took the bus, a huge gash in the flooring afforded us an intimate view of both road conditions and the drive shaft.

The bus first bounces its way into Arraial d'Ajuda (shown on some maps as Nossa Senhora da Ajuda) before descending the final hill to Trancoso. The 22 km trip takes about 1-1/2 hours. Trancoso sits on a bluff above the beach, with a burgeoning number of *pousadas* and organic-chic cafés. The palm-lined beaches just south of Trancoso, however, are nearly deserted and perfect for extended hiking and camping.

As with Morro de São Paulo, it's best to avoid the whole Porto Seguro-Trancoso area during Brazilian holiday season.

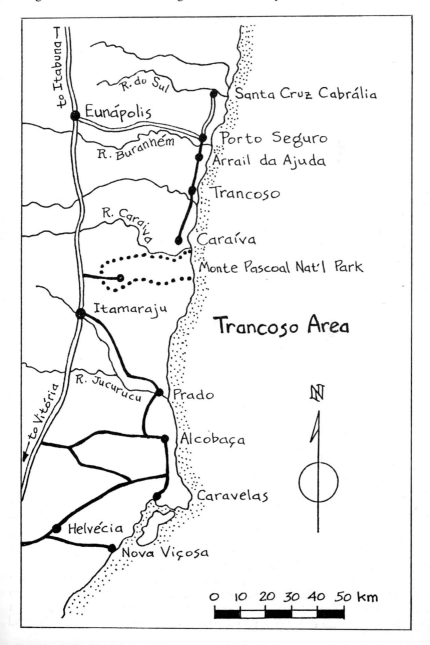

MUSIC AND DANCE IN THE NORTH-EAST BACKCOUNTRY

Nowadays you'll find chic urbanites dancing the *forró* in clubs throughout Brazil. But it's originally a creation of the north-east backcountry, a dance you're sure to experience in its purest form if you spend a weekend in one of the fishing towns mentioned in this chapter. We saw our first *forró* six years ago in Jericoaquara; under a tin-covered shed, villagers had rigged a phonograph to a 12-volt truck battery, and there they danced to the infectious beat of Luiz Gonzaga's accordion. The forró demands a series of quick shuffling steps, and the sounds of perhaps 40 plastic sandals scraping in time over that concrete floor added considerably to the recorded music. The smallest villages — like Jeri — generally rely on record players or even radios for their *forró* music. To really appreciate this local tradition, though, try to catch a live band in the hinterlands. In addition to the ever-present accordion player (*sanfoneira*), you can expect a drummer and a steel-triangle player, often augmented by a tambourine. One or more of the players will sing. We attended one *forró* where a small child spent the entire evening holding a microphone up for the singer, resting his arm between verses. The tunes themselves are fast and rambunctious, sounding a great deal like Mexican music (though I assume that's purely coincidental). Partners cling to each other tightly in this deceptively simple dance. The setting for a good *forrozinho* can often be as intriguing as the music and dancing. We attended one in Peixe Gordo ('Fat Fish'), Ceará, which the band had enclosed within a makeshift barrier of palm fronds to prevent non-paying customers from interloping. On another occasion, the hut where we rented hammock space became the dance hall on Sundays. The name *forró* reportedly originated when English bosses held dances 'for all' their Brazilian and English employees. Most backcountry *forrós* occur on weekends, especially during religious and other holidays. Those with live music will charge you an admission if you're a man (ridiculously cheap); women dance for free.

The backcountry of the north-east also spawned the unique singers known as *repentistas*. Accompanied simply by guitar, tambourine, or triangle, the *repentista* actually makes up lyrics as he goes, singing in a fast, typically harsh monotone. Poverty, politics, drought, and the suffering of the *nordestinos* are common themes, but sly humour plays a big role as well; *repentistas* frequently poke good-natured fun at members of the audience, and a foreigner is always fair game. This isn't dancing music.

If you happen to be visiting around June 23rd, particularly in the state of Maranhão, you may well see the *bumba-meu-boi* festival. The spectacle revolves around an ox, usually portrayed by two local men beneath a fabulously decorated sheet. Dancing, singing, and poetry all play a part in this festival, which may or may not have religious overtones depending on which Brazilian you happen to ask.

Bibliography

General — history, the country, the people

Bastide, Roger (1978). *The African Religions of Brazil*. Johns Hopkins. Rich in detail, this is still the definitive work on the subject. Required reading for anyone visiting the north-east, where Afro-Brazilian religions flourish.

Freyre, Gilberto (1964). Translated by Samuel Putnam. *The Masters and the Slaves*. Alfred A. Knopf, New York. Freyre remains Brazil's best-known sociologist/historian; this is his classic tome interpreting the development of Brazilian society. Fascinating and well-documented, it's nevertheless skewed by Freyre's conservative sympathies (he is an unrepentant supporter of military rule). He looks the other way when it comes to Brazilian racial discrimination, for example.

Skidmore, Thomas E. and Peter H. Smith (1984). *Modern Latin America*. Oxford University Press, New York. Contains an excellent political history of Brazil, with emphasis on developments between 1964 and 1984.

Time/Life Books, editors (1986). *Brazil*. Time/Life Books, Library of Nations Series, Amsterdam. A well-balanced discussion of history, politics, the land, people and their customs. Gorgeous colour photographs.

Wagley, Charles (1971). *An Introduction to Brazil*. Columbia University Press, New York. Somewhat dated, this is still a fine description of social classes, the community, family and education, religion and state.

Natural history

Cousteau, Jacques-Yves and Mose Richards (1984). *Jacques Cousteau's Amazon Journey*. H.N. Abrams, New York. Beautiful photographs.Dunning, J.S. and R.S. Ridgely (1982). *South American Land*

Birds: A Photographic Aid to Identification. Harrowood, London. With 1112 colour photographs, range maps, and identifications of over 2500 species, this is *the* birder's field guide for not only Brazil but the entire continent.

Forsyth, Adrian and Ken Miyata (1984). *Tropical Nature*. Charles Scribner's Sons, New York. A highly readable book for the lay reader on rain forest ecology in Central and South America.

Perry, Donald (1986). *Life Above the Jungle Floor*. Simon and Schuster, New York. Biologist Perry lived for weeks in a platform high amidst the jungle treetops, where hundreds of fascinating plants and animals have gone unappreciated or even unnoticed by traditional biologists.

The Amazon — its people and problems

Denslow, Julie Sloan and Christine Padoch, editors (1988). *People of the Tropical Rainforest*. University of California Press, Berkeley. A host of experts discuss not only jungle people but also agriculture, rain forest ecology, and the politics of exploitation. Much of the book deals with Amazônia. Superb colour photographs. Hemming, John (1978). *Red Gold: The Conquest of the Brazilian Indians*. Harvard University Press, Cambridge. A disturbing historical treatise on Portugal's exploitation and slaughter of Amazonian Indians.

Hemming, John (1987). *Amazon Frontier: the Defeat of the Brazilian Indians*. Harvard University Press, Cambridge. More on the decimation of Amazon tribes, picking up where *Red Gold* left off (1755) and continuing through 1910.

Kandell, Jonathan (1984). *Passage through El Dorado*. William Morrow and Company, New York. An insightful and thoroughly researched look at the development of the Amazon basin, mingled with travelogue.

Kelly, Brian and Mark London (1983). *Amazon*. Harcourt Brace Jovanovich, New York. A compelling account of rain forest politics and destruction.

Shoumatoff, Alex (1978). *The Rivers Amazon*. Sierra Club Books, San Francisco. Shoumatoff is extremely well versed in Amazonian flora and fauna, backcountry travel, Brazilian politics, and Amerindian affairs. He's also a superb travel writer who spends lots of time in remote corners of Brazil. This remains one of the best books on the Amazon.

Stone, Roger D. (1985). *Dreams of Amazonia*. Viking/Penguin, New York. Stone is a member of the World Wildlife Fund with over 20 years experience in Brazilian Amazônia. A well-researched look at exploitation and development within the Amazon basin, from the early Spanish explorers to Henry Ford and Daniel Ludwig.

Wagley, Charles (1976). *Amazon Town: A Study of Man in the Tropics.* Oxford University Press, London. Originally published in 1953, this is a classic study of the *caboclo* way of life in Itá, Amazonas. Fascinating accounts of local customs, religions, myths, and survival along the great river. This edition has an update on the town.

Travel literature

(A great many 'adventure travel' books centred on the Amazon owe more to the imagination than to reality. These are notable exceptions.)Fleming, Peter (1934). *Brazilian Adventure.* Reprinted by J.P. Tarcher/Houghton Mifflin. A travel classic which follows the English journalist on his search for jungle explorer Colonel Fawcett in the Mato Grosso.

Harrison, John (1986). *Up the Creek.* Bradt Publications/Hippocrene Books. A hilarious and harrowing account of a two-man journey up the Jari River by canoe. A good deal of practical advice on jungle camping, canoeing, hunting and fishing. Required reading for anyone considering such a trip; for those of us with more sense, Harrison's vigorous writing makes it fine armchair adventure.

O'Hanlon, Redmond (1989). *In Trouble Again: A Journey Between the Orinoco and the Amazon.* Atlantic Monthly Press, New York. O'Hanlon is a connoisseur of the bizarre, and Amazónia has inspired him to new heights of wit and derring-do.

Holman, Alan (1985). *White River, Brown Water: A Record-Making Kayak Journey Down the Amazon.* The Mountaineers, Seattle. A journal-type account of the longest continuous solo descent of the Amazon. The writing is unremarkable, but there's plenty of practical information for kayak and canoe enthusiasts on what to bring and how to pack.

Shoumatoff, Alex (1986). *In Southern Light: Trekking through Zaire and the Amazon.* Simon and Schuster, New York. No one currently writing can match Shoumatoff when it comes to Amazonian travelogues. The first half of this book recounts his search for the source of the Amazon warrior legend on the Nhamundá River.

Portuguese instruction

(British texts tend to stress European Portuguese; try to get one of the American books, which are invariably slanted toward Brazilian usage.)

Dennis, Ronald D. (1979). *2200 Brazilian Idioms*. Brigham Young University. Brazilians pepper their speech with slang and idiomatic expressions, and this book is lots of fun for those who already know the basics of the language.

Fernández, Oscar (1965). *Living Language Conversational Portuguese*. Crown Publishers, New York. A 2-cassette (or 4-LP) language course that comes with a conversation manual and a dictionary. Uses a phrasebook approach, so it should be supplemented by a grammar text. Several native speakers are used so that you can appreciate regional differences in pronunciation. Retails for about US$15. Make sure you buy the 'South American' version rather than the 'Continental.'

Foreign Service Institute (FSI). *Portuguese Programmatic Course — Brazilian*. Two volumes. U.S. Department of State. The most comprehensive cassette course, with 45 cassettes and 1,400 pages of text. Recommended only for those who really want to immerse themselves in Portuguese. Volume I costs US$130, Volume II sells for US$115. Order from the National Audio Visual Center, Information Services PF, 8700 Edgeworth Drive, Capitol Heights, MD 20743–3701. (Barron's *Mastering Portuguese* course is a slightly modified version of FSI's Volume I. It's a 12–cassette programme with a 620–page text, selling for US$75).

King, Larry D. and Margarita Suñer (1981). Para a Frente!: An Intermediate Course in Portuguese. Cabrilho Press, Los Angeles. Intended for those with some basic knowledge of Portuguese who want more. Lots of slang, idioms, and current Brazilian readings.

Leroy, Claude E. (1964). *Português Para Principiantes*. Two volumes. University of Wisconsin-Extension, Madison. A good text with emphasis on dialogue, grammar, and stories.

Nitti, John J. (1974). *201 Portuguese Verbs*. Barron's Educational Series, Woodbury, New York. Every conjugation for every verb you're likely to need.

Thomas, Earl W. (1974). *A Grammar of Spoken Brazilian Portuguese*. Vanderbilt University Press, Nashville. The best textbook on the subject we've yet seen.

Guidebooks

Box, Ben, editor (published annually). *South American Handbook*. Trade and Travel Publications, Bath. What can you say about 'The Bible'? Easily the most comprehensive guide to Latin America and perhaps the best guidebook ever published anywhere. Regional and town maps, hotel and restaurant listings, travel, health, and background information. The Brazil chapter runs 165 pages.

Herzberg, W. & Schoen M. (1989). *Brazil: a travel survival kit*. Lonely Planet. The usual comprehensive LP information.

Jordan, Tanis and Martin (1982). *South American River Trips*. Bradt Publications. Required reading for anyone planning a river trip on their own. The Jordans do their travelling via inflatables, but kayakers, canoeists, and just plain jungle campers will benefit from the couple's practical advice on everything from staying dry in camp to shooting rapids. Spiced with anecdotes from the authors' river trips in Peru, Suriname, and Venezuela. The Brazilian section is by John Harrison, with advice on the Guaporé and Teles Pires rivers, but the Jordans have added an account of their 1983 trip up the Mapuera to the latest edition.

Quatro Rodas (published annually). *Guia Brasil*. Editora Abril, São Paulo. Over 700 cities and towns, listed alphabetically, with 69 detailed maps. Information includes hotels, restaurants, bus stations, airports, banks, currency exchange houses, tourist bureaux, sights, etc. An invaluable reference, but keep in mind that only the ritzier hotels tend to be listed for the larger cities. You can buy this guide at virtually all newsstands, bookstores, bus stations, and airports in Brazil.

Health and general travel advice

Dawood, Richard (1989). *Traveller's Health*. O.U.P., Oxford. Helpful, concise and up to date information on all aspects of staying healthy abroad.

Hatt, John (1985). *The Tropical Traveller*. Delightfully idiosyncratic but thoroughly useful advice for anyone travelling in the Third World. Full of anecdotes, often hilariously funny, it's worth reading for pleasure as well as the carefully researched information on every relevant subject.

Seah, Stanley S.K., M.D. (1983). *Don't Drink the Water: The Complete Traveler's Guide to Staying Healthy in Warm Climates*. Canadian Public Health Association.

Weinhouse, Beth (1987). *The Healthy Traveler*. Pocket Books, New York.

Fiction

Amado, Jorge (1962). Translated by William L. Grossman and James L. Taylor. *Gabriela, Clove and Cinnamon*. Bard/Avon, New York. Amado has long been Brazil's best-loved novelist. Many of his books deal with city life in Salvador (*Dona Flor and Her Two Husbands*, for example). Yet he can also evoke, better than any sociologist, the flavour and pace of life in small-town Brazil. *Gabriela* takes place in Ilhéus, Bahia, along the north-east coast, and it's one of the world's great love stories. Amado, Jorge (1979). Translated by Barbara Shelby Merello. *Tieta*. Bard/Avon, New York. This time Amado's bawdy heroine does battle with land developers bent on destroying a sleepy fishing village on the north-east coast. The novel's locale, near the Bahia/Sergipe border, remains sleepy, and backcountry travellers may want to visit Mangue Seco, Tieta's favourite wind-swept beach.

Matthiessen, Peter (1965). *At Play in the Fields of the Lord*. Random House, New York. Missionaries versus Indians in the South American rain forest. Evokes the tragedy of cultural interference as powerfully as any non-fiction book on the subject.

Souza, Márcio (1980). Translated by Thomas Colchie. *The Emperor of the Amazon*. Bard/Avon, New York. A wildly picaresque satire set in the rubber-boom era. Souza is a resident of Manaus and one of Brazil's most controversial new authors.

Vierci, Pablo (1987). Translated by Sarah Nelson. *The Impostors*. Bard/Avon, New York. An hilarious novel of river travel, greed, lust, and corruption along the Amazonian backwaters.

OTHER BOOKS ON SOUTH AMERICA FROM BRADT PUBLICATIONS

Backpacking and Trekking in Peru and Bolivia by Hilary Bradt.
Now in its 5th edition (1989) this guide covers all the main hiking areas of the two countries, as well as giving invaluable advice for all travellers.
Maps, photos, drawings. £7.95

Backpacking in Chile and Argentina by Hilary Bradt and others.
Second edition with several new hikes in this spectacular part of the world.
Maps, colour photos, drawings. £8.95.

No Frills Guide to Venezuela by Hilary Bradt and others.
Caracas, the coast and islands, the Angel Falls, Roraima and Amazonia. The No Frills Format allows it to be constantly updated.
Maps, drawings. £5.95.

Climbing and Hiking in Ecuador by Rob Rachowiecki and Betsy Wagenhauser.
Second edition due early 1991.

This is just a few of our books on Latin America. We also sell guides to Costa Rica, Guatemala, No Frills Guides to Peru and Ecuador, a wide selection on the Galapagos Islands, and a comprehensive list of South American Maps.

Send for a catalogue from: Bradt Publications, 41 Nortoft Rd, Chalfont St Peter, Bucks, SL9 OLA, England. Tel: 02407 3478. Fax: 734 509262.

THE GLOBETROTTERS CLUB

An international club which aims to share information on adventurous budget travel through monthly meetings and *Globe* magazine. Published every two months, *Globe* offers a wealth of information, from reports of members' latest adventures to recent travel bargains and tips, plus the invaluable 'Mutual Aid' column where members can swap a house, sell a camper, find a travel companion or offer information on unusual places or hospitality to visiting members.

London meetings are held monthly (Saturdays) and focus on a particular country or continent with illustrated talks.

Enquiries to: The secretary, Globetrotters Club, BCM/Roving, London WC1N 3XX.

186

Index

NOTES

NOTES

NOTES

NOTES

NOTES

NOTES